CW00693427

CRUSADER CASTLES
in the HOLY LAND

*An Illustrated History of the Crusader Fortifications
of the Middle East and Mediterranean*

CRUSADER CASTLES
in the HOLY LAND

An Illustrated History of the Crusader Fortifications
of the Middle East and Mediterranean

DAVID NICOLLE

First published in Great Britain in 2008 by Osprey Publishing,
Midland House, West Way, Botley, Oxford OX2 0PH, United Kingdom.
443 Park Avenue South, New York, NY 10016, USA.

Email: info@ospreypublishing.com

Previously published as David Nicolle, Fortress 21: *Crusader Castles in the Holy Land 1097–1192*; David
Nicolle, Fortress 32: *Crusader Castles in the Holy Land 1192–1302*; and David Nicolle, Fortress 59: *Crusader
Castles in Cyprus, Greece and the Aegean 1191–1571*.

A CIP catalogue record for this book is available from the British Library

ISBN-13: 978 1 84603 349 0

Jacket and page layout by Myriam Bell Design, France
Index by Alison Worthington
Typeset in Arno Pro and Optima
Originated by PDQ Digital Media Solutions, UK
Printed in China through Bookbuilders

08 09 10 11 12   10 9 8 7 6 5 4 3 2 1

For a catalogue of all books published by Osprey please contact:

NORTH AMERICA
Osprey Direct, c/o Random House Distribution Center
400 Hahn Road, Westminster, MD 21157, USA

E-mail: info@ospreydirect.com

ALL OTHER REGIONS
Osprey Direct UK, P.O. Box 140, Wellingborough, Northants, NN8 2FA, UK

E-mail: info@ospreydirect.co.uk

www.ospreypublishing.com

Osprey Publishing is supporting the Woodland Trust, the UK's leading woodland conservation charity,
by funding the dedication of trees.

Front cover, left to right: Kolossi castle © Peter Guttman/Corbis; Palace of the Grand Masters at Rhodes
© Wolfgang Kaehler/Corbis; Genoese castle at Molivos, Lesbos © D. Nicolle
Back cover: (top) Bodrum castle © D. Nicolle; (bottom) Southeastern tower of castle at Molivos, Lesbos
© D. Nicolle
Endpapers: Inner courtyard of Crac des Chevaliers © D. Nicolle

Editor's note:
Measurements are given in metric only throughout this book. To convert these figures to imperial measures, the
following conversion formulas are provided:

1 millimetre (mm) – 0.0394in
1 centimetre (cm) – 0.3937in
1 metre (m) – 1.0936 yards
1 kilometre (km) – 0.6214 miles
1 gram (g) – 0.0353 ounces
1 kilogram (kg) – 2.2046lb
1 tonne (t) – 0.9842 long ton (UK)

CONTENTS

INTRODUCTION

Crusader castles, and the fortifications of cities that the Crusaders once occupied, conjure up images of great fortresses dominating the landscape or walled cities defying the wrath of surrounding Islamic states. In reality, the fortifications taken over, repaired, extended or newly built by the Crusaders from the close of the 11th century existed in a great variety of sizes and styles. Furthermore, most of the towering castles whose photographs illustrate histories of the Crusades actually survive in a 13th-century or even a post-Crusader, that is an Islamic, form. Fortifications dating from the 12th century, when the Crusader States were still a significant military force, are harder to find. Some exist as fragments, walls or towers embedded within later castles or city walls. Others are little more than shattered ruins or foundations in areas where later powers felt little need to maintain Crusader fortifications. The exceptions have all been altered by later occupants.

The First Crusaders who captured Jerusalem in 1099 came to the Middle East with their own established ideas about military architecture. For most of them a castle was a fortification and a residence, though several variations had already emerged. The 10th and 11th centuries had seen the development of sophisticated European timber fortifications, even in areas where good building stone was available. This trend may have reflected a lack of sufficient skilled masons, but it is important to note that within Europe wooden fortresses were not necessarily weaker than those of stone.

Although the Carolingian Empire of Western and Central Europe had not been noted for military architecture, it had built 'royal forts' at strategic points. These had much in common with Late Roman forts, though some also included relatively tall and sturdy towers. Partly as a result of the Scandinavian Viking, Islamic Saracen and Magyar Hungarian raids during the 9th and 10th centuries, the imperial or royal ban on members of the nobility constructing fortresses without authorization gradually waned. At the same time, the crumbling Roman curtain-walls of many towns were repaired.

An increasing number of small rural fortifications became characteristic of 11th-century France, where the motte and bailey castle became a distinctive new form. However, during the 11th century formidable stone castles and towers or keeps also appeared in some regions that had until then been dominated by earth and timber defences. Further south, stone and brick remained the traditional materials when constructing fortifications. Here there is evidence that some existing

The seemingly isolated tower of Burj al-Sabi overlooks the coastal road south of Banyas. It was strong enough to impose tolls upon travellers, but the main fortress in this area was Margat, which rises a short distance inland. This tower is also said to have been linked to Marqab by a long wall. (D. Nicolle)

stone halls were strengthened and heightened to become prototypes of the tall, freestanding donjon tower that typified much 12th-century Western European non-urban fortification. At the same time there was increasing interest in using natural rocky outcrops as defensible sites. Fortified churches similarly became a feature of southern France, an area from which so many participants of the First Crusade would come. Normans would play a very prominent role in the First Crusade, and Normandy and the Anglo-Norman kingdom of England were in some respects in advance of the rest of France in matters of fortification. In fact, the Normans were particularly closely associated with the new motte and bailey style of fortification.

Men from Germany and other parts of what was then simply called 'The Empire' also played a significant role in the spread of military architecture, but slightly different traditions and other new styles of fortification had been developing in their homelands during the 10th and 11th centuries. From the late 10th century onwards, a carefully planned system of provincial fortresses had been erected to control newly conquered Slav-inhabited territories along the eastern frontiers. Yet another series of fortifications could be seen south of the Alps, in Italy. Here cities like Rome had tried to maintain the impressive fortifications inherited from the Roman Empire. Meanwhile the military architecture that emerged in several parts of the country during the 11th century was often technologically more sophisticated than that seen north of the Alps, probably because of the close cultural, political, economic and military proximity of the Byzantine and Islamic worlds, where the art of fortification was even more advanced.

The First Crusaders may have marched east with their own varied traditions of military architecture, but when they reached the Byzantine Empire and then the Islamic states of the Middle East they found themselves facing some of the most massive, sophisticated and expensive fortifications outside China. At this stage the Western European Crusaders were on the offensive, and very rarely felt the need to erect strong fortifications. But as soon as they carved out what are now known as the Crusader States, they began building and were almost immediately influenced by the military architecture they saw around them.

Whether Crusader castles were intended primarily as offensive bases, as defensive bastions, or as statements of power, may never be answered, as these fortifications served several purposes at the same time. The priorities of those who financed, built, garrisoned and defended them similarly changed according to circumstances. One thing was, however, now clear to rulers, churchmen, knights, common soldiers and civilians. Since the fiasco of the Second Crusade in 1148 the Crusader States largely had to rely upon their own resources and on diplomatic as well as military methods of defence. Yet this combination was far from easy to implement. Following the death of the sympathetic Byzantine emperor Manuel in 1180, it proved impossible for the Crusader States to form a genuine alliance with the Byzantine Empire. In fact, increasing diplomatic, political, economic and religious friction between the Orthodox Christian East and the Latin or Catholic West led to a virtual alliance between the Byzantines and the Crusader States' most formidable foe, Saladin.

Consequently, the Crusader States developed a more cautious strategy. The original expansionist spirit largely disappeared and was replaced by a pragmatic emphasis on survival within a largely hostile environment. Paradoxically, however, there was a decline in cooperation amongst the remaining three Crusader States as each concentrated on its own immediate problems.

The Third Crusade was at best only a partial success; nevertheless it achieved more than any subsequent Crusading expedition. Meanwhile, the strengthening of those fortifications that remained in Crusader hands, the building of some new castles and massive efforts to strengthen the defences of Crusader-held towns

Silifke castle on the southern coast of Anatolia was given to the Hospitallers by the Armenian Kingdom of Cilicia to defend the western entrance to the fertile Cilician coastal plain. It had a doubled circuit wall and 23 towers. (D. Nicolle)

9

continued until the final collapse in 1291. In some ways the military situation was now easier, because the Latin or Western European colonists held fewer positions than they had before the disasters of 1187. Several of these fortified sites were immensely strong, and remain impressive pieces of architecture to this day.

Although the abundance of Crusader castles was a sign of the military weakness of the Crusader States, the popular view that the ruling elites and knights of the 13th century Crusader States had 'gone soft' as a result of contact with a supposedly enervating Arab-Islamic culture is nonsense. In reality, the states of Antioch, Tripoli and Jerusalem (the latter so-called in name only, since the Kingdom of Jerusalem rarely controlled the Holy City itself) had developed effective defensive systems. These were based upon experience, realism and an ability to learn from their neighbours. The baronial families of the Crusader States may have regarded France as their cultural ideal, but in international politics as well as everyday life the elites of the Crusader States had more in common with the urbanized and mercantile elites of 13th-century Italy.

Urbanization was similarly a feature of the 13th-century Crusader States. They were now little more than coastal enclaves clinging to the fringe of the Middle East. Of the towns and cities that at various times formed the Kingdom of Jerusalem, only 14 had circuit walls. Of these 12 were already walled before the Crusaders arrived. The two exceptions were Atlit south of Haifa, which was a new Crusader foundation,

THE KINGDOM OF JERUSALEM, C. 1160

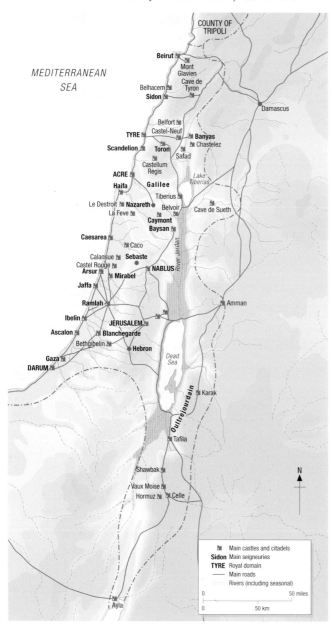

and Acre's similarly new suburb of Montmussard. Elsewhere the Crusaders strengthened what already existed, and most such efforts date from after the Third Crusade. Furthermore, the vast cost of urban refortification projects was often covered by Crusader leaders from Western Europe.

Although the Crusader States never recovered from Saladin's campaigns, they did enjoy a limited respite during the rest of the Ayyubid period, when Saladin's successors adopted a less aggressive policy towards the European settlers. A system of fluctuating alliances often characterized this period, with one or more Crusader States allying themselves with one or more of the fragmented Ayyubid sultanates. This situation had an impact upon the history of specific castles like Belfort, which was lost to Saladin. It was then strengthened by his Ayyubid successors before the Sultan of Damascus agreed to hand it back to the Crusaders as part of an alliance agreement in 1240. The garrison disagreed, however, so the sultan had to besiege his own fortress in order to hand it over to the Christians. The titular lord of Belfort then died and his successor sold the castle to the Templars because this wealthy

The castle of Gaston (Baghras) dominated the strategic Belen Pass through the Amanus Mountains east of Antioch. It consisted of outer and inner circuit walls, both with rounded towers, perched on a very steep hill. After falling to Saladin it passed into the hands of the Armenians before being returned to the Templars in 1216. Ironically, its most important subsequent role was to protect the Principality of Antioch against its fellow-Christian neighbour in the Kingdom of Cilician Armenia. (D. Nicolle)

military order was better able to defend it. During the few years that the Templars held Belfort they were credited with constructing an outwork 250m from the main castle, to stop a besieger dominating the fortress from a nearby hill, probably reflecting the increasing range of stone-throwing siege machines.

These years also saw some 'offensive' building projects, perhaps including work on a new citadel in Tiberius, though there is no evidence that the town was re-colonized. Even Jerusalem was regained by negotiation in 1229, only to be lost permanently 15 years later. During this brief reoccupation, efforts were made to strengthen the fortifications that had been razed by Saladin, including work on two gates. This effort cannot have been effective, as even local Muslim peasants could sometimes break in.

The situation became far more serious during the second half of the 13th century, when the warlike Mamluk sultanate replaced the Ayyubids. This period saw major efforts to strengthen Crusader defences, especially urban fortifications. The castles that had proved quite successful during the first half of the 13th century were now picked off as part of a Mamluk grand strategy initiated by Sultan Baybars. The Christians responded with even stronger fortifications and a massive building programme during the final decades of the Crusader States.

By 1242 changes in the balance of power between the king and his barons resulted in new laws regarding the custody of royal fortresses. Meanwhile, other fortifications were appearing within some Crusader-held coastal cities. Here virtually autonomous Italian merchant communes were playing an increasingly important military and political role, while also importing their own quarrels – rivalries that led to Genoese, Venetians and Pisans attacking each others' fortified towers inside cities like Acre. Similarly, the rivalry between 'imperial' and 'anti-imperial' factions for domination of what remained of the Kingdom of Jerusalem caused not only brawling in the streets, but even small-scale siege warfare. Given such mounting problems, it is not surprising that much of the Crusader aristocracy abandoned Syria, Lebanon and Palestine to seek new opportunities in Crusader-ruled Cyprus and the Crusader States of Greece.

Despite the vulnerable situation in which the Crusader States found themselves, many 13th-century fortifications seem to have been built for offensive as well as defensive purposes. Furthermore, it is wrong to suggest that the Crusader States now had no broad military strategy. Another entrenched myth maintains that Crusader fortifications formed a 'Line of Defence'. Instead they continued to serve

The citadel of Lindos was the second most important fortress on the Hospitaller-ruled island of Rhodes. (D. Nicolle)

as secure centres of administration while providing bases for both offence and defence. These castles, fortified towns, cities and even isolated towers could support one another to some extent. In fact their functions, and the military thinking that lay behind them, were essentially the same in the 13th century as they had been in the 12th. Their eventual failure resulted from the unification of Egypt and Syria under the aggressive leadership of the Mamluk sultans – just as the catastrophe of 1187–88 resulted from the unification of Egypt and Syria under Saladin. By the later 13th century, however, the balance of power had shifted strongly in favour of the Muslims, while interest in Crusading and in the fate of the Crusader States slumped in Western Europe.

Only one significant inland castle was regained in the Kingdom of Jerusalem – Calansue, which was held from 1191 to 1265 – and the settler population was now even more concentrated on the coast than it had been before 1187. For example, the suburb of Montmussard on the northern side of Acre expanded and required fortification. Jaffa had expanded beyond its pre-Crusader walls, while the new castle at Atlit was soon followed by a new town. A comparable process may have taken place further north, around some of the remaining inland castles like Montfort, Safad and Crac des Chevaliers. Trade was another stimulus to fortification, with small castles protecting vulnerable routes through Crusader territory. Here they could levy tolls, as did the isolated Burj al-Sabi tower, next to the coastal road south of Banyas. Meanwhile, fortified towns continued to develop as centres of trade because of the security they offered.

The Principality of Antioch had long been involved in the affairs of the Kingdom of Lesser Armenia in neighbouring Cilicia. During the 13th century, the military orders were also given several castles in this region. Some were existing Byzantine or Islamic structures that the orders strengthened or rebuilt. Others were new foundations. Generally speaking, the Armenians only permitted the Crusading orders to hold castles in the vulnerable south-eastern and south-western border regions, though the Teutonic Knights did play a political role role in support of Armenian rulers, perhaps because they were less of a threat than the longer established Hospitallers and Templars.

The fortifications erected, repaired or reused by the Crusader States in Cyprus and around the Aegean have attracted less interest than those in and around the Holy Land. While the military and political situations that they reflected were also more complex than those in the Middle East, several of the states established by so-called Crusaders in Cyprus and Greece survived much longer than did the Crusader States on the Middle Eastern mainland. Others created in what are now north-western Turkey, Bulgaria, Macedonia and Albania proved more ephemeral.

The citadel at the highest point of the fortifications of the ancient city of Antioch largely dates from the Crusader occupation and includes both 12th- and 13th-century construction. The wall and early half-round towers seen here face inwards, towards the precipitous slope that runs down to the city below. In fact, the upper line of walls is on the crest of the mountain. (D. Nicolle)

The Latin or Catholic Kingdom of Cyprus was established during the course of the Third Crusade, as a consequence of King Richard of England's unprovoked invasion of what was at the time a rebel-held Byzantine island. This was not the first invasion of the Orthodox Christian Byzantine Empire by a Catholic Western European army, but it was the first significant diversion of a major Crusade that had set out to attack Islamic territory. The Fourth Crusade, sometimes described as 'The Great Betrayal', was the most famous such diversion, resulting in the heartlands of the Byzantine Empire being temporarily replaced by a Catholic Christian or Latin 'Empire of Romania'. This, and its subsidiary Kingdom of Thessalonika, was very short-lived, but two other subsidiary states in central and southern Greece endured for centuries and left an architectural legacy in a land better known for Ancient Greek and Roman remains.

Equally important were the widespread colonial outposts planted by the two greatest maritime republics of Italy on the coasts of what had been the Byzantine Empire. First came Venice, whose ships transported the Fourth Crusade to the walls of the Byzantine capital of Constantinople, now named Istanbul. Next came Venice's rival Genoa, largely as an ally of the Byzantines as they fought back against the invading

The Byzantine monastery at Dafni was surrounded by fortified walls during the Crusader occupation. (D. Nicolle)

Crusaders. In fact, the last Western outposts to fall to the Ottoman Turkish Empire – an empire that conquered the mosaic of Orthodox or Catholic Christian and Islamic territories resulting from the Fourth Crusade – were Genoese and Venetian.

The military circumstances of 'Crusader' fortifications in these regions differed significantly from those in and around the Holy Land, yet certain factors remained similar. Most historians highlight Italian naval dominance as being a key strategic consideration. However, as the Christians' naval superiority is too often overstated in relation to the Middle Eastern Crusader States, so the Christians' domination of the Aegean and Black Seas well into the 15th century is similarly exaggerated. Turkish Islamic fleets could rarely challenge Italian or Crusader fleets until the rise of Ottoman naval power in the later 15th century and rarely attempted to do so. Instead pre-Ottoman Turkish, Mamluk (Syrian-Egyptian) and early Ottoman warships used their numerous and almost invariably smaller ships to raid Christian-held islands and coasts while the more powerful but less numerous Italian or Crusader warships were elsewhere. This strategy had a profound impact upon the location, supplying, defence and garrisoning of 'Crusader' fortifications in these regions. Small forces put ashore by Muslim so-called 'pirates' sometimes penetrated deep inland, having an impact upon the internal as well as the coastal fortifications of the Crusader States and those of the larger Italian colonies.

Other geo-political factors are also widely misunderstood. After the fall of the remnants of the Byzantine Empire to the Ottoman Turks in the 15th century, the preceding Byzantine decline came to be seen as inexorable. In reality, Byzantine successes in the early 14th century had made it seem possible that the empire would rebuild a substantial powerbase in the southern Balkans and Greece, while largely abandoning its previous Asian powerbase in Anatolia. For the Crusader States in Greece, the essentially European Byzantine Empire appeared a mortal threat, and was viewed as a serious regional rival by the Catholic rulers of southern Italy and Sicily. In the event this Byzantine revival faded after the Ottoman Turks established a European foothold on the Gallipoli Peninsula. From there the Ottoman state expanded into the Balkans and Greece, becoming the greatest threat not only to the rump Byzantine Empire, other Orthodox Christian states in the Balkans and the Crusader States in Greece, but also to Venetian and Genoese colonial outposts. The Ottoman expansion completely altered the strategic situation faced by the remaining Crusader States and the Italian mercantile outposts.

CHRONOLOGY

1096	Departure of the First Crusade for the Middle East.
1097–98	Siege of Antioch by the First Crusade.
1098	Establishment of the County of Edessa by Baldwin of Boulogne.
1099	First Crusade captures Jerusalem.
1100	Crusaders capture Sidon.
1101	Crusaders capture Arsuf; start of the Crusader siege of Tripoli.
1107	Crusaders capture Vaux Moise (al-Wu'aira) in southern Jordan.
1109	Tripoli surrenders to the Crusaders after an eight-year siege.
1114	Maras is massively damaged by an earthquake.
1115	Muslim army attacks Crusader-held Afamia; Muslim army takes Crusader-held Kafr Tab.
1115–16	Crusader campaign in southern Jordan.
1119	Muslim army attacks and takes the Crusader-held Atharib.
1124	Crusaders capture Tyre.
1129	Crusaders and Kingdom of Jerusalem attack Damascus.
1136	Frontier territory or March granted to the Templars in the Amanus Mountains of north-western Syria.
1144	Crusader-ruled city of Edessa retaken by Zangi; Count Raymond II of Tripoli grants the Hospitallers substantial territories around the Buqai'ah valley.
1147	Second Crusade launched.
1148	Second Crusade defeated outside Damascus.
1151	Last Crusader castle in the County of Edessa surrenders to Nur al-Din.
1153	Crusaders capture Ascalon.
1157	Serious earthquake damages fortifications in north-western Syria.
1163–69	Five invasions of Egypt by the Crusader Kingdom of Jerusalem.
1170	Earthquake damages fortification in north-western Syria; Saladin captures the Crusader castle of Ayla.
1177	Crusaders defeat Saladin at the battle of Mont Gisard.
1179	Saladin captures and destroys the partially built Crusader castle of Vadum Jacob (Yisr Ya'kub).
1183	Campaign by Reynald of Châtillon, Lord of Oultrejourdain, in northern Arabia and the Red Sea area.

1187   Saladin defeats Crusader Kingdom of Jerusalem at the battle of Hattin, retakes Jerusalem and most of the Kingdom of Jerusalem. His siege of Crusader-held Tartus is unsuccessful.

1188–89   Crusader castles in southern Jordan captured by Saladin.

1189–92   The Third Crusade sets off for the Middle East; King Richard I of England seizes Cyprus from the Byzantine Empire; Crusaders retake Acre and defeat Saladin at the battle of Arsuf; Crusaders fail to reach Jerusalem; King Richard agrees a peace treaty with Saladin.

1191   Byzantine Cyprus conquered by King Richard I of England.

1193   Death of Saladin.

1194   Amaury of Lusignan becomes ruler of Cyprus; the following year he is recognized as a king (creation of the Crusader Kingdom of Cyprus).

1197   King Amaury of Cyprus becomes King of Jerusalem (until 1205); German Crusade to the Middle East.

1198   Cilician Armenia becomes a kingdom; German Hospital reconstituted as the Order of Teutonic Knights; proclamation of the Fourth Crusade.

1202–04   Fourth Crusade seizes the Byzantine imperial capital; creation of the Latin Empire of Constantinople; beginning of the Crusader conquest of southern Greece.

1204   Count Baldwin of Flanders elected as first Latin emperor.

1205   Conquest of Morea (Peloponnese, southern Greece) by Geoffrey of Villehardouin and William of Champlitte; establishment of the Crusader States in Greece; Hugh I becomes King of Cyprus (until 1218).

1210   John of Brienne becomes King of Jerusalem (until 1225).

1218   Henry I becomes King of Cyprus (until 1253); Fifth Crusade invades Egypt by sea.

1221   Fifth Crusade is defeated at the first battle of Mansurah.

1225   Emperor Frederick II of Germany and Italy becomes ruler of the Kingdom of Jerusalem (until 1243).

1229–33   Civil war in Crusader Cyprus.

1231–42   Commune of Acre becomes centre of resistance to Emperor Frederick II's rule in the Kingdom of Jerusalem.

1235   John of Brienne saves Crusader Constantinople; defeat of Byzantines and Bulgarians.

1243   Conrad becomes King of Jerusalem (until 1254); Mongols invade Seljuk Anatolia.

1244   Kingdom of Jerusalem forms an alliance with the Ayyubid rulers of Damascus and Jordan against the Ayyubid ruler of Egypt; Khwarazian refugee army from eastern Islam (fleeing advancing Mongols) takes Jerusalem from the Crusader Kingdom; Crusader States defeated at the battle of La Forbie.

1245   Emperor Frederick II deposed.

1250   Crusade of King Louis IX of France invades Egypt; death of Sultan al-Salih Ayub of Egypt; Louis IX defeated at the second battle of Mansurah; effective establishment of the Mamluk sultanate in Egypt.

1253   Hugh II becomes King of Cyprus (until 1267).

1254   Conraddin becomes King of Jerusalem (until 1268; note that Acre was now actual capital of the Kingdom).

1256   Civil war in Acre (until 1258).

1258   Mongols invade Iraq and sack Baghdad.

1259   Crusader Principality of Achaea in Greece defeated by Byzantines at Pelagonia.

1260   Mongols invade Syria; Crusader Principality of Antioch and Kingdom of Cilician Armenia ally with the Mongols; Mamluks defeat Mongols at the battle of Ayn Jalut; Baybars becomes Mamluk Sultan of Egypt.

1261   Byzantine 'Emperor of Nicaea' retakes Crusader-ruled Constantinople; Crusader States also surrender Monemvasia, Mistra and Maina in southern Greece; Byzantine emperor Michael VIII retakes Constantinople from Latin (Crusader) Empire.

1263–66   Mamluks destroy Nazareth, and take Caesarea, Arsuf and Safad.

Bodrum Castle with its tall keep and lower outworks, designed to house and to resist artillery, overlooking the harbour. (D. Nicolle)

1267 Crusader Principality of Achaea recognizes suzerainty of Charles of Anjou, ruler of southern Italy; Hugh III becomes King of Cyprus (until 1284).

1268 Mamluks retake Jaffa, Belfort and Antioch.

1269 King Hugh III of Cyprus becomes ruler of the Kingdom of Jerusalem (until 1284); Aragonese Crusade arrives in Acre.

1271 Charles of Anjou recognized as king in Albania; Mamluks retake Castel Blanc, Crac des Chevaliers and Montfort; Crusade of Prince Edward of England reaches Acre then attacks Caco.

1276–77 King Hugh III abandons Palestine for Cyprus; Mary of Antioch sells the Crown to King Charles of southern Italy; Kingdom of Jerusalem divided between lords who recognize or reject Charles.

1277 Civil war in the County of Tripoli (until 1283).

1278 Death of Prince William of Achaea; Charles of Anjou takes over direct government of Achaea.

1282 'Sicilian Vespers' revolt in Sicily against Charles of Anjou; Peter of Aragon invades Sicily.

1284 John I becomes King of Jerusalem and Cyprus (until 1285).

1285 Death of Charles of Anjou; end of Angevin attempts to create an empire in Italy, Sicily, Greece and the Crusader Kingdom of Jerusalem; Henry II becomes King of Cyprus (nominal ruler until 1324); Mamluks take Margat.

1287–89 Crusade led by Alice of Blois reaches Acre; Mamluks take Latakia and Tripoli.

1290 Northern Italian Crusade to the Holy Land.

1291 Mamluks conquer Acre, Sidon and Beirut; end of the Kingdom of Jerusalem, though the title 'King of Jerusalem' remains, usually held by the Lusignan rulers of Cyprus; Crusaders evacuate Tartus and Atlit.

1299 Mongols defeat a Mamluk army near Homs, leading to temporary revival of Crusading optimism in Europe.

1302 Mamluks retake Arwad island; probable end of Crusader rule at Jbayl.

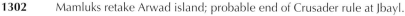

1306   Crusader Order of the Hospitallers invades the Byzantine island of Rhodes.

1309   Hospitallers transfer their headquarters to Rhodes.

1311   Crusader forces in Greece defeated by the freebooting Catalan Company (mercenary army); Catalans take control of Athens and Thebes.

1313–16   Civil war in the Principality of Achaea; Ferdinand of Majorca, leader of the Catalan Company and claimant to Achaea, defeated and killed by Louis of Burgundy, grandson-in-law of William of Villehardouin.

1332   Agreement between Venice, the Hospitallers, and the Byzantine Empire leads to formation of the first 'Crusade League' against the Turks (France and the Papacy join the following year).

1334   The Crusade League fleet defeats the Turks in the Gulf of Edremit.

1344   The Crusade League takes Smyrna (Izmir) from the Turks.

1346   The Genoese take over Chios and Foça from the Byzantines.

1354   Byzantines cede Lesbos to the Genoese; Ottomans seize a European bridgehead at Gallipoli.

1359   Peter I becomes King of Cyprus; Crusade League fleet defeats Turks at Lampacus.

1360–61   Kingdom of Cyprus occupies Corycos and Adalia on the southern coast of Anatolia.

1365   Crusade led by Peter I of Cyprus briefly occupies Alexandria (in Egypt).

1366   Crusade led by Amadeus of Savoy in Thrace and Bulgaria.

1367   Peter I of Cyprus raids Cilicia and Syria.

1369   Assassination of Peter I of Cyprus; Genoese take control of Famagusta in Cyprus, expelling their Venetian rivals.

1371   Ottoman victory at the battle of Maritsa, followed by Ottoman conquest of most of Bulgaria and Macedonia.

1373–74   War between Cyprus and Genoa; Hospitallers take over the defence of Crusader-held Smyrna.

The great Hospitaller fortress of Margat crowns a steep hill overlooking the Mediterranean near Banyas. The site consisted of a fortified town, on the right, and a much more strongly protected citadel, on the left. The southernmost outer bastion of this citadel was rebuilt by the Mamluks after they captured the area. Most of the rest of the fortress dates from the 12th- and 13th-century Crusader period. (D. Nicolle)

1376	Principality of Achaea leased to the Hospitallers, but is taken over by the Navarrese Company (a mercenary army).
1378	The Hospitaller Grand Master is captured by the Ottomans at Arta in Greece.
1379	Navarrese Company takes control of Thebes.
1388	End of Catalan rule in Athens.
1389	Ottoman victory at the first battle of Kosova (Kosovo Field) leaves them as the dominant power in the Balkans.
1396	Large Crusading army destroyed by the Ottomans at the battle of Nicopolis.
1402	Timur-i Lenk (Tamerlane) conquers Smyrna from the Hospitallers.
1406–07	Hospitallers start building a castle at Bodrum on the Anatolian mainland.
1424–25	Mamluks raid Cyprus and capture King Janus.
1432	Thomas Palaeologus, Byzantine despot of the Morea, takes the 'Crusader' Principality of Achaea.
1444	Mamluks unsuccessfully besiege Hospitaller Rhodes; Ottomans defeat a Crusader army at Varna.

1448	Ottomans defeat Hungarians at the second battle of Kosova.
1453	Ottomans conquer Constantinople; end of the Byzantine Empire except for rival Byzantine states, which survive a few more years.
1456	Ottomans take Athens.
1457	A papal fleet raids the Aegean and occupies Samothrace, Thasos and Lemnos.
1458	James 'the Archbishop' becomes King of Cyprus with help from the Mamluk sultan.
1462	Ottomans conquer Genoese Lesbos.
1470	Ottomans conquer Venetian Euboea.
1472	Crusade League attacks Turkish Antalya and Smyrna.
1473	Catherine Cornara, a Venetian noblewoman, becomes regent of Cyprus following the death of her husband King James, and is proclaimed queen the following year.
1480	Unsuccessful Ottoman siege of Hospitaller-ruled Rhodes; Ottoman forces occupy Otranto in southern Italy for a year.
1489	Queen Catherine abdicates and hands the island of Cyprus over to the Venetian Republic.
1516	Ottomans conquer the Mamluk sultanate in Syria and Egypt.
1522	Ottomans conquer Hospitaller-ruled Rhodes.
1570–73	Ottomans conquer Venetian-ruled Cyprus.

The castle of Bilhorod-Dnistrovsky on the Black Sea coast of Ukraine was called Moncastro in the late medieval period. It was also known as Cetatea Alba in Romanian and Ak-Kirman in Turkish. (Author's collection)

PART I

CRUSADER CASTLES IN THE HOLY LAND, 1097–1302

THE DEVELOPMENT OF CRUSADER FORTIFICATIONS

FOUNDATIONS & IMPROVEMENTS

In the 19th and early 20th centuries, historians of the Crusades believed that Crusader military architecture was most strongly influenced by that of the Byzantine Empire. Shortly before World War I, a student from Oxford University conducted field research in the Asiatic provinces of the Ottoman Empire: he then returned to write a thesis in which he argued that the designers of Crusader castles largely based their ideas upon what was then being built in Western Europe. This student's name was T.E. Lawrence, soon to be better known as Lawrence of Arabia. His thesis eventually influenced the next generation of historians of Crusader architecture, but neither they nor Lawrence seriously considered the influence of Islamic traditions of fortification. This idea developed more recently and today it is widely accepted that the military architecture of the Crusader States reflected a broad array of influences, in addition to the inventiveness of those who actually designed it.

The late Nikita Elisséeff, who worked for much of his life in Damascus, maintained that Byzantine forms of military architecture in northern Syria were soon

At al-Wu'aira the builders of the Crusader castle widened and straightened an existing rocky gorge rather than excavating a fosse out of the rock. The anvil-shaped outcrop in the centre of the picture was then pierced with a tunnel to make an outer gate. The stone steps and bridge that now link this outcrop of rock to the castle on the right and the other side of the gorge on the left are modern. In the 12th century there would have been a drawbridge and a removable wooden bridge. (D. Nicolle)

added to the Western European design concepts of the early Crusaders. Within a few decades these newcomers were also learning from their Muslim neighbours, especially in making greater use of topographical features to strengthen a fortified site. More recently the Israeli scholar Ronnie Ellenblum highlighted the fact that Crusader castles were built to deal with specific military situations or threats, and that their designers drew upon what seemed most suitable in the circumstances.

In the early 12th century, each of the newly established Crusader States found itself in a different situation. The Principality of Antioch, for example, was adjacent to the Armenian states of Cilicia, which evolved into the Kingdom of Cilician or Lesser Armenia. Here fortifications ranged from tiny hilltop outposts to major garrison fortresses, while Armenian architects favoured half-round towers that protruded from a curtain-wall far enough to permit archers to enfilade the enemy. Such design ideas influenced castle building in the Principality of Antioch. Furthermore, Antioch attracted few Western European settlers and hence relied to a greater extent on military elites of Armenian, Greek and Syrian origin who may also have influenced the design of local fortifications. The mountainous character of the Principality of Antioch and the County of Tripoli clearly encouraged experimental and daring design ideas, though the castles themselves ranged from very simple, almost rustic structures to huge hilltop fortresses. Meanwhile, building techniques ranged from a typically Byzantine use of small masonry and bricks within one structure, to mixtures of Byzantine, Armenian, Western European and soon also Syrian-Islamic methods of both cutting and shaping stones – each of which had their own distinctive styles. Sometimes variations in ways of mixing cement and mortar also reflected different cultural influences.

Crusader castle building quickly grew more sophisticated. For example, the building of concentric castles first took place in the late 1160s, and although the idea had been around for some time, concentric castles certainly appeared in the Crusader States before they did in Western Europe. On the other hand, most early structures remained relatively small, while the vast sums of money and effort expended on larger and more elaborate fortifications were characteristic of the 13th rather than the 12th century.

One 'supposed' characteristic of Crusader castles was a lack of timber in their construction, with this being attributed to a dearth of suitable timber in the areas where they were built. However, abundant excellent timber was available in neighbouring Cilician Armenia. Although the deforestation of the Kingdom of Jerusalem may have been well advanced by the time of the Crusades, suitable large baulks of timber were available in the mountains of Lebanon and on Mount Carmel. The situation was better in the County of Tripoli, the Principality of Antioch and the northern regions of the County of Edessa. Furthermore, Western Europeans probably enjoyed a technological advantage over their Middle Eastern foes, not only in their tradition of timber architecture but also in their logistical ability to transport large timbers over long distances.

Consequently, it is hardly surprising to find that in reality early Crusader castles made considerable use of wood. Timber roofs, floors, balconies, stairs, ladders and non-defensive storage buildings, barracks or stables were commonplace. Wood was also used for internal fittings, though these do not survive. Other evidence suggests that the newly settled Crusaders rapidly adopted local architectural traditions by being sparing in their use of timber, even in castles erected in relatively well-wooded regions. Of course, it was not simply the availability of wood that mattered: it was the availability of suitably large pieces of timber. Recent archaeological excavations at the unfinished castle of Vadum Jacob also show that timber was used for scaffolding and in other construction processes, though the builders did take advantage of alternative

The tower of Castel Blanc (Burj Safita) dominated the surrounding Syrian town. The 27m high tower is a typical donjon or keep and was rebuilt in the late 12th or early 13th century when it was occupied by the Templars. It is also one of the best-preserved Crusader fortifications in the Middle East. (Institut Français d'Archéologie, Beirut)

techniques where possible – for example the use of temporary earthen ramps to bring building materials to the top of a wall as it was being built.

During the 12th century, the experience of local builders skilled in the construction of substantial stone vaulting, broad arches, domes and other complex load-bearing structures became available to the conquerors: as a result, indigenous Syro-Palestinian architectural influence became more apparent in many aspects of Crusader architecture. In military architecture, the most significant developments were the placing of entrances beneath and through towers rather than through curtain-walls, the construction of defensive towers that protruded further from a wall to permit enfilading fire, and the use of a major tower or keep not as a final redoubt, but as the fulcrum of an overall defensive scheme. Some of these concepts were rare or almost unknown in Western European fortification at the time.

The south-western corner tower of the inner defences of Castel Blanc, tucked away inside the small Syrian town of Safita. (D. Nicolle)

The inability of several Crusader fortifications to withstand enemy sieges became apparent in the 1160s and 1170s. Previously Islamic armies had relied on traditional methods of siege warfare, with direct assaults, blockades, mining and the limited use of relatively light stone-throwing artillery: although Islamic armies had access to superior siege technologies, a limited number of men skilled in heavy carpentry seems to have precluded the greater use of sophisticated artillery. In the 1160s, however, things began to change and a process was set in motion that would eventually result in the Mamluk sultanate's staggering number of huge timber-framed stone-throwing machines, which reached their peak in the late 13th century (see below). Meanwhile, the military setbacks suffered by the Crusader States resulted in the construction of bigger, stronger and notably more expensive castles. The owners of these new castles were not necessarily any richer, however, a fact that contributed to the rising military orders being asked to take over several castles because they were better able to garrison, maintain and defend them.

There was reduced reliance on a donjon and a greater emphasis on an enceinte or curtain-wall strengthened by towers. Yet there was also a tendency to increase the number of existing defensive features while shying away from incorporating new ones. Hence walls, towers and fosse ditches were multiplied while the natural defensive features of a site were enhanced by excavation and what could almost be called 'landscaping'. Walls became thicker and the originally Islamic concept of the *talus* (an additional sloping front) along the lower parts of walls and towers was adopted.

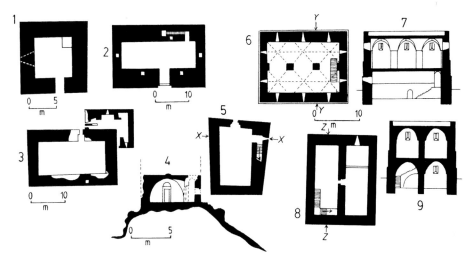

A selection of tower castles.
1 – Casal des Plains, Yazur (after Leach).
2 – Tal al-Badawiyah, basement (after Pease).
3 – Khirbat Rushmiyah, tower with forebuilding (after Pease).
4–5 – Bayt Jubr al-Tahtani, plan and section.
6 – Turris Rubea, Burj al-Ahmar, first floor.
7 – Turris Rubea, section Z–Z.
8 – Turris Rubea, basement
9 – Turris Rubea, section Y–Y (6–9 after Pease).

Ancient stone columns were added to walls as horizontal bonding, tying together the carefully laid outer and inner layers through a core filled with rubble and mortar. The number of embrasures for archery or observation was increased and single or superimposed horizontal defensive galleries, again with loopholes, became more common. Various forms of projecting machicolation appeared, which permitted arrows to be shot at, or missiles to be dropped on, enemies beneath. (Both Byzantine and Islamic fortifications had, of course, made use of machicolations long before the Crusaders arrived.) Meanwhile, towers began to get bigger and more closely spaced, though the massive projecting artillery bastion towers of the early 13th century had not yet appeared.

Below and opposite: The outer wall of the small castle of Castel Rouge (al-Qal'at Yahmur) has only one corner tower. Its barrel vaulted interior is rather cramped, but it was provided with arrow slits for crossbowmen. (D. Nicolle)

THE TYPES OF CRUSADER FORTIFICATION

By the end of the 12th century there were several basic forms of what can loosely be called Crusader fortifications. However, there was considerable overlap between them and no clear line of development even within these forms. The simplest was

the freestanding (or almost freestanding) tower, an idea brought to the Middle East by the Crusaders. Single towers were found in many areas, most commonly in the more settled regions. The second was the castrum or enclosure within a fortified wall, usually rectangular with corner towers: these too were more common in settled areas. The double-castrum was a development of this simple castrum and could be seen as the earliest manifestation of the concentric castle: these tended to be built in more vulnerable frontier regions. Third, the Crusaders used hilltop and spur-castles, the latter being sited upon a promontory attached to a hill by a narrow neck of land that could be cut off by a fosse or ditch. These were also common in unsettled areas. A fourth and characteristically Western European form of fortification has recently been added to this list: the motte and bailey castle. Originally of earth and timber, it was not previously thought to have been used in the Middle East.

A more sophisticated typology has been suggested by Adrian Boas who subdivides the towers into isolated towers, towers with outworks, and donjons as parts of larger castles. Castra are subdivided into simple castra, 'castrum and keep' castles that combined a castrum with a main tower or keep, and 'defended' castra with additional outworks. Double-castra or early concentric castles, hilltop and spur-castles remained separate categories.

TOWERS

At least 75 tower castles have been identified in the Crusader Kingdom of Jerusalem alone, and they are far more numerous than small-scale fortifications from the pre-Crusader and post-Crusader periods. Although defensive towers had previously been attached to some earlier monasteries in this area, they were rare. Nor was there anything comparable in previous Byzantine, Armenian or Islamic military architecture. The majority of these Crusader towers date from the 12th century and while some were related to early feudal lordships, several were later integrated into more elaborate fortifications.

THE CASTRUM

The existing Islamic castra north of Caesarea were used by Crusader forces from the time of their arrival in Palestine. Kfar Lam was an irregular four-sided structure built of sandstone ashlar (stone cut into regular rectangular blocks) with round corner towers and additional towers flanking a gate on its southern side. Its walls were then strengthened with small external buttresses, and under Crusader occupation the gate was both narrowed and lowered.

The invading Crusaders soon built castra of their own in southern Palestine, supposedly to contain a perceived threat from Ascalon, which was held by Fatimid forces until the mid 12th century. The example at al-Darum had one of its corner towers bigger than the others whereas those at Ibelin (Yibna) and Blanchegarde (Tal al-Safiyah) had four equal towers. Others in the centre and north of the Kingdom included Coliat (al-Qalai'ah), which was a simple castrum except that one tower was again larger and there were barrel-vaulted undercrofts along the northern and perhaps southern walls. The 'Sea Castle' at Sidon may originally have been a form of castrum, though it was later altered.

The Crusader castrum at Bethgibelin (Bayt Jibrin) was large and complex. It lies in a valley near freshwater springs and a road. Two main stages of construction have been identified. The first in 1136 used part of the existing Roman and Byzantine city wall and towers, strengthened with new wall construction. In the centre was an inner ward based upon an early Islamic Umayyad structure. When first built, Bethgibelin was described as a *praesidium* with a high wall, an antemurabilus (outer wall), towers and a moat. The ruins indicate an enclosure about 50m square with four corner towers, the entire layout being set inside the north-west corner of the ancient city walls. A second stage of construction saw the erection of outer walls and the excavation of a moat to create a larger defended area. This changed a simple square fortress into a complex concentric one. Both the inner and outer walls were strengthened with salient towers. The Israeli archaeologist Michael Cohen has recently suggested that Bethgibelin may have served as a model for future Crusader concentric castles.

Though one tower appears rather larger than the rest, there was no central keep at Bethgibelin. At Daron (al-Darum) there was a dominant tower. Here the outworks were eventually strengthened and by the late 12th century included no fewer than 17 towers. Jubayl had projecting corner towers plus an additional tower

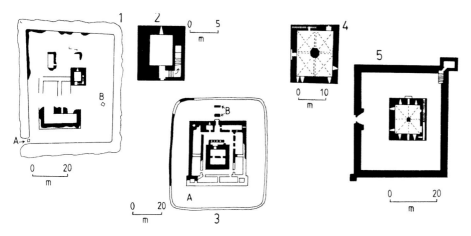

A selection of castra.
1. Cisterna Rubea (Qal'at al-Damm): (A) probable site of gate, (B) cistern (after Pease).
2. Cisterna Rubea, ground floor of central tower (after Pringle).
3. Bethsan (Baysan): (A) moat, (B) supports for bridge (after Seligman).
4. Castel Rouge (al-Qal'at Yahmur), plan of first floor (after Lawrence).
5. Castel Rouge (al-Qal'at Yahmur) (after Müller-Wiener).

on the eastern side of the north gate. Inside the courtyard was a keep, two storeys high with its entrance at first-floor level. This marriage of a castrum and a dominant keep seems to have been a significant advance in military architecture that could be credited to the Crusader States. The idea reached its full flowering at the Hospitaller castle of Belvoir, which was built shortly after 1168. It should also be noted though that some mid 12th-century Islamic fortifications gave a dominant tower a more independent role in defence.

HILLTOP & SPUR-CASTLES

Crusader hilltop castles shared few characteristics other than their setting. For example, Judin (Qal'at Jiddin) in western Galilee consisted of two great towers enclosed by curtain-walls, with the massive eastern tower perhaps being the earliest. The entrance to this tower was at ground-floor level, leading to a passage within the thickness of the wall, which perhaps led to a latrine. A second door in the entrance passage led to a staircase to the first floor. Like the ground floor, this was barrel vaulted. Another staircase led from here to a second floor or the roof. The second tower at Judin was unusual for such Crusader fortifications because it had three floors.

The spur-castles obviously shared certain features, principally in having the strongest part of their defences face a promontory that linked the 'spur' to the body of a neighbouring hill. Several of these spur-castles had a deep fosse or ditch cut across the promontory. However, some castles that were never occupied by the Crusaders, such as Shayzar, also had such rock-cut fosses.

Saone (Sahyun), in the southern part of the Principality of Antioch, is the least altered of the large 12th-century Crusader spur-castles. Here a tower keep was added to an existing Byzantine fortification before 1132 to dominate the curtain-wall with its smaller towers. The merlons of the crenellated wall are not pierced for archers or crossbowmen, as was typical of Islamic fortification, and most of the embrasures at Saone are also high up. Nor is there any direct communication between the keep and the curtain-wall, nor between some of the larger towers and the curtain-wall. These 'primitive' features might indicate residual Byzantine influence. Finally, the main tower at Saone is quite low, perhaps because it was built wholly of stone by designers who felt more comfortable using timber.

In 1031 the ruler of the Islamic city of Hims (in Syria) built a small castle at what was later known as Crac des Chevaliers. None of this first structure, however, has yet been found. Massively damaged by earthquakes in 1157 and 1170, Crac des Chevaliers was almost entirely rebuilt before being further extended by both the Hospitallers and the Mamluks in the 13th century, resulting in the magnificent castle seen today. Other than Saone, the oldest parts of Crac, 'Akkar in Lebanon and Karak in Jordan, the majority of existing spur-castles in what had been Crusader territory date from after the catastrophic battle of Hattin in 1187.

A fortified outpost on top of an isolated rock called al-Habis overlooking the ruins of ancient Petra in southern Jordan has recently been identified as the 'lost' Crusader castle of Celle. (D. Nicolle)

The fortifications of Celle overlooking Petra were not particularly strong. This position was, of course, a minor outpost of the Crusader Kingdom of Jerusalem and its virtually inaccessible location meant that it could be held by a small garrison. (D. Nicolle)

MOTTE & BAILEY CASTLES

Motte and bailey castles were typical of northern France and Norman England, while earthwork and motte fortifications were also seen in both northern and southern Italy. The man-made tals (or tells) that mark the sites of millenia-long human habitation in the Middle East already existed and were frequently used as centres of resistance, with or without formal fortifications on top: they were used in the same way as existing natural hills. More recently, Denys Pringle has identified at least one man-made motte in the Crusader States, on the site of the 'Land Castle'

A selection of spur-castles.
1 – Saone (Sahyun): (A) deep rock-cut fosse, (B) donjon, (C) Byzantine castle, (D) shallow fosse between upper and lower fortresses (after Deschamps & Müller-Wiener).
2 – Saone donjon, ground floor (after Lawrence).
3 – Saone donjon, first floor (after Lawrence).
4 – Castellum Regis, al-Mi'ilyah (after Pease).
5 – Arima (al-Araymah), probable early structures shown in black: (A) donjon, (B) main gate of inner citadel, (C) outer gate (after Müller-Wiener).
6 – Burj al-Malih (after Conder).
7 – Ravendel (Ravanda): (C) cisterns, (E) main entrance, (W) well (after Morray).

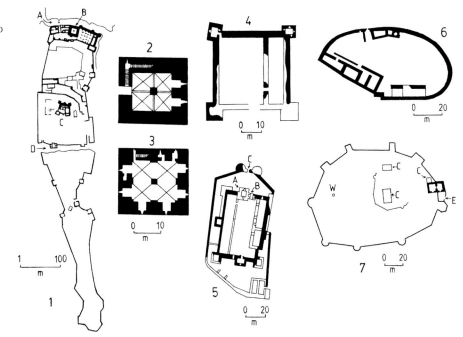

of Sidon. It seems to date from the 12th century, but was largely destroyed during the construction of a larger castle in the 13th century.

CAVE-FORTRESSES

Ledge- and cave-fortresses are not usually included in the typologies of Crusader castles because they rely almost entirely upon their natural locations for defence, with man-made structures playing a secondary role. The only 12th-century ledge-fortress to have been studied in detail is near al-Naqa, not far from Petra in southern Jordan. This has been identified as Hormuz (al-Naqa II), the third Crusader fort in the Petra region, the others being al-Wu'aira and al-Habis. It is part way up a precipice that forms part of the Jabal Bayda mountain. For some time the ruins were regarded as the remains of a fortified 12th–13th-century Arab-Islamic village, but they have now been identified as an isolated Crusader outpost facing west, across the Wadi Araba. Most other Crusader castles in southern Jordan were primarily concerned with threats from the east, north or south.

Crusader Hormuz consisted of about 15 rooms on the edge of a precipice. The walls comprised sandstone blocks from a nearby quarry and there was a gate through a narrow gorge or crack in the rock on the south-western side. Inside the site German archaeologists have found locally made Islamic pottery of a type also used by Crusader garrisons at other castles in southern Jordan. They also found millstones to grind flour. Water running off rocks on the upper part of the plateau was diverted into a cistern by a stone wall. Another round rock-cut cistern perhaps served as a filter pond, as its water then flowed into a larger catchment basin. Clearly the collection, retention and clarification of drinking water were of primary concern in such isolated desert outposts. The troops in Hormuz could control movement along the tracks that wound up from the Wadi Araba and Egypt beyond, while the larger garrisons at Karak des Moabites (al-Karak) and Montréal (Shawbak) could threaten the main road from Syria to western Arabia and Egypt.

Caves had been used as places of refuge from earliest times and were still used as centres of defence in the Middle East. For example, an underground church at Jumlayn in what became the Crusader County of Edessa had been fortified with a curtain-wall and ditch in the mid 11th century before the Crusaders arrived. A brief Crusader occupation resulted in no major changes, but what became the strategic castle of Qal'at Jumlayn (Çimdine Kalesi) was considerably strengthened after being taken by Islamic forces. In Lebanon the Cave de Tyron was used by the Crusaders as a simple fort, but little study has yet been made of this site. The most famous and best-recorded cave-fortress of the Crusader States is the Cave de Sueth in Jordan.

CAVE DE SUETH

The Cave de Sueth, now known in Arabic as 'Ain al-Habis or 'Spring of the Hermit's Retreat', overlooks a gorge from the plateau into the Yarmouk valley. A seasonal stream forms an occasional waterfall down an overhanging cliff known as 'Araq al-Habis. The caves in this cliff were excavated as a hermitage or monastic retreat long before being used as a military outpost in the 12th century, when the Crusaders knew the site as the Cave de Sueth.

The history of this cave-fortress begins with the Crusaders' fortification of the lower Yarmouk valley in 1105. The invaders knew the area as the Terre de Suethe, from the Arabic word *sawad* meaning 'cultivated zone', in contrast to the semi-desert further east. That same year the area was ravaged by the ruler of Damascus, who also destroyed a new Crusader outpost on the Golan Heights. Instead of provoking further retaliation by building a castle on the Heights, the Crusader

The Cave de Sueth ('Ain al-Habis) was cut from the soft limestone of a massive cliff and was accessed along a single path that ran across the sloping lower part of this cliff. Written records suggest that there was a gatehouse or wall at each end of the path. In fact, four or five courses of dressed masonry are visible at the western end of the path, the lowest three courses consisting of dark grey stone that does not come from the immediate vicinity. (D. Nicolle)

Prince of Galilee garrisoned the naturally defensible site of the Cave de Sueth on the southern side of the river, primarily as an observation post.

A peaceful arrangement lasted until 1111 when the Cave de Sueth fell to a force from Damascus. Two years later it reverted to Crusader control but in 1118 it again fell to the Muslims before being almost immediately retaken by King Baldwin of Jerusalem. Thereafter the entire Yarmouk valley was held by the Crusaders, to be used as a base for further raids. Around this time another cave-fortress was established at Cavea Roob, probably near al-Mughayir or al-Shajarah 15km south-east of 'Ain al-Habis: here there are cisterns plus the remains of an associated medieval settlement.

Many of the surviving defences probably date from after Nur al-Din unsuccessfully besieged the cave-fortress in 1158. Wooden stairs, ladders and walkways almost

certainly linked the three levels of caves, presumably being partially removable in an emergency. The Crusader chronicler William of Tyre described the Cave de Sueth as being set in a vertical cliff, inaccessible from above or below and reached solely by a precipitous path across the mountainside. The caves, he said, consisted of rooms fully supplied with the necessities of life plus plenty of good water. It is even possible that the garrison was supplied with livestock stabled in the lower caves, which are still used by Jordanian shepherds.

URBAN FORTIFICATIONS

The urban fortifications of the Crusader States were similar to those of neighbouring Islamic cities and, in fact, largely consisted of walls, towers and gates constructed before the Crusaders arrived. When these were repaired by the Christian conquerors, limited modifications were introduced, such as varied styles of stonework and the shape or position of new

The Cave de Sueth ('Ain al-Habis) was a Crusader cave fortress that made use of an earlier rock-cut Byzantine monastic retreat overlooking the precipitous valley of the River Yarmouk. Here the southernmost third and perhaps fourth level of man-made caves include two probable entrance points (centre-left) through which water from a seasonal waterfall was channelled into a cistern. (D. Nicolle)

towers. Acre, for example, still only had a single circuit wall at the time of the Third Crusade. At the smaller fortified coastal town of Arsuf the builders embedded their fortified wall in sand, as was also the case with several buildings inside the town. This may have helped the structures absorb earthquake shocks while also draining water away from the base of the fortifications. Furthermore a besieger would have encountered great difficulty trying to mine through sand. (For more explanation of urban defences, see the 'Feudal, Religious and Urban Defences' chapter below.)

13TH-CENTURY DEVELOPMENTS

The 13th century saw a number of significant changes in the design of both European and Islamic fortifications, the most significant of which first appeared in the Middle East. Consequently, the development of military architecture within the Crusader States played an important role in the history of medieval castles. The biggest design changes became apparent in the early part of the century, reflecting developments in urban and citadel construction in neighbouring Syria. (Simple rectangular towers were still built during the 13th century, though, one example being Qal'at Jiddin.)

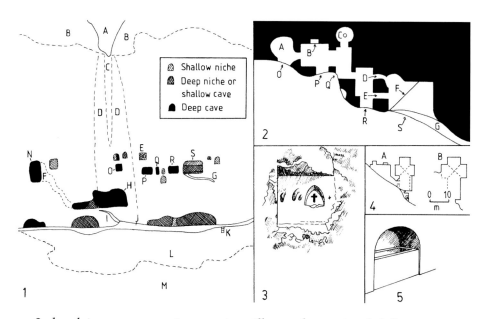

In low-lying or open regions, castra still served as regional defences against raiding or small-scale invasions, though most dated from before the battle of Hattin (1187). The original Sea Castle at Sidon may be such a castrum. The gate of this unusual fort faced the land, with a broad outer and a narrower inner arch, and with a slit for a portcullis between. Above the outer arch was a large machicolation supported by four stone brackets. Beneath each outer bracket was a carved lion, with human figures on the inner brackets. A bridge to the gate was supported by massive rectangular piers with triangular eastern sides to break the force of the waves. Stone arches spanned the gaps, except for the innermost, which orginally had a wooden drawbridge raised by chains from the machicolation.

Most double-castra, hilltop and spur-castles were sited in border areas, serving as garrison bases or protected depots containing supplies for field armies. Nevertheless, some scholars have misunderstood their function, dismissing some mountain castles as 'not very impressive' and failing to appreciate the importance of location. In fact, most complex spur and hilltop Crusader fortifications date from the 13th century. This might reflect new military priorities, although most Crusader inland territory now consisted of mountainous or upland terrain.

The most detailed documentary source about the construction of a 13th-century fortification deals with a hilltop castle. The *De constructione castri Saphet* discusses the Templar rebuilding of Saphet (Safad) after 1240. The huge costs came to 1.1 million 'Saracen bezants' for the first two-and-a-half years, followed by 40,000 per year thereafter. A peacetime garrison was to include 50 brother knights, 30 brother sergeants, 50 turcopoles, 300 archers, 820 workmen and other staff, and 400 slaves; in wartime their number was expected to reach 2,200.

The fortified monastery of St Simeon the Younger, in the mountains west of Antioch, was presumably a much less expensive fortification. The best-preserved fragment is the western gateway in an outer wall, which formed one of three concentric barriers. Its crude construction made use of material from the inner wall. A third construction programme on a western gateway using well-cut ashlar blocks probably dates from the late Crusader period.

The majority of 13th-century Crusader spur-castles are in the northern and eastern regions, where the largest dominated passes or important roads. Several could accommodate large garrisons and one of the biggest problems faced by their designers was guaranteeing adequate water supplies. According to the Arab chronicler al-Dimashqi, writing about 1300, Gibelcar (Jabal 'Akkar) had a 'channel of water coming right into the castle, brought down from the hills above, and sufficient both for domestic purposes and for drinking.' Its remains can still be seen. At Montfort (Qa'lat al-Qurayn) the keep was built above a massive cistern. Water might have been a problem in some spur-castles, but their locations on steep

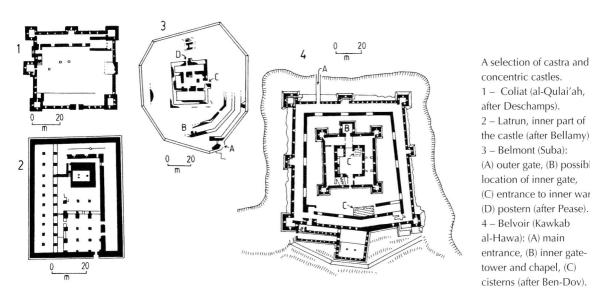

A selection of castra and concentric castles.
1 – Coliat (al-Qulai'ah, after Deschamps).
2 – Latrun, inner part of the castle (after Bellamy).
3 – Belmont (Suba): (A) outer gate, (B) possible location of inner gate, (C) entrance to inner ward, (D) postern (after Pease).
4 – Belvoir (Kawkab al-Hawa): (A) main entrance, (B) inner gate-tower and chapel, (C) cisterns (after Ben-Dov).

The strongest parts of
the fortifications of Saone
(Sahyun) castle were at the
eastern end. These walls
and towers, seen from inside
the castle, overlooked the
rock-cut fosse or ditch that
separated the castle from
the rest of the promontory.
(D. Nicolle)

promontories gave designers a clear topographical advantage. This was usually enhanced by cutting a fosse across the spur, separating the castle from the neighbouring hill.

The most dramatic and expensive changes in 13th-century Crusader fortifications came in the early decades, and were responses to a large-scale adoption of powerful counterweight trebuchets. The principle of the counterweight stone-throwing machine had probably been known for considerably longer than is generally realized, but it was only from the late 12th century onwards that such weapons were used in large numbers. Furthermore, the counterweight trebuchet initially made its greatest impact in defence rather than attack, as a counter-battery weapon that was most effective when mounted on top of a tower.

The emergence of such weapons led to a sudden appearance of larger, broader and deeper fortification towers, serving as artillery emplacements. Some fortresses had one such 'great tower' placed on the most vulnerable side, sometimes as a further development of the main keep. Where a larger area was enclosed the result could be a series of massive towers linked by relatively traditional curtain-walls. It was a true revolution in fortification, and it was not until the widespread adoption of siege cannon in the 15th century that anything as fundamental would be seen again.

Another important development was a multiplication of existing defensive features, including doubled walls, more numerous towers and an abundance of embrasures. Tiers of superimposed defensive galleries with loopholes were installed, along with various forms of projecting machicolation. While greater efforts were made to use naturally defensive features, walls also become thicker. Ancient columns were often laid horizontally through such walls, binding their inner and outer layers together, and there was increasing use of the Islamic talus, or sloping additional base, along the outer foot of a wall.

DESIGN INFLUENCES

Despite the increasing sophistication of 13th-century Crusader fortifications, their designs still reflected the immediate circumstances; efforts to impose distinctive categories upon Templar or Hospitaller military architecture are misleading. Much more depended on local conditions, available local stone and the origins, backgrounds and traditions of architects, masons and even labourers.

The castle of 'Akkar in Lebanon, known to the Crusaders as Gibelcar, defied the First Crusade on its march south to Jerusalem. It fell later and became an important outpost in the County of Tripoli. Like many 12th-century Crusader castles, it relied on an exceptionally rugged location rather than on its walls and a small keep, neither of which were particularly strong or sophisticated. Here the lower or northern end of the fortifications overlooks the 'Akkar river. (D. Nicolle)

It has sometimes been suggested that the adoption of round towers in the early 13th century reflected Armenian influence. Yet influences flowed in several directions and while there was Armenian impact on castles in the Principality of Antioch, there was comparable Crusader influence upon Armenian fortifications in neighbouring Cilicia. Elsewhere in the Kingdom of Cilician Armenia, the large castle of Silifke was largely built by or for the Hospitallers, who also rebuilt Toprakkale (Tal Hamdun), where a Mamluk castle later largely replaced the Hospitaller one. The Templars built a castle at Amoude, were largely responsible for a castle at Trapesac, and made minor alterations to the existing Islamic castle at Haruniya; all of which were at various times within the Armenian kingdom. However, these tended to be different from one another, again reflecting the primacy of local considerations.

Islamic influence is more obvious, though the identity of those responsible for a specific structure can remain problematic. For example, the castle of Belfort (Shaqif Arnun) overlooking the western side of the Litani gorge in southern Lebanon began as a simple 12th-century tower-keep, approximately 12m square. Later additions included a vaulted hall and a broad enclosed area with rounded towers. A rock-cut fosse contained cisterns and during the 13th century further outworks strengthened the southern side of Belfort. This resulted in a barbican in the upper ward dominating the lower ward. A new chapel was added and eventually both wards were almost filled with vaulted structures. However, archaeological work has shown that by the time the Crusaders finally lost the castle of Belfort, it already included a hexagonal tower added by the Ayyubids during their previous domination of the site. Much of the outer works and the entrance ramp is now lost. However, relics of a vast strengthening programme carried out by the Mamluks during the second half of the 13th century remain.

There were as yet no European parallels for the cramped, box-type machicolations seen at Crac des Chevaliers, though these did exist in the Islamic citadels of Aleppo, Damascus and elsewhere. In fact, the similarities are so striking that the same stonemasons might have been employed by both Muslims and Christians. Some doubts have been raised about the windmill on a tower at Crac des Chevaliers, though the evidence is strong. Windmills originated in Iran and spread to Europe during the Middle Ages, so perhaps Crusader castles like Crac des Chevaliers played a part in this process of technological transfer.

Opposite: The upper part of the main entrance ramp of the castle of Crac des Chevaliers (Hisn al-Akrad), after the abrupt dog-leg turn, had embrasures on one side which meant that it could also serve as a defensive gallery. (D. Nicolle)

METHODS OF CONSTRUCTION

Until recently little research had been done on the techniques, materials, sources of timber and stone, and material transportation methods used in the construction of Crusader fortifications. Even less research had been undertaken into how fortifications were demolished or how materials from razed castles were reused. It is unclear how early settlers from different countries enagaged their different traditions and experience in the building of castles, or to what extent they employed local labourers, skilled personel and architects. It is worth noting that several ancient building techniques were still in use in this part of the Middle East at the time of the Crusades.

Three basic stones were available: hard limestone, softer limestone and very hard volcanic basalt. Each had their characteristics and limitations. Normally Middle Eastern builders used what was locally available, stone only being transported long distances for a specific structural reason or for aesthetic considerations. Ablaq, the mixing of creamy white limestone and the darkest basalt, was a traditional form of decoration in Bilad al-Sham, the geographical and cultural area of Greater Syria.

The remaining lower parts of the south-western tower of the outer wall of the Hospitaller castle of Belvoir (Kawkab al-Hawa). Note that the sloping talus against the western wall (left) does not continue as far as the base of the tower itself, because there is a small postern gate hidden in the shadow at this point. (D. Nicolle)

THE BUILDING OF THE CASTLE OF BETHGIBELIN, 1136

Archaeological research has confirmed that the early Crusader castle of Bethgibelin (Bayt Jibrin) was built in two main stages, the most important work being done in 1136. The first builders naturally made use of surviving walls and foundations from part of an ancient Romano-Byzantine fortified city, but also added new walls (as the Crusader castle covered only part of the old city). The strongest or central part of the castle consisted of an inner ward based upon the ruins of another existing structure, this time an early Islamic so-called 'palace' or perhaps administrative centre dating from the Umayyad period. The second stage of Crusader building saw the construction of outer walls and a fosse that enclosed a significantly larger area. The result was, by accident or design,

a very early example of what became known as a concentric castle. Medieval building techniques and tools are illustrated in great detail in many manuscripts. They include wheelbarrows supported by a sturdy strap across the labourer's shoulders, hods, pallets, cold-chisels, special axes for smoothing stone and masonry hammers. Walls were kept vertical and level with plumb-lines and spirit-levels (which incorporated small plumb-lines rather than the 'bubble in a curved glass tube' used in modern examples). The items illustrated here are largely based on early 13th-century sources. The crane is powered by what was called a 'squirrel's cage', a surviving medieval example having been found in Beauvais Cathedral in France. (Adam Hook © Osprey Publishing)

Naturally the builders of castles, and those who paid the costs, tried to obtain suitable masonry from a local quarry or from the construction site itself. In the latter case, rock excavated from a man-made fosse or ditch could be used for the walls above. An estimated 17,000 tons of rock were, for example, removed to create the fosse at Saone. Similarly, rock from an underground water-storage cistern beneath a castle or its courtyard might be used to build a tower above.

In naturally defensible sites such as hilltop or spur-castles, masons often shaped the rock to provide the walls with a firm footing. On other occasions they laid a shaped cement bedding. Considerable attention was given to providing good drainage systems to protect the foot of a wall and to collect drinking water. Existing rock formations could be used, or improved and then used, as buttresses. Other cracks or gaps in the rock might be integrated into the design, sometimes as a starting point for further excavation.

Though local stone was preferred for the bulk of a fortified structure, this was not always possible. Some local materials were unsuitable, at least for load-bearing parts of a building, and fine stone could be transported over substantial distances for structural or decorative purposes. The chapel at Belvoir (Kawkab al-Hawa) is largely of fine stone whereas the rest of the castle is almost entirely of roughly hewn basalt from the surrounding ditch. Basalt, being extremely hard, is difficult to cut into complex shapes.

Most research attention has focused on the finely built castles of the central and northern regions of the Crusader States. However, many other fortifications were erected with remarkable speed and little apparent expense. The most obvious examples are those in the virtually autonomous province of Oultrejourdain: al-Salt, Karak, Tafila, Montréal, Hormuz, Celle, Le Vaux Moise (al-Wu'aira) and Ayla (now believed to be on the Egyptian Sinai island of Jazirat Fara'un). This line of castles was built with limited money and labour, using rubble, ancient Nabatean masonry and a minimal amount of newly dressed stone. Refinement, it seems, was not considered necessary whereas the provision of reliable sources of water was much more significant. The reuse of existing materials from destroyed buildings was widespread: the insertion of antique columns as a form of horizontal bonding, noted previously, was already a characteristic of Islamic fortifications. The Crusader attitude to such matters was summed up by the chronicler William of Tyre when he described the building of Ibelin (Yibna) in 1144: 'First of all they laid the foundations, then they made four towers. Stones were to be found in sufficiency in those places where there had formerly been fortresses for, as they say, "A castle destroyed is a castle half remade."'

Middle Eastern architects traditionally tried to link stones together where the masonry supported vertical loads or the sideways stresses of arches. Otherwise, the use of dry-stone ashlar or finely cut blocks of stone without mortar continued until modern times. A less visible technique was the laying of horizontal ashlar across a wall, through a rubble core, to bind the entire structure together.

Some historians have pointed to the massive size of the blocks occasionally used in Crusader castles. This scale, however, was little different from what was being used on the Islamic side of the frontier. Furthermore, care must be taken with the idea that masonry with different surface finishes can distinguish Crusader and Islamic workmanship. Both used a variety of picks, hammers, cold-chisels and axes with heavy, thick heads, sometimes with a straight edge, sometimes with a notched edge. Each gave a different surface effect, especially on easily worked limestone. However, Denys Pringle looked at the question in greater detail and wrote that ashlar bearing both diagonal dressing and masonry marks can almost always be attributed to the

The citadel of the castle of Gibelet (Jubayl) consists of a four-sided enclosure with corner towers and a separate keep in the centre. It was initially built by the Crusaders early in the 12th century and although changes were made in the 13th century the overall character of Gibelet's fortifications remains simple. (D. Pringle)

Crusader period while diagonal tooling and certain types of masonry marks are also found, though not together, on buildings of the Islamic Ayyubid period.

So many variations were involved in the buildings that it is difficult to distinguish Crusader and Islamic work. However, one idea that does seem to have spread from east to west was the use of embossed masonry. This had been known in the Middle East since ancient times but did not appear in Western Europe – with the possible exception of Alsace – before the 13th century. It offered additional protection against missiles, since the bosses ensured that mangonel balls rarely struck a wall square but normally hit a glancing blow. Their appearance at Acre and Tyre at the start of the 13th century might be further evidence for the increasing importance of large trebuchets in siege warfare.

Where architects did not rely on dry-stone construction, various materials were used to tie the masonry together. The most common were various forms of mortar and cement, but other methods were also seen. For example, bitumen or petroleum

The Israeli archaeologists who excavated the unfinished 12th-century Crusader castle of Vadum Jacob (Jisr Ya'kub) found a number of mysteries. One was this as yet unexplained massive stone platform with carefully constructed hollow chambers beneath. Perhaps it was part of the pre-Crusader, Islamic sacred site whose conversion into a fortress so incensed Saladin. (D. Nicolle)

tar comparable to that used to make modern roads was used to bind stones taken from an Islamic cemetery to make the Mahommeries Tower during the First Crusade's siege of Antioch. This apparently inflammable construction method was, in fact, more characteristic of medieval Iraq than Syria. On other occasions the laying of stone walls involved the use of metal tenons, cramps or pins, sometimes bedded in lead, a construction technique stretching back to the time of the ancient Greeks. It certainly made the resulting structure difficult to demolish, and there were references to its use in the Tower of David in Jerusalem, as well as in the fortifications of Maraclea, Sidon and Beirut. Perhaps it is worth noting that, with the exception of Jerusalem, all these sites are on the Mediterranean coast, the most Greek-influenced part of Greater Syria.

Recent excavations at the site of the unfinished castle of Vadum Jacob have shed remarkable light on how a 12th-century Crusader fortress was built. First the foundations were dug and the waste removed. Only then did building begin. Work actually started, in violation of an agreement with Saladin, about half a year before Saladin attacked the site. What happened next was described by Saladin's secretary, the Qadi al-Fadl:

The width of the wall surpassed ten cubits [about 5m]. It was built of stones of enormous size of which each block was seven cubits, more or less. The number of these dressed stones exceeded 20,000 and each stone, put in place and sealed into the masonry, cost not less than four dinars [high-value Islamic coinage] and even more. Between the two walls extended a line of massive blocks raised up to the proud summit of the mountains. The lime which was poured around the stone in order to seal it was mixed and incorporated into it, giving it a strength and solidity superior to the stone itself, and frustrating with more success than that of metal all attempts to destroy it.

The Hospitaller Convent or headquarters in Acre, sometimes called the Citadel, was built on and around earlier structures. These included some Fatimid fortifications, probably dating from the 11th century. Here the Islamic walls can still be seen inside the more massive western wall of the Hospitaller fortification. (D. Nicolle)

The Qadi and other sources indicate that the site was well stocked with food, and the construction of a citadel was planned over a large water cistern. Many men were, in fact, still working on Vadum Jacob when Saladin attacked, including a hundred Muslim slaves and many horses. Islamic accounts of the resulting siege state that the Crusader defenders lit fires behind the unfinished gates as a defence against sudden assault. In fact, so much wood was piled up against the interior of the walls that the resulting fires caused the partially completed wall to crumble.

Archaeological evidence confirms several details of this attack. At the time Vadum Jacob consisted of half-finished walls and incomplete vaults, probably with wooden scaffolding in place. There were also several temporary walls, as well as piles of mortar and lime, dressed stones and earth ramps in various places. Around the walls were tracks hardened with layers of plaster where ox-carts could haul stone from a nearby quarry. Stone troughs to feed and water the oxen were placed alongside these tracks. There were earth ramps on both sides of the walls as well as large numbers of tools lying around. These included axes and chisels for cutting stone, spades, hoes, and spatulas for laying mortar and plaster. Inside one of the gates was a pile of lime with tools still embedded in it, as well as iron hubs that may have belonged to a wooden cart. Hundreds of arrowheads were found amongst these tools, showing that the defenders suffered hails of arrows.

On the northern, western and eastern sides of the site were small gates with stepped entrances, boltholes and beam channels for doors. Their purpose remains a mystery, since they opened inwards and would have been vulnerable to a battering ram. Perhaps they were intended for towers that had not yet been started. An artificial slope made of layers of rubble and soil probably taken from the interior of the fortress was piled against the sides of the castle wall. This slope was levelled and included several hard layers of lime. Oxen presumably hauled stones across this reinforced surface to the base of the wall from where the stones were lifted into position. Perhaps the builders intended to leave the material of the outer slopes as the basis of a later talus, or it could have been intended to raise the level of a proposed outer bailey. Material piled against the inner side of the walls raised the ground level during construction, thus minimizing the use of scarce timber for scaffolding, though scaffolding remained necessary higher up. Timber formers were similarly needed during the constructing of barrel vaults, which were initially laid upon a half-wheel framework set into holes in the upper parts of the wall.

Construction techniques inevitably differed according to the nature of the terrain, and archaeological excavations show some unusual variations. For example, when the Crusaders refortified Ascalon ('Asqalan) they built thick walls with narrow courses of dressed ashlar around a poured concrete core with through columns. These were raised on a sloping artificial mound, largely of sand, and rising to a height of up to 10m with horizontal offsets at approximately 1m or 2m intervals. The mound was then lined with stone to form a glacis.

More detailed information about 13th-century construction techniques was uncovered at the so-called Courthouse site in Acre, which exposed part of the Crusader city's outer wall, a tower and part of the moat with a masonry counterscarp. The tower was made of ashlar, pieces of which featured traces of plaster, suggesting they had previously been used elsewhere. The outer ashlar was finely finished and was laid in mortar 3cm thick. But the ashlar stones of the inner face were not so well dressed, with smaller stones being added to level the courses or fill gaps. This inner face was then plastered. The core of the wall was almost 2m thick, consisting of concrete into which rough 'field' stones and dressed stones were irregularly set. Evidence from other Crusader sites indicates that such inner cores were not just dumped inside the outer facings. In many cases they were carefully made and proved just as strong as the regular facings. The city wall of Acre, as exposed at the Courthouse site, was about 3m thick at its base, tapering slightly as it rose. It was laid upon bedrock, which is today not only below the water table but below the current sea level. However, the sea level has changed since the 13th century. The lower three courses were of large dressed stones, and a vertical seam, which does not continue in the higher courses, shows that the planners decided to enlarge the tower after work had already begun. The bottom of the moat corresponded to the third course of stones, and above these foundations the upper part of the wall was built of smooth ashlar.

MASONS & ENGIGNEORS

Skilled masons in the Crusader States included Greeks, Armenians, Syrian Christians and Western Europeans. Given the importance of such men and the vital need for fortifications one would assume that they would be well treated. This was not always the case, however. According to one chronicler, Michael the Syrian, Count Baldwin II

The French King Louis VII offered to pay for the construction of the refectory in the Hospitallers' main Convent or headquarters at Acre. This fact may account for the presence of at least two carved fleurs-de-lys, the French royal coat-of-arms, in the otherwise undecorated Convent hall. (D. Nicolle)

of Edessa began reconstructing the walls of Kesoun shortly before his death, but treated his workers so badly that the work was delayed and, indeed, remained unfinished. The numerous slaves and prisoners of war who were employed in the construction of Crusader fortifications could not expect good treatment and are unlikely to have been entrusted with skilled work.

Meanwhile, documentary sources shed an interesting light on the men who actually designed or supervised the construction of Crusader fortifications – the *engigneors*. These men were not merely military engineers, but were often multi-talented individuals with numerous different skills. They could have high status, though not members of the aristocratic elite, and appear to have been recruited from various ethnic groups, including Greeks, Armenians and Jews and Western Europeans.

Other specialists included men whose task was to feed and clothe the people on the building site. In addition to those involved in building work, soldiers defended the place and the resulting numbers could run into the tens of thousands. Perhaps because some projects were now so huge, these numbers had increased during the early 13th century, resulting in the effective conscription of some local populations who were then organized into what was almost an army of militarized artisan-soldiers. Prisoners of war could also be used as slave labour, but they required close supervision and were not entrusted with responsible tasks.

THE PRINCIPLES OF DEFENCE

The first line of defence for a castle or fortified city under siege was a ditch. These moats or fosses ranged from a shallow excavation, sometimes down to sea level where the fortification was on the coast, to a huge gash cut across the spur of a hill or mountain. The Crusader States seem to have taken the existing Byzantine and Islamic concept of a rock-cut ditch to much greater depths and widths.

Beyond the ditch would be one or more walls strengthened by towers. During the 12th century many such defensive circuits were built with dimensions very similar to those used in the late Roman fortification of Syria. These remained the norm during the early Islamic period when advances in siege technology largely focused on anti-personnel weapons rather than machines to destroy walls or towers. Even the adoption of beam-sling stone-throwing manjaniqs or mangonels had more impact on the uppermost parts of a fortification whose function was to protect the soldiers manning the walls, rather than on the main structure of a wall or tower. As a result towers still averaged around 5–6m in width and projected 3.5–4m ahead of a curtain-wall. As in late Roman fortifications, towers were normally placed at approximately 30m intervals, which was suitable for providing enfilading fire by archers and crossbowmen. Small towers of this type were also adequate for accommodating early forms of man-powered stone-throwing mangonels. Most urban defensive walls in the Crusader States were strengthened by rectangular towers, though rounded towers were occasionally seen, as were a few pointed or triangular towers.

The primary defensive focus was still on gates, though these were rarely attacked, presumably because their defences were so effective. Such gates could incorporate a portcullis of iron or timber and iron, which was raised and lowered along grooves in the side walls, as well as a drawbridge that was normally raised by chains. Interestingly enough, the portcullis does not seem to have been favoured by Byzantine and Islamic military architects, even though it had been used by the Romans. Further protection was provided by panels in the gates, and embrasures in the side walls and roofs of gateways through which archers or crossbowmen could shoot at the enemy. During the 12th century, the gates of Crusader-ruled cities were either flanked by towers or went beneath large towers or bastions. Posterns or postern gates were smaller openings in the outer defences. Their primary purpose was to enable defenders to attack the flanks of any enemy troops that came too close to the walls. They would presumably also enable messengers to come and go in relative secrecy, as well as permitting small numbers of fugitives or relieving troops to enter a fortress.

The castle of Ravendel (Ravanda) was a typical hilltop fortress. In such a location the defenders relied as much on the length and height of the slope as on its steepness. Early stone-throwing mangonels could not reach such a range and any troops assaulting the walls would have needed a secure jumping off point near the summit. (D. Nicolle)

At this stage, stone-throwing mangonels were more effective in defensive than offensive siege warfare. However, the late 12th century saw early forms of counterweight mangonel enter more widespread use. The earliest clear account of such a weapon, in a book written for Saladin by Murda al-Tarsusi, stated that it needed a hole or trench through which its counterweight could swing. This problem was later overcome by raising the height of the frame. However, an otherwise unexplained trench still exists in the summit of the largest tower of the French castle of Bressuire, which probably dates from the late 12th or early 13th century – after the Plantagenet ruler of south-western France, King Richard the Lionhearted of England, had returned from Crusade.

Apart from stone-throwing machines, the main form of active defence in Crusader castles was archery. The latter included not only hand-drawn bows, mostly of composite construction like those used by neighbouring Islamic and Byzantine armies, but also crossbows. The effectiveness of defensive archery, if the fortifications had an adequate garrison, could be impressive. The chronicler Baha al-Din said that the Hospitaller castle of Belvoir was so actively defended that no Muslim besieger could 'appear at the entrance of his tent without putting on his armour.'

Archery was usually employed from the tops of the walls and towers that were crenellated, sometimes with pierced stone merlons through which an archer or crossbowman could shoot in relative safety. Other embrasures in the sides of walls and towers offered even better protection, though their arcs of fire were necessarily limited. Stone machicolations enabled defenders to shoot vertically upon an enemy or drop rocks, heated sand or boiling water upon him. Heated oil and pitch were useful weapons against enemy siege

At least two stages in the construction of Krak des Moabites (al-Karak) castle are seen here. In the foreground are the remains of the walls and towers built during the Second Crusader phase around 1168. Beyond and below it is a massive barbican dating from the Mamluk era in the later 13th and 14th centuries. (D. Nicolle)

machines made of wood, since they could be ignited by a burning brand or a fire-arrow. The simple stone corbels still visible at Saone and elsewhere show that some form of machicolation was used by Crusader architects in the 12th century. The structures supported by these corbels were probably of stone, though wooden hoardings (brattices) may have been possible. At Crac des Chevaliers the only square tower to survive in its original 12th-century form has three arched slot machicolations, above which lies a line of small openings that probably gave access to a projecting machicolation added during the 13th century. A slot machicolation consisted of a broad groove down the face of a tower or wall, instead of a stone projection supported by corbels. It is also interesting to note that slot machicolations are seen at Château Gaillard in Normandy, built by King Richard I after he returned from Crusade.

Many fortified walls and towers were provided with an additional defence against enemy mining: the talus. This sloping base increased the thickness of the structure but was not itself a load-bearing part of the wall or tower. Since 12th-century siege

At al-Wu'aira the builders of the castle which the Crusaders knew as Le Vaux Moise used the natural location to maximize the site's defensive potential. Here, on the eastern site of the castle, one of the remaining towers and a crumbling stretch of curtain wall overlook the near vertical gorge of the Wadi al-Wu'aira. (D. Nicolle)

mining still focused on attacking the base of a wall rather than sinking a mine and tunnelling beneath the fortifications, a talus served as an additional time-consuming obstacle whose collapse did not threaten the stability of the primary structure. The construction of double walls provided further obstruction to a besieger's progress, while also forming a 'killing zone' between the two walls until such time as the enemy took full possession of the outer defences. The inner wall and towers were built to a greater height than the outer ones, so that men on the inner defences could shoot over the outer wall and retained a height advantage if the outer wall was lost. Finally, the siting of the inner towers was usually such that they overlooked part of the outer wall between two of the latter's towers to provide a clear field of fire.

STRATEGIC CHANGES

The 13th century was not only a period of revolutionary change in the design of Crusader fortifications, but also in strategic priorities. The main efforts were now focused upon the protection of people rather than territory and in some places the numbers to be defended were very high. Acre was the biggest city, but Crusader-ruled Antioch still had a population of around 100,000 people,

FORTIFICATIONS OF THE CRUSADER STATES OF THE MIDDLE EAST, C. 1241

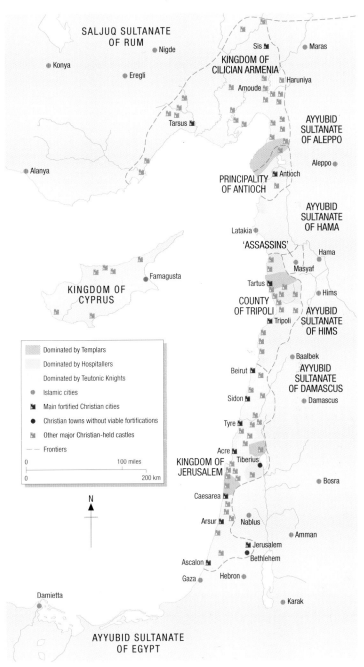

mostly Greeks and other non-Catholic Christians. Another feature of this period was the growth of suburbs next to major fortresses, mostly defended by a single wall. Crusader-held territory now consisted of parts of the eastern Mediterranean coast with the sea to the west and hills or mountains to the east. This strip had, in fact, been cut in two by Saladin's reconquest of some of the coast north of Latakia. Some castles were sited to cover the few east–west routes through which Islamic armies might enter Crusader territory, but it was just as important to locate fortifications on the coast, to hinder movement by invaders who reached it. Furthermore, the Crusader States were now entirely dependent upon contact with, and support from, Europe.

The protection of ports and harbours was thus essential. By the 13th century, European fleets dominated the Mediterranean, and without them the Crusader States could not have survived as long as they did. Nevertheless, this domination was not complete and the Mamluks made several efforts to revive the Egyptian navy. Meanwhile, smaller Turkish fleets based along what are now the Mediterreanean and Aegean coasts of Turkey grew increasingly daring.

The perennial problem of ensuring reliable supplies of drinking water resulted in extraordinary care being taken in the fortified Hospitaller headquarters in Acre, with every drop of rain from the wet season being stored. This was not only for drinking but also for hygiene, such as the flushing of the communal toilets; the two parallel water systems were kept scrupulously separate. However, Islamic architects always demonstrated a little more sophistication in such matters, and in many fortifications the most impressive water storage cisterns date from Mamluk rebuilding rather than from the Crusader period. One example is in the castle at Safad where a circular large cistern, excavated from rock then covered by a masonry dome, lay beneath the great Mamluk tower at the southern part of the site.

The Crusader States' shortage of military manpower was also growing more acute. Architectural and engineering skills could help greatly, but could not solve this problem definitively; as a result, most 13th-century Crusader fortifications were designed for small garrisons. Large garrisons existed, though rarely, and they were usually mustered for offensive purposes. In fact, many Crusader castles were gravely undermanned when the final crisis came. Belfort is said to have had 22 knights and 400 other men when it was besieged by a Mamluk army in 1268. Even so, the Mamluk sultan Baybars still felt the need to bring 28 powerful siege machines against it.

Whether a reliance on fortification made the Crusader States vulnerable to the Mamluks' highly developed forms of psychological warfare seems doubtful. This interpretation of events probably reflects the attitudes of 19th- and 20th-century military historians rather than the realities of 13th-century Middle Eastern warfare. Another myth concerns a supposed system of visible communication between Crusader castles. According to this theory, those in Cilicia formed part of an elaborate network. Yet most were not in actual or useful line-of-sight with each other and the Crusader States' hypothetical chain of signal beacons probably never existed. The good visibility enjoyed by such garrisons stemmed from the fact that they were stationed on hilltops for defensive reasons, not for communication.

Height was always sought after, although the emphasis on defending the weakest slope meant that the strongest part of a fortification was not necessarily at its highest point. On the other hand, locating a castle on a high place often limited its internal space. Haruniya, for example, was given to the Teutonic Knights in 1236. Here a largely 10th-century Islamic fort was in the hands of a Latin lord by the late 12th century. It consisted of a cramped central courtyard within a shell keep with two floors of shooting galleries and a rounded tower. The Teutonic Knights probably repaired the tower and perhaps used it as a chapel, but did little else. The northern Lebanese castle of Gibelcar was similarly cramped and rudimentary. Yet the site is so inaccessible that Sultan Baybars found it as difficult to take as the far larger and more sophisticated castle at Crac des Chevaliers. In the event Baybars' sense of achievement when Gibelcar finally fell is reflected in a letter he wrote to Prince Bohemond VI of Antioch: 'We have transported the mangonels there through mountains where the birds think it too difficult to nest; how patiently we have hauled them, troubled by mud and struggling against rain.'

The top of a rock-cut cistern next to the fortified manor house at Khirbat Rushmiyah, on Mount Carmel above Haifa. The carefully carved edge of the opening shows that it was designed to have a lid, perhaps of wood or stone. The chamber inside expands into a sort of large bottle shape. (D. Nicolle)

The castle of Ravendel (Ravanda) was a significant defence in the northern part of the Crusader County of Edessa. Though it was considerably strengthened in the 13th century, the main layout seems to date from the 12th century. Here two ruined towers can be seen, while the slope between them marks the position of the outer curtain wall. The site has not been excavated by archaeologists and so the internal structures and much of the wall are buried beneath debris. (D. Nicolle)

TACTICAL ARRANGEMENTS

The citadels that defended a town or served as places of refuge for the inhabitants faced different problems. They were almost always easier to access than mountaintop or spur-castles and could be vulnerable to attack from within the town if it fell to an enemy. In fact urban areas often provided good positions for mangonels to hurl stones against a citadel. A different problem was caused if a suburb extended around or beyond the citadel, leaving the latter as a fortified enclave within the urban area. This happened at Acre, where the Castle of the King's Constable and the Convent of the Hospitallers lost much of their original value following the fortification of Montmussard.

Crusader urban defences usually had an outer ditch, often with a counterscarp wall. In many places all or part of the city wall was revetted with a sloping talus. Outer walls and barbicans were not universal in the Crusader States and do not seem to have been used in Western Europe before the 13th century. In most places the walls themselves consisted of the previous Islamic defences, more or less improved, as was the case at Arsuf, though here the existing city walls were considerably strengthened. The main changes were usually the addition of larger towers along the curtain-wall, and occasionally the building of a second wall. At Acre the resulting

THE ENTRANCE COMPLEX OF CRAC DES CHEVALIERS, MID 13TH CENTURY

Some of the smaller or less important Crusader castles had small resident garrisons, and in some cases no permanent garrisons at all. However, major fortified locations like Crac des Chevaliers housed a considerable number of people and animals, and this number could reach a remarkable level in times of crisis. Consequently even Crac des Chevaliers could get crowded. Small postern gates in the outer walls of such castles were not normally used for entry and exit, so at Crac des Chevaliers everything had to use the main east gate. Behind this was a long, covered, dog-leg entrance ramp (shown here) leading to the centre of the castle. It also went past what are believed to have been the main stables. Here, two war-horses are being brought out of the inner stables by their grooms; having been inside the stables for some time, one of the horses has reared up, as its owner watches, to the right. Behind the horse, a column of baggage donkeys coming down the exit ramp with their handlers has been held up by the commotion. (Adam Hook © Osprey Publishing)

defences were particularly impressive, so much so that during the final siege of 1291, the Mamluk army needed a massive and prolonged bombardment using a very large number of the most powerful trebuchets before they could break into the city.

These new-style towers were much more formidable than those built in the 12th century, clearly impressing pilgrims like Wilbrand von Oldenburg, who visited Acre in 1212:

> This is a fine and strong city situated on the seashore in such a way that, while it is quadrangular in shape, two of its sides forming an angle are girdled and protected by the sea. The other two are encompassed by a fine, wide and deep ditch, stone lined to the very bottom, and by a double wall fortified with towers according to a fine arrangement, in such a way that the first wall with its towers does not overtop the main (second) wall and is commanded and defended by the second and inner wall, the towers of which are tall and very strong.

This arrangement meant that arrows shot from the inner wall could be aimed over the outer wall, which was about one-third lower than the inner. The towers were also staggered so that those in front did not obstruct archers in the rear towers.

Although the Crusader military architects who designed the new fortifications of the town of Arsus (Arsuf) followed the lines of the existing Islamic defences, they added several stronger walls and towers. Here the lower part of the south-eastern corner tower has been excavated, along with part of the moat and a retaining wall on the far right. (D. Nicolle)

The great castle of Crac des Chevaliers was similarly ringed by an outer wall, which is generally believed to date from the early 13th century. The normal interpretation of Crac des Chevaliers' fortification maintains that the inner defences were strengthened after this outer wall was added, while the southern side of the castle was given massive new-style towers around this time, almost certainly serving as artillery emplacements.

The defences of Atlit castle were similarly designed with defensive artillery in mind. Here three rectangular gate towers were placed approximately 44m apart. They had two floors and were surmounted by a platform enclosed by a parapet. All three projected about 12m from the curtain-wall. Behind them was an inner wall with two huge towers approximately 28m long by 18m deep, both of which were originally over 34m high. Their great size and height reflected their role as artillery bastions to bombard enemy artillery, or at least keep it at a reasonable distance.

The greatly increased number of archery embrasures, niches, machicolations and other wall features indicated that crossbows played a very significant role in the defence of 13th-century Crusader fortifications. Some sources refer to 'underground vaults' where 'great-crossbows' could be sited; these were found in Louis IX's city walls of Caesarea, probably in the citadel of Arsuf, and perhaps forming a continuous

1 – Caesarea Maritima: (1) north gate, (2) east gate, (3) sea gate, (4) excavated Crusader building, (5) excavated Crusader houses, (6) Cathedral of St Peter, (7) port, (8) citadel (after Benvenisti and Kaufmann). 2 – Atlit: (1) inner ward of the citadel, (2) harbour, (3) north great tower, (4) south great tower, (5) outer wall, (6) north beach gate, (7) south beach gate, (8) urban fortified wall, (9) baths, (10) faubourg, or town, (11) unfinished church, (12) stables (after Johns and Pringle). 3 – Section through the citadel of Atlit (surviving structures are shown in black): (1) north-west tower, (2) north-west hall, (3) west undercroft, (4) inner ward, (5) east quarters, (6) north gate tower, (7) east bailey, (8) outer wall, (9) fosse (after Pringle).

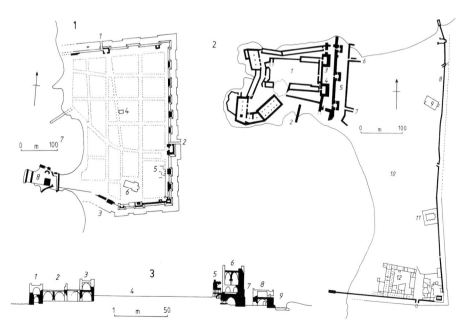

line of niched embrasures in curtain-walls and towers. It is also interesting to note the similarity in some details of design and construction, which almost suggest a conscious programme of refortification in the mid 13th-century Kingdom of Jerusalem.

Comparable details are found in Crac des Chevaliers, where the outer wall and towers had archery slits to minimize the area of dead ground. These were staggered to avoid weakening the wall and to enable archers to command the area in front of the walls. Similarly a stone-vaulted *chemin de ronde* gave access to box machicolations. However, the cramped interiors of these machicolations meant that crossbowmen squatted or knelt to shoot. The entrance to Crac des Chevaliers was greatly strengthened, resulting in a highly developed bent entrance system, the whole length of which had 'murder holes' overlooking it. Although Crac des Chevaliers was a large castle, the space between its inner and outer walls remained so narrow that it could not be used as an outer bailey. The vulnerable south-eastern side of this gap consisted of an open water tank fed by an aqueduct from the neighbouring hill, both as a water supply

The Tower of Flies once guarded the entrance to the outer harbour of Acre. A mole may originally have enclosed the southern side of this harbour, extending from the base of the tower to the seaward end of the inner eastern wall of the city. (D. Nicolle)

and perhaps to inhibit mining. The massive inner walls followed those of the 12th-century castle, but were built slightly outside the earlier fortification, leaving a narrow passage that was developed as a shooting gallery on the western and southern sides. The southern and western walls were the most impressive, rising from a sloping glacis from which huge round towers emerged. There was even a shooting chamber within some parts of this glacis. Unfortunately, most of the wall-head defences have gone, though traces along the southern wall show no machicolations. Instead there were arrow slits and larger rectangular openings, perhaps for great-crossbows or espringals.

The design of the walls of Acre meant that any part of the curtain-wall that was breached was still covered by crossbowmen in the neighbouring towers. Considerable emphasis was also placed on the fortification of gates; so much so that these were rarely attacked. They could include a drawbridge, portcullis and panels in the doors, plus embrasures to increase the number of shooting positions within the gateway. Limitations of space may have been why bent-gates were not always employed. At Atlit the three gate towers had straight-through entrances, two with a portcullis and one possibly having a slit machicolation. In contrast, two of the three gates at Caesarea (al-Qaisariyah) were certainly bent. Each had a slit machicolation and a portcullis protecting the doors while the inner doors were defended by a slit machicolation. Most town gates, however strongly fortified, were less complicated than those of castles or citadels. The latter tended to have adjacent towers while access to the interior was usually via one or more right-angle bends, often through gate chambers that could be sealed off by the defenders.

Postern gates allowed sorties by the defenders if any attackers came too close. One of the last Hospitaller constructions at Crac des Chevaliers was a postern, built between 1254 and 1269. It had a tower on each side plus a portcullis and probably machicolations. The small castle of Cursat (Qusair) may have included an unusual postern, which seems to have been associated with a cistern, several underground apartments and a vertical shaft cut into the rock. This led from a subterranean complex in the eastern part of the castle, down to a lower chamber at the level of the base of the ramparts. The associated masonry probably dates from the late 12th or early 13th century and the vertical shaft may have been excavated after an upper firing platform was already in place. Perhaps archers climbed down the shaft to cover a small postern gate. Elsewhere some posterns opened several metres above the base of the wall, and were only reached by ropes or a ladder.

The complex at Cursat apparently made use of an existing crack in the rock that was subsequently enlarged; Crusader military architects often made use of available natural features. On the coast these included the sea itself. At Atlit a small promontory was cut by a moat, and although the available technology did not permit the excavation of deep sea-filled moats, the rock could be cut away to just below sea level. Since then, however, part of the coast has sunk, leaving some 'sea moats' deeper than they were in the Middle Ages.

The few safe harbours along the coast were vital for the survival of the Crusader States, and so were given special attention. Most consisted of small bays, sometimes sheltered by reefs or rocks. Man-made harbours (moles) existed at Acre, Arsuf, Atlit, Caesarea, Beirut, Sidon and Tyre in the Kingdom of Jerusalem, while others served the County of Tripoli and the Principality of Antioch. In several places towers stood at the ends of moles, one such being the Tower of Flies at Acre. This was garrisoned by guards who checked the identities of ships, the arrival of which was indicated by the tolling of a bell, perhaps in this tower. Towers could also be armed with anti-shipping siege machines, which threatened to sink vessels that attacked the boom. Other towers served as anchor points for chains or booms to close a harbour entrance, like the floating wooden 'chain' constructed across Acre harbour by the Genoese during their quarrel with the Venetians in 1258.

Harbours were themselves usually separated from a town by a wall. However, quays were rare and small boats usually carried goods between the beach and ships moored in the harbour. Elsewhere, Jaffa had a very exposed port, which had been refortified by the early Crusaders. It was strengthened during the following century, but still fell to the Mamluks in 1268. The Citadel of Arsuf is sometimes said to tower above a small harbour enclosed by two moles and a breakwater. However, the area in question may actually have been just above water during the Crusader occupation. So perhaps the moles and breakwater enclosed a flat area of flimsy buildings serving as a sort of foreshore beneath the castle and city.

TOUR OF THE CASTLES

Given the wide variation in Crusader fortifications, no single example can be described as typical. A selection of ten castles has been made here: Ravendel (Ravanda), Saone, Gibelcar, Belvoir, Le Vaux Moise, Margat (al-Marqab), Crac de Chevaliers, Atlit, Caesarea Maritima and Arsus (Arsuf).

RAVENDEL

Ravendel castle was described by the Arab geographer Ibn Adim of Aleppo in the first half of the 13th century, after it had returned to Islamic rule. By then the castle had been repaired and strengthened but not greatly altered: 'It is a small castle on the top of a high hill, isolated in its situation. Neither mangonels nor arrows can reach it.' Ibn Adim had, in fact, highlighted the importance of location for this sort of relatively small castle in which a garrison could defy an enemy equipped with still primitive stone-throwing engines. Ibn Adim continued: 'It is one of the strongest castles, and most favoured spots. A valley runs north and west of the castle, like a fosse. It contains a permanent river.' Just as the author did in the early 1970s, the chronicler from Aleppo found the ascent far from easy: 'I made it up to the castle on horseback, but experienced great difficulty owing to its height, and the narrowness of the track to it.' The castle has a single curtain-wall on top of a long, steep slope. A short section of wall is doubled to form an angled rather than bent gate, to foil a battering ram. Some lower parts of the main wall and gate are made of irregular blocks of basalt with large spaces filled with mortar, while the upper parts are of neat ashlar. In addition to arrow slits there are still corbels, which once supported a brattice or machicolation above the gate.

The outer wall includes four rectangular towers, which project quite a way from the wall, and four rounded towers that do not protrude so far, plus a substantial polygonal tower next to the entrance. Inside the outer wall there is a large open area or enceinte around the remains of a much smaller inner wall with small rounded towers or salients that only project a short distance. Part of this inner fortification may date from the Byzantine or earlier Islamic periods. Within the inner wall are two cisterns while a third cistern is next to the main entrance.

This needle of rock was left in place when the Crusaders, or more likely the slaves and prisoners of war they obliged to work for them, excavated the remarkable fosse at Saone (Sahyun). The fosse separated the castle, on the left, from the rest of the hill on the right, while the pillar itself originally supported a bridge. (D. Nicolle)

SAONE

Saone is a far larger and more impressive structure than Ravendel, covering 5 hectares of a rocky spur about 25km from Latakia. The castle was virtually surrounded by steep cliffs except at the eastern end where a narrow neck of land, linking the site to the neighbouring hill, was cut by a stupendous man-made fosse over 155m long, almost 30m deep, and 15–20m wide. In the middle of the northern end of the fosse a needle of rock was left to support a bridge that led to a gatehouse in the wall. This gatehouse had two projecting, rounded towers. The strongest defences were concentrated at this western end, which formed a massive citadel dominated by a keep, just south of the gatehouse. On the other side of the keep were extensive vaulted stables, a cistern and three rounded towers. In the southern wall were large rectangular towers with a second gateway in the third tower from the east.

THE CASTLE OF SAONE

The castle of Saone holds a particularly important place in the history of Crusader military architecture because it was not recaptured after falling to Saladin in the wake of the sultan's great victory at Hattin in 1187. Minor repairs and additions were made in later years, and these are clearly identifiable, the most obvious being a small Islamic palace, a mosque and a *hamam* or public bath in the centre of the fortified complex. By 1119 the existing small Byzantine castle (1) belonged to one of the great lords of the Principality of Antioch. By 1132 a massive though rather low donjon (2) had been added outside the existing eastern

wall of the Byzantine fortified area. The most astonishing defensive feature, though, was a rock-cut fosse (3) across the neck of the promontory linking Saone to the neighbouring hill. The fortress eventually comprised an elongated walled hilltop, consisting of an Upper Ward (4) and a huge Lower Ward (5), separated by a wall and a shallow fosse. The defences of the Lower Ward were relatively weak. The strongest fortified structures were concentrated in the east, overlooking the great fosse, and to a lesser extent along the southern side of the Upper Ward where there was another strong entrance tower. (Adam Hook © Osprey Publishing)

The top of the rock 'needle' In the fosse of Saone (Sahyun) castle. It is seen from the gate where a drawbridge would have been lowered onto the masonry on top of the pillar. A bridge would then have linked the pillar to a buttress-like extension of rock and the plateau beyond. (D. Nicolle)

A chemin de ronde ran around the curtain-walls at Saone. This was not uncommon but at Saone the chemin de ronde has no access to the towers, which could only be reached by stairs from inside the courtyard, as was also the case with the walkway along the top of the curtain-wall. This was a feature of Byzantine castles, but was not generally adopted in later Crusader fortification. Nor can the multiple lines of Byzantine and Crusader fortifications at Saone be described as truly concentric, since the inner Byzantine defences are overlooked by the outer Crusader ones and were too far apart for mutual support. Another old-fashioned feature at Saone was a lack of arrow slits in the walls, except for a few at the base of the towers. Consequently the walls of Saone had to be defended from their parapets. Most of Saone castle consists of what is now the Upper Ward, which contains the ruins of an earlier Byzantine citadel. A wall virtually cuts the Upper Ward in half while the western end of the site, separated by a shallow fosse, forms the Lower Ward. This was probably not fortified before the Crusaders arrived, relying primarily on the precipitous cliffs for security, but is now surrounded by weaker walls and small towers.

GIBELCAR

Gibelcar in Lebanon is one of the least-known Crusader castles. It stands on a narrow spur of land at the northern end of the Mount Lebanon Range with steep gorges on both sides and a view that is said to reach Crac des Chevaliers in Syria. Like Crac, Gibelcar is separated from the mountainside by a shallow rock-cut fosse. Outside this fosse a rock-cut channel once brought water to the castle. The fosse is dominated by a tall but relatively narrow tower keep. Otherwise the site is surrounded by a single curtain-wall on top of cliffs that, though not high, appear to have been cut away to make them smoother. Spaced around this wall are four rectangular towers. The towers, keep and parts of the curtain-wall were pierced by embrasures and inside the castle there was at least one cistern. The area within the curtain-wall was again divided into upper and lower wards, perhaps once separated by a trench. Sadly no recent archaeological work has been done on this dramatic and beautiful site.

BELVOIR

In complete contrast to Gibelcar, the castle of Belvoir has been entirely cleared and fully studied. In fact, the Palestine village that once stood on this site was actually obliterated and its inhabitants expelled so that archaeologists could uncover the remains of the castle. It is surrounded on three sides by a rock-cut fosse, the eastern ends of which open onto a steep slope down to the Jordan valley. On the rectangular platform inside the fosse was a rectangular concentric castle largely built of basalt with some small decorative elements in limestone. It covered an area of approximately 100m by 140m with four rectangular corner towers plus slightly smaller towers in the middle of the northern, western and southern walls. The eastern wall, overlooking the Jordan valley, was protected by a large and slightly irregular barbican culminating in a substantial bastion. The main entrance was through the southern end of this barbican where the wall was doubled to form a long dog's-leg path before entering the main wall of the castle. In addition, there were posterns through several towers.

Whether the multiple concentric plan of Belvoir was designed entirely for defensive reasons or partially reflected the fact that the Hospitallers were a monastic order who required a cloistered or enclosed area remains a matter of debate. The result was a strong outer wall with towers, then a large vaulted space that included storage, stables, a cistern and a large communal bath within a simple inner wall. These in turn enclosed a narrow courtyard surrounding a taller inner fortress with four corner towers and an even taller western tower over its entrance. The inner castle consisted of vaulted chambers, including a kitchen, refectory, chapel and perhaps dormitories for the Brothers of the Order, surrounding a small inner courtyard.

The Hospitaller castle of Belvoir (Kawkab al-Hawa) is perched on the edge of a steep slope dipping down to the Jordan valley, with the hills of Jordan rising beyond. Its designers, therefore, only had to add a rock-cut fosse on three sides. The relatively shallow trench seen here is on the northern side of the castle. (D. Nicolle)

LE VAUX MOISE

Le Vaux Moise has now been identified as al-Wu'aira, a few kilometres from Petra in southern Jordan, where construction is generally believed to have started after 1115. It consists of an irregular, four-sided fortified enclosure whose shape is largely dictated by the extremely rocky nature of the site. The outer walls stand on top of natural sandstone ridges overlooking water-worn gorges. The ravine on the eastern side of the castle was artificially deepened to create a highly effective vertical fosse, while a rocky pinnacle was left to support a bridge to the barbican and gate at the south-eastern corner of the castle. This is similar in concept to the amazing pinnacle at Saone, though much smaller, and has a tunnel cut through its top to form an outer gateway. The actual entrance to the castle was through a narrow rock-hewn passage near the south-eastern corner, which was itself originally reached by a wooden bridge across the al-Wu'aira gorge.

The outer wall had several towers but the main bastions were the west tower, midway between the north-western and south-western corners of the castle, plus the north-eastern tower that overlooks the Wadi al-Wu'aira ravine. Additional outworks strengthened the northern and southern walls. Within the walls, part of the floor of the enclosure was plastered with clay. Four finely carved white limestone blocks, two of which were decorated with Christian crosses, were inserted in the top course of the wall. They probably came either from a chapel built when the Crusaders first took over the site shortly after 1108, or from a pre-Crusader monastery. Other structures were placed around the insides of the main curtain-wall, leaving a large but irregular courtyard in the centre.

MARGAT

Wilbrand von Oldenburg described Margat as follows:

> A huge and very strong castle, defended by a double wall and protected by several towers. It stands on a high mountain… Every night four Knights of the Hospital and 28 soldiers keep guard there… The provisions stored there are sufficient for five years.

An embrasure in the largest surviving tower at Le Vaux Moise (al-Wu'aira) castle. Some features at al-Wu'aira are particularly important because they are early examples of Crusader military architecture in a castle that was then abandoned rather than being altered following the Islamic reconquest. (D. Nicolle)

Margat's hilltop location is linked by a neck of land to a larger hill to the south, this potentially vulnerable approach being defended by a rock-cut reservoir to discourage mining. Margat itself is divided into two areas consisting of the castle and the fortified town, divided by a ditch and wall. The outer walls were defended by a dozen towers, of which all but four are round and probably date from after the Hospitallers had taken control.

Though plain and undecorated, the church inside the citadel of Margat (al-Marqab) is an impressive structure built of finely cut white limestone, in stark contrast to the roughly cut black basalt of the rest of the castle. (D. Nicolle)

Margat's defences are remarkably varied. On the eastern front, a wall and several round towers create a huge hillside terrace, behind which is a glacis crowned by an inner wall. How far this inner wall originally extended is, however, unclear. The north of the site has a single wall dominated by a square tower, probably from the 12th century. On the western side was an enclosure strengthened by four early 13th-century round towers whose wall-head defences are now lost. The main castle dominated the southern end of the enclosure, and was approached through a square gatehouse in the outer wall. Above the entrance arch are the corbels, which supported a machicolation; there is also a groove for a portcullis. The resulting complex entrance has alternative angled routes into the castle, though there was no access to the upper floors from the gate. Another fortified gate linked the fortress and the town, while the exterior of the citadel was protected by a double wall. On its western side are three square towers, again probably dating from the 12th century. The wall connecting them has a covered 'shooting gallery', but on the other side there are no towers because the slope is so steep that simple walls were considered adequate. At the very southern tip of this roughly triangular citadel was what the Crusaders called the Tower of the Spur, which was replaced by the great Mamluk tower that dominates the southern end of Margat.

These outer defences are overlooked by cliff-like inner walls, which surround the inner court; the latter is largely surrounded by vaulted halls used for storage and shelter. On the southern side is a more elegant, vaulted chamber, which was probably the Knights' Hall. Nearby is a grand but austere chapel whose eastern end was incorporated into the castle wall. It was probably built shortly after the Hospitallers gained possession of Margat, although the halls on each side are from a later period.

Numerous changes were made to the plan during the construction of Margat, and it seems almost as if the masons were working continuously, year after year. The result is ingenious if rather confusing, with the most impressive elements of the citadel being two massive round towers. The smaller of these, at the north-eastern corner, still has its wall-head defences, which consist at the lower level of arrow slits and one large rectangular opening for a counter-siege machine. Above them a wall walk has merlons pierced with arrow slits. At the southern end, where the natural defences are weakest, the Hospitallers constructed a round keep, 200m in diameter and 24m high. It was comparable to the great circular keeps of Western Europe, though somewhat squatter, perhaps because of the threat of earthquakes.

Otherwise the castle of Margat is remarkable for its use of superimposed halls and vaults, provided with arrow slits to turn them into huge shooting galleries, linked by a maze of often unlit staircases within the wall. Most probably served as storerooms or barracks though one contained ovens and some seem to have been stables. Above them is an extensive roof terrace, perhaps intended for stone-throwing siege machines of the type which defended Margat in 1285. In fact, numerous arrowheads embedded in the mortar around certain arrow slits probably date from the final siege.

Today the western side of the fortress-town of Margat (al-Marqab) looks less impressive than the eastern and southern defences. The west was, however, the original approach and it was protected by two strong enclosure walls plus a dry moat. Most of what is visible here forms the inner wall with the mass of the main citadel rising on the right. (D. Nicolle)

CRAC DES CHEVALIERS

Crac des Chevaliers, with its finely cut white limestone masonry, is less forbidding than the dark and roughly cut basalt mass of Margat. It is, however, more cramped, with approximately three-quarters of the area within the inner walls being built over. A chapel stands at one end of a small courtyard, while at the other a large

CRAC DES CHEVALIERS IN THE MID 13TH CENTURY

Much of what remains of Crac des Chevaliers today is actually Mamluk, and dates from after the castle fell to Sultan Baybars in 1271. This is certainly true of the eastern side (1); this was the most vulnerable stretch of wall, and most often damaged by sieges. The changes were even more dramatic on the southern side (2), facing a neighbouring hill across a deep fosse. This bore the brunt of the final Mamluk attack; both its main rounded towers being so damaged that they had to be rebuilt. In 1285 construction began on a massive new

rectangular tower, which today dominates this southern wall. A stone aqueduct (2a) brought water from a tunnel in the hillside into the internal moat. In contrast, the western wall (3), with its protruding box machicolations (3a), overlooks a very steep valley and consists of virtually unaltered Crusader work, as does the inner fortress; dating from before 1170, it is protected by a moat (4), a talus (4a), massive walls, and towers built after Crac des Chevaliers had been handed over to the Hospitallers. (Adam Hook © Osprey Publishing)

raised platform rests on vaults, which were probably used for storage, inner stabling and as shelter from incoming stones and arrows. On the western side of this courtyard is the magnificent Hall of the Knights, perhaps largely 12th century with 13th-century interior vaulting and ribs. However, even this was not the most remarkable aspect of Crac des Chevaliers. To quote the historian Hugh Kennedy:

> The most striking feature is the gallery on the courtyard side, which probably dates from the 1230s; elegant, with delicate, slender pillars and tracery, it shows all the refinement of the high Gothic of the thirteenth century and is a perfect complement to the massive fortifications. There is a short Latin verse inscribed on one of the arches: *Sit tibi copia, Sit sapiencia, Formaque detur, Inquinat omnia sola, Superbia si comitetur.* (Have richness, have wisdom, have beauty but beware of pride, which spoils all it comes into contact with.)

In stern contrast to the delicacy of this carved gallery or cloister, are the great towers of the southern wall. These provided accommodation for the 60 or so knights who were the aristocracy of the community. The south-west tower also has a vaulted circular chamber, which may later have been modified to provide the Grand Master with some privacy. On top are the remains of a small watchtower.

LEFT
The Templar castle of Atlit or Pilgrims' Castle, seen from the ruins of the 12th-century castle of Le Destroit (Qal'at Dustray) which it replaced. Atlit castle was in a very strong position that could be directly resupplied and supported from the sea. Consequently, it resisted long after the now abandoned town of Atlit (to the left of this picture) had fallen to the Mamluks. The Templars also gained considerable revenues from valuable salt-evaporation pans in the foreground. (D. Nicolle)

FOLLOWING PAGE
One of the most remarkable features inside the castle of Crac des Chevaliers (Hisn al-Akrad) is an open cistern or moat between the extremely strong southern outer wall, on the left, and the even more massive southern glacis of the inner citadel on the right. In addition to serving as a secure source of water, its existence may have inhibited mining operations against the vulnerable southern side of the castle. (D. Nicolle)

ATLIT

The dramatic coastal castle of Atlit is now a closed military zone, and it remains to be seen how much damage is being caused by its use as a training area for Israeli marine commandos. However, it was well recorded during the British Mandate of the 1930s.

THE TEMPLAR STABLES IN THE CITY OF ATLIT, 13TH CENTURY

The extensive stables that were built against the southern wall of Atlit were not reused after the fortified city was destroyed by the Mamluks in 1265. This reconstruction attempts to illustrate one corner of the Templars' stable area next to the southern city gate of Atlit town, as it probably looked early in the 13th century before various modifications were undertaken; a section of the stable walls has been removed in the illustration. The whole area contained permanent stabling for over 200 animals, including war-horses, smaller horses for turcopole cavalry or to be used as baggage animals, plus draught oxen and even camels. Oxen seem to have fed from continuous troughs, whereas horse-troughs or mangers were usually divided into individual sections. There were also wells, drainage systems, grain chutes, tethering points and rooms that might have served as storage, offices or accommodation. (Adam Hook © Osprey Publishing)

Otherwise known as Pilgrims' Castle, Atlit stands on a low promontory and was built from 1217 onwards. A fortified town was added later. The concentric defences of the castle itself are separated from the mainland by a rock-cut ditch and counterscarp wall in front of two massive walls. The inner wall is 12m thick and was over 30m high, being flanked by two rectangular towers. The outer is over 6m thick and was 15m high with three towers.

Beyond the castle, the town wall had a ditch and counterscarp, three gatehouses, each with a portcullis and probably slot machicolations. There were wooden bridges over the ditch, and an additional postern. A small harbour south of the castle provided limited protection from storms, and on the far side of the town was a stone-faced earthen rampart, which marked the southern edge of the precious salt-pans that brought considerable revenue to Atlit. The seaward end of this rampart also had a moated tower.

CAESAREA MARITIMA

Caesarea Maritima on the Palestinian coast boasts the best-preserved Crusader urban defences, largely because this site was abandoned for centuries after it had been retaken by the Mamluks. The main city gate was on its eastern side and had a drawbridge supported by a stone vault, which has been reconstructed. The lines of the town's fortifications follow those of the early medieval Islamic defences, though the walls themselves received their final form when Louis IX of France had the city refortified in 1252. The original height of this mid 13th-century wall is unknown, but in several places there were casemated arrow slits with sloping sills; the whole was fronted by a talus rising 8m from the base of a dry ditch 7–8m wide and 4–6m deep. The vertical counterscarp remains, along with 14 projecting towers. One tower on each of the landward sides of Caesarea had a bent entrance. The ruins of a castle were found on the southern harbour mole, consisting of a keep behind a wall with rectangular towers fronted by a sea-level rock-cut moat.

ARSUF

Archaeological investigations at Arsuf are much more recent and a great deal remains to be published. The site differed from that at Caesarea Maritima, as Arsuf

Much of the ruins of the medieval Crusader city of Arsus (Arsuf) remains unexcavated, because the ground has been polluted by chemicals from a neighbouring Israeli armaments factory. However, the foundations of the ruined east gate have been uncovered. Here the Crusaders followed the line of the previous Fatimid city fortifications, but added a stronger gate. (D. Nicolle)

THE CITY AND CITADEL OF ARSUF IN THE MID 13TH CENTURY

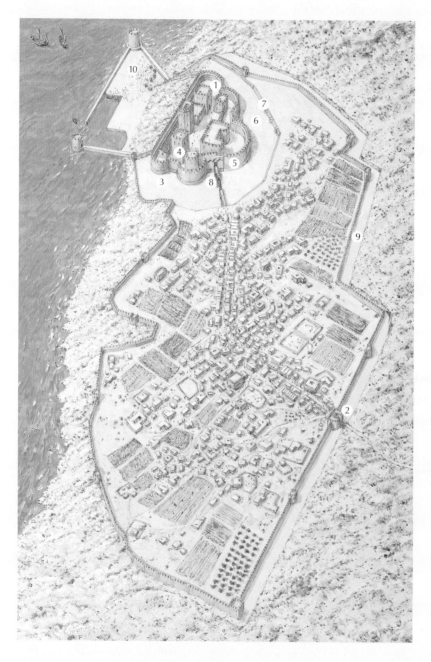

Arsuf was a thriving commercial centre before the Crusaders arrived in 1101. It already had urban fortifications, but apparently lacked a citadel, though the remains of a small early Islamic tower may have been found beneath the castle added by the Crusaders in the early 13th century (1). During the Crusader occupation the existing Islamic urban defences were repaired and in the south-eastern corner these were greatly strengthened. A new city gate (2) was similarly built on the eastern side. The Crusader citadel (3) was an impressive structure consisting of a courtyard surrounded by a high inner wall with rectangular and semicircular towers (4). Massive outer bastions (5) were placed immediately in front of the inner towers. Beyond these was a deep fosse (6) surrounded by a carefully constructed retaining wall (7), needed because of the sandy nature of the soil. A drawbridge tower (8) provided access to the citadel. The city itself was protected by a wall with an outer fosse (9). The true nature of the 'harbour' at the base of the cliff (10) is still the subject of debate. Leased to the Hospitallers in 1261, the castle was considerably strengthened, yet Arsuf fell to the Mamluks only four years later. (After Roll and Smertenko, with additions by Nicolle; Adam Hook © Osprey Publishing)

takes advantage of a sandstone bluff overlooking a shallow natural haven near the modern Israeli town of Herzliya.

The city had reached its greatest extent during the pre-Islamic Byzantine period when it had an important Samaritan community, though not, it appears, a Jewish one. During the early Islamic period the extent, though not necessarily the population, of Arsuf was reduced, apparently in response to the threat of Byzantine naval attack. Arsuf was now, for the first time, given a fortified wall. This was the city that the Crusaders seized early in the 12th century, after which the conquerors continued to use the existing Islamic fortifications, restoring them and adding a new gate. During the early 13th century, the Crusaders added a castle on the edge of a cliff overlooking the sea. This included a courtyard surrounded by a high inner wall with two rectangular and four semi-circular towers. An outer wall had five larger and lower bastions, the largest of which projected directly ahead of the twin gate-towers. This doubled-wall system was in turn surrounded by a deep moat strengthened by outer retaining walls forming a polygon. The seaward ends of this retaining system have, like much of the western side of the castle, collapsed as a result of cliff erosion.

A bridge on two piers led into the south-eastern side of the castle. It would originally have had a drawbridge into a short wall between the southern and easternmost outer towers. Some large circular structures in the north-eastern corner of the castle may have been ovens in a kitchen area, and on the western side was a polygonal keep over a vaulted hall. Much of the western side of the castle and all of its straight western wall have fallen down the cliff.

At the base of this cliff was what some have identified as a harbour with jetties and corner towers. An alternative interpretation suggests that it included a flat area of land, just above sea level, which may have served as a wharf. A tunnel led from the fortress to the supposed 'port', perhaps as a final means of escape, while another tunnel led south from the courtyard into the moat. This could have served as a postern, enabling the garrison to attack an enemy in the moat.

FEUDAL, RELIGIOUS & URBAN DEFENCES

FEUDAL TOWER BUILDING

For a while, during the Crusader 12th century, there seems to have been a castle-dwelling knightly aristocracy. When a piece of land was granted to a knight or group of knights in the newly established Kingdom of Jerusalem, many of these new fief holders did what was normal in Western Europe by erecting fortified towers or donjons. This may have been common during the optimistic first half of the 12th century, although such an interpretation relies almost entirely on archaeological evidence since so few documentary sources survive. When feudal landholders later withdrew to the relative safety of fortified coastal cities, the knight or lord still sent representatives to supervise his fiefs, ensure the collection of rents, impose law and garrison local fortifications.

Towers built by the early feudal elite of the Crusader States varied considerably. Most had an outwork enclosing a courtyard around the tower. However, defence was largely passive and these fortifications were too small to house large garrisons. Some had halls that could have been used as administrative centres while others included large storage areas, perhaps for local agricultural produce. At the same time towers served as symbols of a new Crusader authority.

Most of the towers lay in fertile regions and their locations varied from flat land to hilltops. Some were very small, though even these could incorporate strong defences. One such tower was Mirabel (Mijdal Afiq), which was probably built in 1152. It had very thick walls plus outworks that included an enclosure with a sloping talus and towers. Most towers like this had walls with few openings, the towers themselves usually being two storeys high, which probably reflected weight problems with stone vaulting. Lighting was largely through arrow slits. Some towers also had machicolations above a single entrance, or a portcullis, or occasionally both. There was often a water cistern beneath the ground floor and some towers had latrines built into their walls.

ROYAL & LARGE-SCALE CASTLES

In addition to the practice of building small towers, the more powerful members of the new Crusader aristocracy took over, rebuilt or constructed new and more impressive castles. Belhacem (Qal'at Abu'l-Hasan), for example, was an Islamic castle occupied by a Crusader lord in 1128. It had two wards or open areas defended by a curtain-wall and rectangular towers. Like Gibelcar in northern Lebanon, it stood on a rocky spur protected by a gorge on three sides.

In southern Palestine, the building of Bethgibelin castle initially seems to have been a local and communal affair in which the king was not directly involved. On the eastern side of the Dead Sea the castle of Karak des Moabites was founded by Payen the Butler, Lord of Montréal, in 1142. Far to the north, overlooking the Syrian coast, the first Crusader castle of Margat was built by the Mazoir family, but all that remains of their original castle is part of the curtain-wall with the rectangular towers. By the mid 12th century some feudal castles were quite large. At Montdidier (Madd al-Dayr) the donjon measured some 20m by 15m, with an outer wall enclosing a bailey about 60m square.

It might be assumed that royal castles would be larger than feudal castles and would be sited in more strategic locations. However, neither was the case. For example the first Crusader enlargement of the existing Islamic castle at Crac des Chevaliers was apparently carried out by Tancred as ruler of the Principality of

Small fragments of wall paintings have been found in several 13th-century Crusader castles. Most are in a distinctive style that combined Western European, Byzantine and Syrian Christian elements. But to get a better idea of what these paintings once looked like it is necessary to travel beyond the area conquered by the Crusaders, to the remarkable monastery of Mar Musa al-Habashi in the hills north-east of Damascus. The interior of the church is almost covered with paintings of mounted warrior saints and Biblical scenes in the same mixed style. Here, for example, St Bacchus uses a Western European form of saddle, which is even painted with heraldic decorations. (D. Nicolle)

Antioch. Montréal in southern Jordan became the seat of the Lord of Oultrejordain, but the first Crusader castle was started in 1115 for King Baldwin I of Jerusalem. One of the most important features at Montréal was its water supply system, which reportedly consisted of a sloping underground tunnel with 365 steps leading to cisterns fed by underground springs inside the castle hill. It is also possible that the seasonal Wadi al-Bustan below Montréal castle was irrigated by water diverted from other springs and there may have been water mills to process sugar cane brought from the Wadi Araba oases.

THE HOSPITALLERS TAKE OVER THE CASTLE OF TURRIS RUBEA IN THE 1190S

There were many reasons why castles and landed estates were handed over to the military orders by their feudal owners. Families might no longer feel capable of maintaining, garrisoning or defending such fortified properties, or they may have donated valuable assets to a religious order for the good of their souls. The death of the head of a noble family could, if he left no sons to succeed him, be reason enough. Turris Rubea (Burj al-Ahmar) had been given to the Abbey of St Mary Latina by 1158, and was then leased to the Hospitallers some time between 1187 and 1191, probably because of the virtual collapse of the Kingdom of Jerusalem following its catastrophic defeat at the battle of Hattin. In later years Turris Rubea was in the hands of the rival military order of the Templars. Though not one of the biggest castles in the kingdom, it consisted of a fortified enclosure approximately 60m square that contained a massive donjon (1) plus other buildings. The walls of the donjon were over 2m thick and about 14m high. The basement or slightly sunken ground floor consisted of two parallel barrel-vaulted storage chambers (2). From here stairs ran up to an impressive hall, shown here, which seems to have consisted of six groin-vaulted bays with two massive central pillars. Lighting came from relatively narrow slit-windows (3), which were, however, too high in the walls to serve as arrow slits. Any active defence would have been conducted from the roof, though whether or not this was originally crenellated is unknown. (Adam Hook © Osprey Publishing)

One clearly royal fortress was the so-called Tower of David, or Citadel, in the north-western corner of the fortified Old City of Jerusalem. It served as a royal palace until 1104 when the court moved to the Aqsa Mosque on the Haram al-Sharif, and was strong enough to resist a bombardment from outside and inside the city during a Crusader civil war in 1152. During the 1160s and 1170s the Citadel was strengthened with additional towers and and a curtain-wall to create a substantial fortified enclosure. Around 1172, it was described by Theoderich as being protected by ditches and outworks, while some decades later William of Tyre referred to its towers, walls and forewalls.

More is known about the organization of royal than feudal castles. Naturally rulers tried to keep the largest and most important fortifications in their own hands. They also preferred to give the most powerful fiefs to their relatives. These princely castles were under the command of *châtelains* appointed by the prince or count. Other châtelains were appointed by leading nobles. The importance of each châtelain reflected the importance of the castle he commanded. Meanwhile in cities and major towns other châtelains controlled the citadel and its garrison. In the Kingdom of Jerusalem a senior royal official called the *Sénéchal* (also called the *Dapifer Regis*) inspected castles in the king's name and organized their provisions. He had the authority to change garrisons but not the baillis or châtelains who commanded the castles, since these were appointed by the king himself.

The inner courtyard of the great castle of Crac des Chevaliers is remarkably small because so much of its area has been covered by additional structures. Of these the most famous is the fine carved Gothic arcade on the right, which formed a covered cloister for the brothers of the Hospitaller military order. (D. Nicolle)

RELIGIOUS CENTRES & MILITARY ORDERS

Relatively few fortifications were built specifically to protect religious centres. Of these Jerusalem was the most important, and during the 15 years when it was again under Crusader control, efforts were made to restore some defences. The city walls had been dismantled by Saladin, but a barbican in front of St Stephen's Gate was repaired, along with the Citadel, whose existing glacis may date from this period. However, there is some argument over where a castle constructed in 1240 was located. Some historians believe it was next to what was then called the Gaza Gate, where the Tower of the Maidens and the Tower of the Hospital were sited, but others maintain that the castle of 1240 was at the north-western corner of the Old City. Other fortifications were sited in an attempt to encourage the development of specific locations as centres of pilgrimage. However, by the 13th century security had deteriorated to such an extent that local bishops would evacuate threatened towns for the relative safety of these nearby fortresses.

The most significant 'religious' fortifications were, of course, those of the military orders. These included towns that were under an order's control. In such places the citadel would normally be used as the order's local headquarters. In Acre, however, the headquarters of the Hospitallers and of the Templars formed separate enclaves, each capable of individual defence.

The castles of the increasingly powerful military orders were distinct even in the 12th century. Most already consisted of substantial enclosure fortresses rather than simple towers, except for the simple fortifications that served as places of refuge and patrol bases along important pilgrim roads. The early enclosure castles of the military orders were usually rectangular with vaulted chambers around the insides of their walls, normally with a chapel, refectory and other conventual or monastic rooms in the upper floors over vaulted storage chambers and stables.

The Hospitallers seem to have selected more isolated locations for their castles during the 12th century than did the Templars. As a result, more Hospitaller castles survive reasonably intact. Many guarded the order's ever-increasing landed estates. Perhaps a majority had originally been feudal castles handed over to the order, along with large pieces of land, by families that could no longer maintain or garrison them. The castle of Calansue (al-Qalansuwa) was, for example, built by a local lord but was already in Hospitaller hands by 1128. The order then added a hall and other structures to the existing tower. Bethgibelin was the second castle known to have been granted

Montfort (Qal'at al-Qurayn) in northern Galilee was a typical and very dramatic spur-castle, located on an easily defensible extension of one of the surrounding hills. This position was further strengthened by the excavation of dry ditches or fosses, separating the castle from the main hill. The Crusader fortification of Montfort all dates from the 13th century and the place served as the headquarters of the Order of Teutonic Knights until it fell to the Mamluks in 1271. (D. Pringle)

to the Hospitallers. The third was Belmont, a more elaborate fortress on top of a hill. It consisted of an outer wall without flanking towers, enclosing an area approximately 100m by 115m. There was a gatehouse in this outer wall, while a vaulted passage ran around the inside. Within the enclosed courtyard was a rectangular inner bailey but no dominating tower or donjon.

The Hospitallers and Templars were also given castles and estates in the County of Tripoli before the middle of the 12th century. Castel Rouge (al-Qal'at Yahmur) was, for example, handed over to the Hospitallers by Count Raymond II of Tripoli while the castle's original owners, the Montopieu family, were awarded 400 bezants in compensation. The Hospitallers certainly put considerable effort and money into their holdings in the County of Tripoli after 1144, when Count Raymond granted them a virtually independent lordship in the east. This was a dangerous, yet strategically important area around the fertile Buqai'ah valley. Though blessed with adequate rainfull, it lacked natural defences and was very exposed to raiding. On the other hand, the Hospitallers' new estates in the Buqai'ah valley formed a useful base from which to raid Islamic territory, so the order established its headquarters at Crac des Chevaliers.

By 1160 the Hospitallers had seven or eight castles in Syria, gaining a further 11 or 12 during the following decade. One of the strongest was Margat, which lay within the Principality of Antioch. It had been the centre of the Mazoir family's extensive properties after 1130, but was sold to the Hospitallers in 1186. At the same time, the military order aquired various lesser castles and a patchwork of estates and territories. Like Crac des Chevaliers in the County of Tripoli, Margat in the Principality of Antioch developed as the military centre of what became a virtually autonomous palatinate.

THE FORTIFIED CHURCH AND TOWN OF SAFITA (CASTEL BLANC) IN THE MID 13TH CENTURY

The great tower or keep (1) of Castel Blanc in the Syrian coastal mountains was a massively fortified church rather than simply a castle. The lower chamber (2) formed the church with a semi-domed apse at its eastern end (3); a function that continues to this day. The upper chamber (4) consists of a two-aisled hall supported by three columns. Access to this upper chamber from the church was within the south-western corner (5) and was not particularly convenient for military purposes, while access to the roof was by stairs against the western wall of the upper chamber. A rock-cut cistern lay beneath the church (6). An extensive platform surrounds the church, and appears to have had a defensive wall that formed an inner enceinte (7). Apart from the platform, the only substantial surviving element of these inner defences is the small south-western tower (8). Even less remains of the outer fortifications of Castel Blanc, recreated in the lower illustration, with the notable exception of part of a great entrance tower on the eastern side of the hill (9). Photographs taken before the modern village of Safita expanded into a small but thriving town, indicate that this formed only part of a complex of fortifications around the entrance to the Crusader town. (Adam Hook © Osprey Publishing)

The castellans of the main Hospitaller castles were under the authority of the marshal. In peacetime the 'Castellans of Syria' answered to the marshal and to the Chapter General of the Order, though in time of war the marshal's authority was more direct, particularly if he was personally present within their bailiwick, or district. However, some smaller castles may not have had castellans and were instead garrisoned by mercenaries.

With regard to the number of personnel present in each castle, the evidence can be confusing. Eighty Hospitaller brethren were said to have been killed or captured when Arsuf fell to the Mamluks in 1265, whereas the complete garrison totalled around 1,000 men. Fifteen years later the Hospitallers were said to have had 600 cavalry in Margat, whereas a source from 1211 indicated that the complete garrison consisted of 2,000 men. In 1255 a Papal document maintained that the order had only 60 mounted troops in Crac des Chevaliers, and proposed stationing 40 more in a new castle to be built on Mount Tabor. To further confuse the issue, a letter from the Hospitaller Grand Master, written in 1268, stated that the order had only 300 brethren in the whole of Syria, so it is clearly impossible to present firm figures for the garrisons of specific castles.

The Templars' most important possession, and their headquarters, was on the Haram al-Sharif in Jerusalem – the site of the Temple of Solomon, from which they took their name. This stood at the south-eastern corner of the walled city of Jerusalem. A recently cleared tunnel near the south-eastern corner of the Haram

Most of the wall-head defences and crenellations now visible on Crusader castles are either modern reconstructions or dated from Mamluk rebuilding. However, photographs from the early 20th century show that some of the original crenellations on the fortified church at Castel Blanc (Burj Safita) still existed. They are seen here in greater detail. The upper gaps were for observation while the tapering slots at floor level were for shooting through. (D. Nicolle)

al-Sharif was perhaps a 'secret' entrance to the Templars' fortified headquarters, used during emergencies.

The highly detailed Rule of the military order of the Templars does not make a clear distinction between a proper castle and an unfortified 'house' where brethren lived and administered the order's estates. Both were under a commander in charge of all supplies and of the sergeants who guarded their gates. In fact the Rule of the Templars makes few references to castles or their role in warfare. By the second half of the 12th century most Templar castles were concentrated in the northern part of the Principality of Antioch and in the south of the Kingdom of Jerusalem. In the north these Templar castles formed a frontier march based upon Gaston (Baghras), Roche Guillaume, Roche de Roissel and Darbsak. In the south, some were close to Ascalon, which was held by the Fatimids until 1153. However, most Templar castles in the Kingdom of Jerusalem guarded pilgrim routes. They ensured that pilgrims had food, tents, animal transport and protection. One small Templar castle was Citerne Rouge (Cisterna Rubea), which defended a *caravanserai* or hostel on the road to the River Jordan. Also known as Maldoim (Qal'at al-Damm), it was a four-sided fort built by the Templars before 1169 to protect the Jerusalem–Jericho road.

By the mid 12th century the Templars were in the process of forming a sort of autonomous palatinate around Tartus, just as the Hospitallers would do around Crac des Chevaliers. Within this expanding Templar palatinate, the castle of Castel Blanc was an impressive église-donjon, or fortified church, that dominated the surrounding castle. It was built in the final quarter of the 12th century, but was subsequently repaired extensively. Access from the ground-floor church to the upper chamber and roof is so awkward that the building cannot have been permanently garrisoned. However, it was very defensible and had a slit machicolation over the main church door.

In 1217–18 the Templars demolished the late 12th-century fort of Le Destroit (Qal'at Dustray) and replaced it with the much larger castle of Atlit. The latter was largely built with pilgrim manpower, and became known as Château Pelerin. It was so strong that it survived the fall of Atlit town in 1265 and was only abandoned in August 1291, after the fall of Acre itself. A variation on the way Crusader builders reused ancient materials occurred in 1218, when the Templars cut a moat across the narrow isthmus at Atlit. They not only found ancient walls, which offered a ready supply of cut stones, but also gold coins with which they paid their workers.

The town that was later built outside Atlit castle was defended by much weaker fortifications, although the huge stables were very impressive. These seem to have been based upon the traditional design of an Islamic *khan*, or protected lodging place, for merchants. Here archaeologists found evidence for the everyday working life of a garrison, including tethering points and sockets for halter-rings for animals, and a courtyard well with a drain leading outside the buildings. The flat roofs that covered this remarkably large area rested on piers and wooden beams and consisted of boards. A concrete crust consisted of gravel and lime, rendered smooth with lime plaster, just as in traditional Palestinian domestic architecture. Most of the timber came from Mount Carmel, though some fragments of cedar were also found in the ruins, possibly shipped in from Lebanon or Cyprus.

The Atlit garrison relied on shallow dug wells, which produced slightly brackish but drinkable water, and one well in the middle of the stable yard remained in use until modern times. Other neighbouring buildings were not linked to the interior of the main stable structure, but were accessed from the beach. The northern gateway of the complex was intended for heavier traffic than the other entrances, and had a roadway paved with diagonal slabs. The impressive door was approached by a metalled slope and seems to have been the only entrance to the main stable

The island of Ru'ad lies a kilometre or so off the Syrian coast near Tartus. A small castle overlooking the little harbour was constructed after the Crusaders were driven from the island in 1302, but another larger castle seen here lies almost hidden within the village that now covers Ru'ad. It is a simple 13th-century rectangular enclosure with rounded corner towers, yet it enabled a Templar garrison to hold the island for more than a decade after the fall of the last Crusader outposts on the mainland. (D. Nicolle)

yard. Carts probably remained outside in a shaded area or shed. Stone 'grain chutes' made it easier to get the grain into various storage bins. Other rooms were possibly used as stores for the harnesses. However, only one room was specifically designed

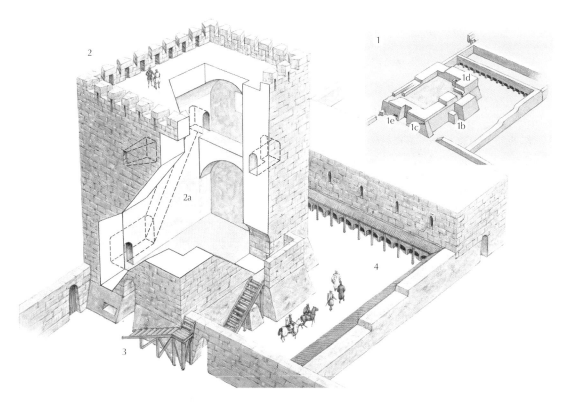

THE FORTIFIED WAY-STATION OF LE DESTROIT IN THE LATE 12TH CENTURY

Le Destroit was built on a system of foundations excavated from the rock. It commanded a defile through a low ridge parallel to the shore, along which the north–south road ran until modern times. These fortifications played a vital role during the Third Crusade, but in 1220 Le Destroit was demolished by the Templars and was replaced by the stronger fortress of Atlit. Today only the rock-cut foundations (1) and some of the lower course of masonry remains. The tower (2) originally consisted of a vaulted chamber with a staircase within its north wall (2a) leading to an upper chamber; this hypothetical reconstruction is based upon similar towers within the Kingdom of Jerusalem. The stone-cut foundation plinth contained cisterns on its eastern (1d) and western (1e) sides, plus rock-cut supports for an entrance stair on the south (1b). Peg-holes on the western slope (1c) may have been for a wooden stair to a wall between two main yards (3). The inner yard (4) contained rows of rock-cut mangers, once covered by simple wooden roofs. Whether any of the outer rock-cut areas were roofed is unknown. (After Dikijian and Nicolle; Adam Hook © Osprey Publishing)

On the mainland next to the castle of Atlit is one of the rarest sights in the Middle East: a largely undisturbed Crusader cemetery. Some of the most decorated gravestones have been removed, and most that remain are quite plain, but amongst them are a few with carved crosses. The identity of those buried beneath are unknown, but they may have been senior members of the Hospitaller garrison. (D. Nicolle)

for larger horses, presumably the war-horses of the Brother Knights. It had sufficient space for animals to lie down, perhaps in separate wooden stalls.

Meanwhile, the grooms were provided with comfortable living quarters next to the stables. Much broken pottery was found here along with a steel 'striker' to be used with flint and tinder to start a cooking fire, while their drinking water was cooled in the semi-porous jars that remain traditional throughout much of the Middle East. Most of the ceramics were locally made, though some finer ware had been imported from Cyprus or Italy. A blacksmith also worked somewhere around the site, though the exact spot could not be identified.

THE TEUTONIC KNIGHTS

The Teutonic Knights possessed several important fortresses in the Middle East. These included Montfort in Galilee, which had a separate hall, built in the second quarter of the 13th century next to the Wadi al-Qarn. It stands north of the castle, at the bottom of a steep slope. The hall is a rectangular structure, 40m long by 10–12m wide, over a barrel-vaulted undercroft. It was probably constructed in at least two stages and is attached to a dam across the wadi; this dam having sluices to control the flow of water. Part of the structure originally served as a mill, probably for processing sugar cane, where a horizontal millwheel seems to have been powered by water directed through wooden channels. The main hall above could

A winepress was amongst the varied evidence for agricultural and indeed industrial production at the Teutonic Knights castle of Montfort in Galilee. (D. Pringle)

not have been used for storing food as it was in a vulnerable position outside the castle. So perhaps the undercroft served as a stable or kitchen after the upper hall was added, the whole structure then forming a guesthouse for high-ranking visitors to the Teutonic Knights' castle. During the final phase of the Crusader occupation of Montfort, a faubourg, or suburb, may also have grown up outside the castle.

The first castle donated to the Teutonic Knights in Cilicia was at Amoude, which was handed over by the Armenian king in 1212. Situated on a rocky outcrop in the middle of the Cilician plain, it was a simple fortified enclosure to which the Teutonic Knights added a three-storey keep. Another possible reason for the selection of Amoude was the abundant availability of fish from the nearby Ceyhan River; this still clearly being the case when the German traveller Wilbrand von Oldenburg visited Amoude some years later.

RELIGIOUS HOUSES & HOLY SITES

During the 12th century Catholic Western European religious houses were often fortified in the Crusader States. One was the convent of Benedictine nuns founded at Bethany in 1138. According to William of Tyre it consisted of 'a strongly fortified tower of hewn and polished stone. This was devoted to the necessary purpose of defence, that the maidens dedicated to God might have an impregnable fortress as a protection against the enemy.' In Bethlehem the Crusader occupiers even surrounded the Church of the Holy Nativity and its associated buildings with a fortified enclosure. This had strong gates and a massive donjon on its south-eastern corner, which might have contained the Bishop of Bethlehem's residence. The important Crusader site at Castel Blanc may have been an église-donjon or fortified church. Here the central elongated rectangular tower was unusual, most other such keeps being almost square. Its outer defences included two outworks, an inner wall of uncertain shape and an outer polygonal curtain-wall with at least two towers and several vaulted chambers.

The original name of the Crusader manor house at Khirbat Rushmiyah is uncertain. The complex consists of a tower whose basement is partly groin-vaulted and partly barrel-vaulted. A rectangular forebuilding was added later, perhaps in the 13th century, and may originally have contained a staircase. Meanwhile, the main door was protected by arrowslits. (D. Nicolle)

URBAN DEFENCES

Most cities and towns of the Crusader States still had plenty of open spaces inside their fortified walls during the 12th century. These were used for market gardens and orchards. It was not until the late 12th and 13th centuries that the remaining Crusader-held cities along the Mediterranean coast began to fill up with settlers fleeing from lost territories in the interior. In fact, several early 12th-century Crusader towns were not fortified, though they might contain a castle or fortified church, and within the Kingdom of Jerusalem only 14 towns had circuit-walls. Of these, 12 were walled before the Crusaders arrived.

Many existing walls, towers and gates were considerably strengthened under Western-European Crusader occupation, though mostly after the Third Crusade in the 1190s and during the 13th century. Their garrisons were drawn from a variety of different groups, especially during the first half of the 12th century. In the County of Edessa urban burgesses provided most of the non-noble troops who defended such cities. Many were Armenian. Unfortunately little is known about the troops who manned rural fortifications, though most were probably drawn from the European settler population or professional mercenaries.

BRINGING LOCAL PRODUCE INTO THE FORTIFIED MANOR HOUSE OF AQUA BELLA ('EN HEMED), MID 12TH CENTURY

Many though not all of the isolated manor houses that dotted the more fertile regions of the Crusader Kingdom of Jerusalem were fortified. Whether this was done for reasons of local insecurity, fear of enemy raiding or, as in Western Europe, merely because it was considered normal practice to fortify such buildings, remains unclear. They were, after all, statements of feudal power and authority as well as functioning farms and agricultural storage facilities. The manor house of Aqua Bella is one of the best preserved in Palestine. It was perhaps built for a secular lord during the first half of the 12th century, but belonged to the Hospitallers by the second half of the 1160s. Built around a courtyard on quite a steep slope overlooking a valley, it was also close to the main medieval road between Jerusalem and the port of Jaffa. Part of the ground-floor level was cut into the hillside, with the resulting stone being used for the building above. In the centre was the roughly square courtyard (1) with an entrance on its eastern side. The three other sides of this yard led into barrel-vaulted chambers that would presumably have been used for storage or for the stabling of animals (2). The vault on the southern side (3) also included a press to make olive oil. A staircase on the southern side led to the upper part of the buildings, which included a chapel (4). Other vaulted chambers on this upper level probably served as kitchens, accommodation and additional storage areas (5). (Adam Hook © Osprey Publishing)

During the 1920s, when this photograph was taken, the eastern end of the hilltop of Safita was largely bare of buildings except for the remains of a tall gate. Behind it rose the stern rectangular fortified church which the Crusaders called Castel Blanc. Today this, like the rest of the hill, is almost entirely covered with attractive stone houses, many made from masonry from the collapsed outer fortifications of the Crusader castle. (Institut Français d'Archéologie, Beirut)

During the 13th century, construction efforts were initially focused upon citadels rather than the walls around a town. Most such work was done during the decades of relative peace, when Egypt and Syria were ruled by the Ayyubids. Examples include the Castle of Richard of Cornwall, built in 1241 in the north-western corner of a revitalized Ascalon, which the Crusaders briefly regained. In earlier times, parts of the Fatimid defences at Ascalon included so much timber they they caught fire during the siege of 1153, which resulted in the city falling to the Crusaders. Almost 40 years later sufficient timber was available for Saladin to have the towers and walls 'filled' with wood and then burned down to deny them to the approaching enemy. Yet the partially demolished defences of Ascalon were already so strong that late 12th- and 13th-century Crusader work largely consisted of repairs and embellishments. The redeveloped Ascalon of the 13th century featured a new concentric citadel with a rock-cut ditch to the south and east. To the north was the city wall, fronted by a masonry talus, and some marble slabs crudely carved with the arms of Sir Hugh Wake of Lincolnshire date from this period. The construction included outworks with occasional casemates, four towers with indirect access and at least 14 other towers of rectangular, half-round or triangular plan, some strengthened with reused or horizontally laid ancient or early medieval columns. The town's four gates similarly incorporated reused Roman and early Islamic elements.

A few years later the French King Louis IX built a second castle at Sidon, known as the Land Castle to distinguish it from Sidon's more famous Sea Castle. It was built upon the massive remains of a Romano-Byzantine theatre and used the ancient stone seats as building blocks. In addition, Louis IX built massive walls around the town itself, with a deep moat and an entrance known as the Tyre Gate between two strong towers. Most of this has been lost, but Louis' walls around Caesarea Maritima on the Palestinian coast largely survive. They have been excavated by Israeli archaeologists and now stand as the finest existing examples of 13th-century Crusader urban fortification.

From Louis IX's Crusade onwards, greater efforts were put into fortifying the urban areas. Previously citizens had been vulnerable to enemy raiding, sometimes even being plundered by local bedouin. It was assumed that such raiders merely wanted portable loot, and would leave once satisfied. Meanwhile, the town's inhabitants took refuge in a citadel with their most valuable property, then returned to their homes in the largely unprotected outer city once the raiders departed. The rise of the Mamluk sultanate changed this, and the determined campaigns of reconquest launched by Mamluk armies resulted in more efforts to surround the remaining Crusader towns with proper fortifications, including some massive gates. The towers spaced along curtain-walls were usually rectangular, though there was one rounded tower at Atlit, while Ascalon had both rounded and triangular ones.

Until the Third Crusade, Acre had only a single wall, but in its aftermath the city and its expanding northern suburb of Montmussard were given doubled walls, numerous massive towers and a deep ditch or moat. These were further strengthened by King Louis IX. Sadly almost all have now disappeared and even their position remains a matter of debate. Recent archaeological excavation and new analysis of the documentary sources are clarifying the issue. The northern walls were probably further north than believed and Acre, plus Montmussard, were much larger than had been realized.

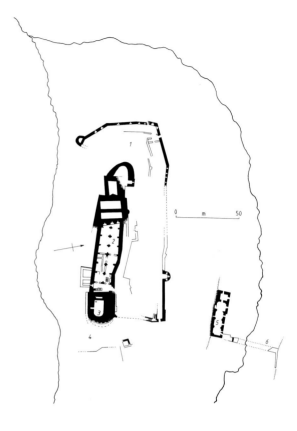

The castle of Montfort: (1) outer ward, (2) upper castle, (3) donjon built over a huge cistern, (4) fosse, (5) presumed 'guest house' built on earlier mill, (6) remains of a dam across the Wadi al-Qarn (after Dean, Hubatsch, Frankel and Pringle).

Some of the most useful evidence comes from aerial photography before what is now called the Old City of Acre expanded. These include reconnaissance photographs taken by the Ottoman Turkish Air Force during World War I, which clearly show the foundations of a wall that looks like the northern defences of Acre-Montmussard. They also show the coastal marsh, now drained, which lay just beyond that wall. A short section of wall uncovered in 1935 lay on this line, while a remarkable number of stone mangonel balls were found on a small promontory where it reached the sea – almost certainly dating from the 1291 siege.

Within the Old City were several large fortified structures, plus the torre (tall fortified towers) of the Italian merchant communes. They included the Castle of the King's Constable and the massive Convent or Headquarters of the Hospitallers, both adjacent to the 12th-century city wall separating Acre proper from Montmussard. Close to the main harbour stood the Court of the Chain and the Venetian 'market', both massive enough to be fortifications in their own right. The Templar Burgus or Castle stood on the shore at the south-western corner of the city. Early aerial photography and recent archaeological investigations indicate that the eastern wall lay further east than once thought. As a result it now seems that later 13th-century Acre

The walls and towers of the abandoned city of Ascalon ('Asqalan) were built upon a largely man-made rampart, much of it sand. Several towers dating from, or substantially rebuilt during, the Crusader period incorporate antique columns laid horizontally to bind the inner and outer layers of the walls. (D. Nicolle)

enclosed an area considerably larger than pre-Crusader Islamic Acre, whose layout had been established in the 9th century.

The most significant recent excavation concerning the fortifications of Crusader Acre took place in what is called the Courthouse site, outside what had been regarded as the 13th-century city. Here a team of Israeli archaeologists uncovered a postern gate and a tower, both probably built between 1198 and 1212. A wide pilaster in a corner of the tower may have supported wooden stairs to the upper floors. A plaster-lined water basin was constructed inside one corner of the tower and the designers even inserted a well shaft within the core of the circuit wall, suggesting that the tower served as a service area as well as a fortification. Furthermore, the archaeologists discovered fragments of Crusader pottery, including a cooking pot, an amphora, a drinking jug, some bowls containing chicken bones and two decorated glass vessels plus evidence of a cooking fire. Perhaps the tower was a kitchen. Its walls were vertical

The Citadel near the north-western corner of the walled Old City of Jerusalem was known to the Crusaders as the Tower of David. It was built on the foundations of a vast Herodian structure and formed the strongest point in the city's fortifications long before the arrival of the First Crusade. During the Crusader occupation it was strengthened and, after damage by wars and earthquakes, was rebuilt more than once after that. (D. Nicolle)

with no glacis, and beyond them a moat was cut through earlier Hellenistic and Byzantine remains. The plastered upper floor of the tower had not been carried on stone vaults, as was usual, but on wooden joists, and the upper chamber itself was probably used as soldiers' living quarters.

These remains formed part of the outer wall of 13th-century Acre, but were well beyond the line of the inner wall, as excavated in the mid 1980s. The tower itself is likely to have been one of those between the doubled wall around Montmussard and the north-eastern corner of the city proper. According to written sources, there were three towers here: the Venetian Tower, the English Tower and the King's Tower. Of these the King's Tower was the most important, marking the north-eastern corner itself. However, it was round, whereas the tower at the Courthouse site was square. Though it was destroyed by fire, there is no evidence of a major attack upon this structure, and because it seems to be so close to Montmussard it should probably be identified as the Venetian rather than the English Tower.

THE CITY OF JERUSALEM

The Crusaders' rebuilding of the walls of Jerusalem has been studied for over a century. It is clear that they not only re-used available masonry but also laid newly cut ashlar blocks. Shortly before the battle of Hattin, the barons of the Kingdom of Jerusalem were obliged to pay for the reinforcement and maintenance of the Holy City's fortifications. Nevertheless, the overall layout remained as it had been when the First Crusade arrived, with the significant exception of the greatly strengthened Tower of David Citadel.

By the time Jerusalem was retaken by Saladin's army, the area immediately outside the Citadel seems to have been enclosed within a network of fosses or moats, while a wall had been built within the riverbed that joined the north-western corner of the Citadel to a continuation of the curtain-wall. David's Gate (now called the Jaffa Gate) was rebuilt slightly west of its original position and was reconstructed as part of a new city wall. The original Fatimid tower in the north-western corner of the city was expanded by the Crusaders, who knew it as Tancred's Tower. Meanwhile, a network of defensive ditches excavated in the 11th century along the north side of the city continued to function and may have been deepened. Here there were three gates, with St Mary Magdalene's Postern (Herod's Gate) being the furthest east. On one of the towers east of this gate there was reportedly a large cross marking the place where the First Crusade broke in to butcher the Muslim and Jewish inhabitants. In the centre of the northern walls was St Stephen's Gate (Damascus Gate), while to the west of this gate was a smaller entrance called St Lazarus' Postern. The most complex defences on the northern wall lay around St Stephen's Gate, which had an external and inner entrance, with an angled passage between them. The inner part of this gate included a chapel and what seems to have been a customs post.

The eastern and western circuit-walls of Jerusalem were built along the lines of the ancient walls. The eastern wall had only one major entrance, the Gate of Jehoshapat (now the Lion's Gate). Less is known about the southern wall during the Crusader period, though it was perhaps a few metres inside today's wall. Here three gates and smaller posterns are known:

The Laqlaq Tower at the north-eastern corner of the walled Old City of Jerusalem. The First Crusade broke in just west of this tower and during the 12th century their point of entry was marked by a large cross. Although most of the fortifications were later rebuilt during the Ottoman period, much of the lower part of the walls and towers incorporate Crusader masonry. (D. Nicolle)

ST STEPHEN'S GATE IN JERUSALEM

The strongly fortified main gate in the northern wall of Jerusalem was called St Stephen's Gate under Crusader occupation. It was on the site of what is now known as the Damascus Gate, and in the previous Arab-Islamic period had been called the Gate of the Column.

This had been defended by two large towers dating from the late-Roman and early-Byzantine periods, though it was later repaired and strengthened following various earthquakes. Water cisterns were built in front of one or perhaps originally both of these ancient towers during the early Islamic period. The city walls on either side also followed the old Romano-Byzantine line. The two ancient towers (1 and 2) were now incorporated into the Crusader gate, that on the western side now being strengthened with an additional lower wall. Most significant, however, were the new outer structures, including a third tower (3) near the existing eastern tower, which formed a small barbican (4) and a bent entrance that made the entire gate complex much stronger. Between the new and eastern towers was a large building, entered by stairs, which may have served as an administrative or customs post (5). The massive Umayyad period water cistern in front of the eastern tower was now beneath this (presumed customs) building, and it continued to supply the inhabitants of Jerusalem during the Crusader period. Next to the western tower and facing the 'customs' building was a small chapel whose interior was decorated with coloured plaster (6). (Adam Hook © Osprey Publishing)

the Postern of the Tannery west of the existing Dung Gate, the Zion Gate and Belcayre's Postern. There was also a large tower built of limestone ashlar at the south-western corner of the city walls.

The Haram al-Sharif was also fortified. Its three southern entrances, now called the Double Gate, the Triple Gate and the Single Gate, were strongly reinforced by the now lost Templar's Wall, which enclosed them like a barbican. This contained an outer gate that was part of the structures adjacent to the southern side of the Aqsa Mosque. North of the Haram al-Sharif a quarter had been allocated to the native or Syrian Christians, largely consisting of people transferred from what is now southern Jordan after 1116. It occupied what had previously been the Jewish quarter and was protected by a new wall behind the Church of Mary Magdalene. This wall turned south-eastwards from the main wall to meet the eastern wall about 150m north of the present St Stephen's Gate, creating a double-wall defensive system in the vulnerable north-eastern corner of the city.

The rectangular area of very shallow water in the centre of this photograph is sheltered by the foundations of walls dating from the 13th-century Crusader occupation of Arsus (Arsuf). It has sometimes been interpreted as the remains of a small harbour, though it might also have been a wharf that was later flooded by a slight change in sea level. The massive pieces of masonry on the right are from the collapsed western side of the citadel overlooking this harbour or wharf. (D. Nicolle)

THE FORTIFICATIONS OF OTHER CITIES & TOWNS

Beyond Jerusalem, few other large inland towns boasted fortifications. Only Tiberius appears to have a proper circuit wall. At Ramlah, the capital of Palestine in the earlier Islamic period, the Crusaders reportedly built a moated and fortified stronghold, but nothing now remains. At Nablus the only fortification from the Crusader period was a small tower serving as a place of refuge. In the other Crusader States to the north, Edessa was strongly fortified but its defences almost all pre-dated the Crusader conquest. The same was true at Harran, where some impressive fortifications had been constructed around 1059, but the Crusaders were said to have rebuilt the structures thrown down by an earthquake in 1114. In Antioch, most of the fortifications are Byzantine, and although much of the Crusader Citadel survives most of it dates from the 13th century. The town and defences of Tripoli were severely damaged in another earthquake in 1170 and had to be repaired in the late 12th or 13th centuries. At Jaffa the small port was safe only in summer; nevertheless its location as the closest port to Jerusalem caused the Crusaders to refortify the town immediately after they captured it.

PORTS & HARBOURS

Naval communications between the Crusader States and Western Europe were so important that considerable effort went into making the ports of Palestine, Lebanon, Syria and the Hatay province of Turkey secure. Several harbours were given special defence installations. Man-made harbours existed at Acre, Arsuf, 'Atlit, Caesarea, Beirut, Sidon and Tyre, plus several others in the County of Tripoli and the Principality of Antioch. The towers built on the moles that sheltered open harbours also served as anchorages for booms across the entrances. Some could also serve as locations for anti-shipping, stone-throwing engines like those used in siege warfare. The harbours themselves were usually separated from the town by a fortified wall, though these were not as strong as the walls on the landward sides of these ports.

The medieval harbour of Acre has been studied in detail. It had a mole and a quay, which were improved by Ibn Tulun, the ruler of Egypt in the 9th century. The sea level was 2m lower during the Middle Ages than today, whereas in Roman times it had been higher. Two maritime castles protected the entrance to the Crusader port. The first was the Tower of the Flies standing in the middle of the bay of Acre and commanding the south-eastern side of the entrance. First built in the Hellenistic period, it had several medieval layers, the earliest now being below sea level. This Crusader tower also served as a lighthouse for vessels entering the port. A second tower stood at the eastern end of the southern quay. Its remains are now a metre below sea level but it originally commanded the south-western side of the entrance to the port. A chain or boom protecting the port extended between this tower and the Tower of the Flies.

FORTIFIED RURAL VILLAGES & HOUSES

Before the Crusader conquest, most agricultural land in the Islamic Middle East was owned by *fallahin* peasants as freehold. However, this did not suit the feudal system introduced by the Western European conquerors, and as a result most of the indigenous peasants who remained became serfs while ownership of their lands transferred to the new Crusader aristocratic and settler elites. During the 12th century there was intensive Western European settlement, especially in the area north of Jerusalem. Here new towns, religious establishments, castles, towers and semi-fortified building complexes served as rural residences and granges or storage facilities for lesser

Crusader lords and their vassals. In fact many non-military buildings in the Kingdom of Jerusalem included defensive elements, primarily because of the fear of raiding and of rebellion by the indigenous population. At the same time the inclusion of such fortified elements was traditional in many of those countries from which the Crusaders came.

In contrast, some new 'planned' Crusader villages consisted of buildings along a single main street, forming an elongated settlement that was difficult to defend; the indigenous villages of Palestine were settlements clustered around an open central area, with their outer buildings often forming a continuous defensive wall. Excavations at the Crusader village of Caymont (Tal Qaimun) show that the village was in places double-walled. However the fortifications were not strong, the outer being less than 1.25m thick while the inner was 1.50m thick. There were no towers in the surrounding wall, though the village did contain one tower refuge. Another Crusader tower at al-Ram was later incorporated into a courtyard with surrounding vaults that included a wine press: Al-Ram has been identified as the grange of a 'new town' founded by the Canons of the Holy Sepulchre before 1160. In contrast, Forbelet (al-Taiyiba) is an example of a Crusader *bovaria* 'farm' in open countryside. It is a quasi-military structure built on Roman foundations but with no other defensive devices incorporated into its simple fortified wall.

Under Crusader occupation there was more intensive building in the rural regions of Palestine than at any other time since Umayyad rule in the 7th and 8th centuries. After the Crusaders were driven out, the construction work that characterized the Mamluk period focused on cities and strategic fortresses plus roads, bridges and facilities for merchants or pilgrims; villages were largely left to their own devices and most small castles were abandoned.

LIFE IN THE HOLY LAND CASTLES

Very few Crusader lords formed part of a village or rural community. Instead they lived in the cities where their way of life had more in common with the aristocratic elites of Italy than of France or Germany. Many members of the aristocracy no longer held much (or indeed any) land. Instead they maintained themselves by other forms of 'feudal rent'. Meanwhile, the castles were under authority of professional châtelains. Most of the strategically significant castles were also passing into the hands of the military orders.

CASTLES & SOCIAL ORDER

As in Italy, the knightly class of the Crusader States tried to preserve their social status and live what was seen as a knightly way of life. This did not mean that castles became mere fortresses garrisoned by low-status troops, whose comfort or cultural interests were neglected. Many castles provided a remarkably sophisticated and comfortable environment, no matter who actually lived in them. The remains of what would today be called 'Turkish baths' were found at Atlit and there may have been extensive

One fragment of wall painting from the chapel of the Hospitaller castle of Crac des Chevaliers (Hisn al-Akrad) probably illustrates the Virgin Mary presenting the infant Jesus to Simeon at the Temple in Jerusalem. (Archaeological Museum, Tartus, Syria; DGMS)

gardens at Montfort. According to Wilbrand von Oldenburg, the citadel of Beirut had mosaic floors that looked like gently rolling waves, while one room contained a fountain in the shape of a dragon. Even some smaller castles still contain traces of mosaics and painted plaster. Nevertheless, most of the sculptural decoration found at Safad dates from the 12th rather than the 13th century. It has also been assumed that the refined lifestyle seen in Crusader castles reflected Arab-Islamic and Byzantine cultural influences, and there is little reason to doubt this was true.

The most striking decoration was probably reserved for chapels, which included decorative stone panelling, floor mosaics and wall paintings. Here a distinctive style developed that was a mixture of Western European and Byzantine artistic styles while including Islamic decorative elements. Quite a lot survives in castle chapels, though it is likely that wall paintings were also seen in other important parts of a castle.

The most detailed description of a seigneurial chapel was of that in the castle of Tyre, as rebuilt around 1212. It is found in an account of the assassination of Philip of Montfort, Lord of Tyre, in 1270. The killer had entered Philip's service and the murder took place when he was talking to some burgesses from Tyre in the outer lobby of the chapel. Another mass had started, but as there were so few people in the chapel the assassin seized his opportunity and struck Philip with a dagger. He then attacked Philip's son John with a sword, but the youngster hid inside the altar, the front of which consisted of a wooden panel decorated with saints. The assassin's sword stuck in this panel, whereupon other people arrived and overpowered the killer. Philip, though mortally wounded, staggered to a stone bench in front of the entrance to his private chamber. Other evidence indicates that the chapel

was probably at first-floor level, and had a staircase as well as a lobby. Castle chapels were often placed close to the lord's private rooms, not merely for convenience but also because they also served as administrative meeting places.

Looking from the kitchens of Crac des Chevaliers (Hisn al-Akrad), along the main dining hall or chamber, a series of water-flushed latrines can be seen in the distance. (D. Nicolle)

Despite the Crusader States' loss of territory, castles and smaller fortifications continued to be centres of rural and agricultural administration, storage or distribution. More importantly they provided security, enabling agriculture to continue. Yet the poverty of so many of the 13th-century Crusader aristocracy meant that their garrisons were rarely as effective as those of the military orders, and even rulers were sometimes unable to pay or feed their own garrisons. This was particularly acute in the Principality of Antioch and the County of Tripoli, which rarely benefited from Papal appeals for money in support of the Kingdom of Jerusalem. Consequently it was common for garrisons to take part in agricultural activities to maintain themselves.

Amongst the smaller rural fortifications that continued to function was the Castle of Roger the Lombard in what is now Natanya. Caco, another rural fortification consisting of a tower and a reused Byzantine cistern, was not far away from this site. Khirbat Kurdana was different, consisting of a mill with a feeder dam and a defensive tower whose timber lower floor rested on stone corbels. It had one splayed arrow slit in the southern wall, and three in the north. During a second phase of construction after 1267, two floors were inserted on groin vaults, whose

Archaeologists excavating the early 12th-century Crusader castle at al-Wu'aira in southern Jordan found several neatly cut blocks of limestone, which probably served as keystones for arches in an earlier church. They were then incorporated into a much more roughly made Crusader wall. Each stone had a two-armed Christian Cross, though these had been partially defaced at some later period. (D. Nicolle)

corner pilasters blocked three of the arrow slits. A large pointed arch on the west side was now defended by a box machicolation, while the tower itself was flanked by two barrel-vaulted wheel chambers for a mill with a mill room above. These rural fortifications were small, but some others were more complex, including the Hospitaller castle of Coliat (al-Qulai'ah) north of Tripoli.

Most cities and larger towns within the Crusader States had a castle as the residence of a ruler, his castellan or a local lord. By the mid 13th century the King of Jerusalem's sénéschal had considerable authority over the royal fortresses, which played a significant role during the struggles between pro- and anti-imperial factions for control of the dwindling kingdom in the 1240s. The princely castles of Antioch and Tripoli were similarly under the authority of châtelains.

Apart from their military role protecting against invasion and during internal conflicts, the major castles were also used to receive important overseas visitors, as well as providing locations for politically significant weddings or festivals. Such events probably took place in their great halls and out of doors when weather permitted. They also served as courts of justice, and centres of administration and for the raising of taxes. High-status prisoners could normally expect to be held in such castles, though not necessarily in any comfort. In fact, elite prisoners were

The lower chambers of Crusader castles were almost invariably much plainer than the sometimes decorated and better illuminated upper chambers. Those seen here are in Crac des Chevaliers (Hisn al-Akrad) and are sometimes described as barracks. However, they are more likely to have been used as store rooms for food for the garrison and its horses, or for munitions. (D. Nicolle)

sometimes kept in extremely poor conditions until they died, though others were treated with respect and consideration until release or ransom.

Another group of smaller fortifications were those of the competing Italian merchant republics: Pisa, Genoa and Venice. These foreign powers had become significant landholders within the Crusader States, with the Venetians rivalling the King of Jerusalem as seigneurs around 13th-century Tyre. However, it was the great seaport of Acre that most concerned the Italians. Here considerable efforts were made, until the mid 13th century, to keep the quarters of the quarrelsome Italian merchant communes separated by neutral ground. Yet this did not stop the rivals from building ever taller towers for reasons of prestige as well as defence against rivals. The Pisans apparently had two such towers in their part of Acre during the first half of the 13th century. The Genoese, whose quarter was in the centre of Acre, had what was described as a 'great tower' called the Lamonçoia, until this was destroyed following Genoa's defeat by Venice and Pisa during the so-called War of St Sabas. A Genoese 'new tower' mentioned in 1249 may have been a replacement following the burning of the previous one. It was within crossbow range of the Pisan tower and, given the volatile relations between rival mercantile communes, Genoa not surprisingly sent military equipment from Italy to be used by their consul in Acre.

THE CASTLES AT WAR

The men who designed, built, garrisoned and attacked Crusader castles did so within military traditions that both inspired and limited their actions. Though the Crusader States were increasingly influenced by their Byzantine and Islamic rivals, their concepts of siege warfare remained rooted in their own Western European heritages. During the 12th century the science of warfare in Europe was primarily focused upon the taking and holding of fortified places, including towns and castles. The possession of territory, rather than the fighting of unpredictable set-piece battles, was what normally won wars within this tradition. Another secondary but still important strategy was raiding and devastation as a form of economic warfare.

Under such circumstances, the defenders' primary aim was to limit damage done by the enemy and to attack the raiders' supply lines, or to assemble an army to attack these invaders while they were scattered. Risking battle was apparently considered more worthwhile in societies where fortifications were poorly developed, but this was no longer the case in Europe or the Middle East. Furthermore, it is important to note that medieval Western European, Byzantine and Middle Eastern Islamic warfare all called for large numbers of military specialists or at least experienced soldiers. These would include garrison troops, artillerymen to operate stone-throwing war-machines, and engineers. All were normally included amongst the infantry and were further evidence that the idea of horsemen 'dominating' warfare during the medieval period is very misleading.

12TH-CENTURY STRATEGIES

Given the sophistication of 12th-century warfare in both Western Europe and the Middle East, it is not surprising to find that some castles or fortified places were given specific strategic roles. Reynaud de Châtillon, Lord of the virtually autonomous eastern fiefdom of Oultrejordain in the Kingdom of Jerusalem, decided to use his castles as springboards from which to extend his domination southwards into the Hijaz or western part of the Arabian peninsula. His strongly fortified lordship could, perhaps, also have been developed into an effective military barrier between the main Islamic political, economic and military power centres of Syria and Egypt. So it is hardly surprising that the removal of this threat, and of Reynaud de Châtillon himself, almost became an obsession for Saladin.

Further north the Terre de Suethe formed another smaller and more vulnerable extension of Crusader-held territory east of the River Jordan in what are now the Kingdom of Jordan and southern Syria. Here, for much of the 12th century, the garrison of the Crusader cave-fortress of the Cave de Sueth attempted to dominate the surrounding Arab villagers and bedouin. Their strong position at 'Ain al-Habis, overlooking the Yarmouk river, also enabled them to threaten the strategic road from Damascus to Arabia and Egypt.

An ability to threaten the enemy's communication from the relative safety of a castle offered several military, political and commercial advantages. For example, the Crusader castles in southern Jordan normally allowed Muslim pilgrims to use the ancient Haj road to the Islamic holy cities of Mecca and Medina in Arabia, but the Hajis or pilgrims often had to pay tolls. While the Crusaders held the so-called 'castle of Ayla', the same applied to Hajis travelling from Egypt across the Sinai Peninsula and the southern tip of Palestine. However, it is now thought that the Crusader castle of Ayla was on the island of Jazirat Fara'un rather than the mainland: this little island was recaptured by Saladin in 1170 and its fortifications were thereafter substantially enlarged. As a result there is, as yet, no clear archaeological evidence of Crusader architecture on Jazirat Fara'un. On the other hand, substantial Islamic forces, pilgrim caravans with adequate military escorts, and full-scale Islamic armies could cross such territories unhindered while the small garrisons of isolated Crusader castles dared not intervene.

In addition to threatening enemy communications, these Crusader castles could act as garrisoned strongpoints to secure the Crusaders' own lines of contact. This was considered extremely important, and the reason King Richard advanced so slowly towards Jerusalem during the final phase of the Third Crusade was his need to repair castles that Saladin had carefully destroyed along Richard's route. Unless these could be secured, the Crusaders could not be confident of protecting their extended supply lines. In the end the failure to secure the road to Jerusalem resulted in King Richard's advance failing, and Saladin retained control.

A tower or castle could also blockade a particularly stubborn enemy position. In such circumstances it was almost a case of 'castle versus castle'. This situation started very early in the history of the Crusades, with the erection of three strong towers

The remains of what was probably a rock-cut channel for water still lead from the stream in a steep valley running along the western side of the castle of Gibelcar ('Akkar), into the castle which is to the left of the observer. Though it could be blocked by a besieger, it was used to fill the castle's cisterns before a siege occurred. (D. Nicolle)

during the First Crusade's siege of Antioch. The fact that two were built after the arrival of allied fleets on the nearby coast might suggest that they were made of timber from the ships in question, and perhaps also earth. In northern Italy tall timber 'counter-towers' were already a feature of siege warfare. However, the written accounts make it clear that at least one of these 'counter-forts', the Mahommeries Tower, was partially or wholly built of stone, despite the fact that it had been erected after the arrival of a Byzantine fleet manned by Anglo-Saxon exiles. Taking all the evidence into consideration it seems most likely that the Crusader counter-towers outside Antioch used whatever materials were available, be these stones from an Islamic cemetery, earth, rubble or timber from dismantled ships.

During the Crusader siege of Tripoli in 1101, the largely southern French or Provençal army of Raymond of St Gilles built a more substantial blockade castle overlooking the low-lying neck of land on which the port-city of Tripoli lay. This castle stood on a hill known to the Crusaders as Mons Peregrinus. It was subsequently

The oval-shaped open water cistern near the Crusader citadel at the summit of the fortifications of Antioch. The retaining wall would originally have gone all the way around. (D. Nicolle)

called Jabal Sanjil in Arabic, or the 'Hill of St Gilles'. A small settlement soon developed around the base of the hill and in 1109 the Islamic port-city of Tripoli finally surrendered. This castle was extended considerably during the 12th and 13th centuries. However, the original city remained the main centre of population and it was not until after the Crusaders were expelled in the late 13th century that the ancient centre was largely abandoned and a new city developed around the castle. This became today's bustling city of Tripoli, while the old seaport declined into a sleepy suburb called al-Mina.

The Arab chronicler Ibn al-Athir seems to have regarded the Crusader castle of Montferrand (Ba'rin) not far from the Islamic city of Hama as a sort of counter-castle or means of blockading Hama, rather like the castle built earlier to overlook Tripoli. On the other hand the well-known theory that several early Crusader castles in south-western Palestine were intended to contain raiding from Fatimid-held Ascalon is now widely discredited.

When used as bases for defensive operations, the castles of the Crusader States were often very well stocked with food and other supplies, not merely for their own garrisons but for use by a field army operating in the locality or camped close to the castle. This, according to William of Tyre, was the case with Artah and some other small neighbouring towns during 1119. On other occasions in the 12th century, the castle of Trapesac (Darbsak) appears to have served as a regional armoury or mobilization store. Arima (al-Araymah) in the County of Tripoli similarly seems to have been used as a storage base or distribution centre for military supplies during the mid 12th century. Fortified cities, of course, frequently fulfilled the same role, and the huge quantities of military material that fell into Saladin's hands when he conquered Acre in 1187 were surely not only for the city garrison's use.

The field armies that depended upon such well-protected stores did not necessarily have to win a battle to defeat an enemy invasion. In the autumn of 1183 the army of the Kingdom of Jerusalem successfully shadowed Saladin's invading force, first using Saffuriyah (Sephorie) and then al-Fula as secure bases. Eventually Saladin was obliged to withdraw, though only after ravaging large parts of the Crusader Kingdom. The castle of Saffuriyah was, in fact, an obvious place for the army of Jerusalem to gather if an enemy assembled around Damascus. Saffuriyah had plenty of water for a defending army as it waited to see if the enemy chose to cross the Jordan north or south of Lake Tiberius, both of which approaches could

The rock-cut fosse that separated the spur-castle at Krak des Moabites (al-Karak) from the rest of the hill on the right is shallow compared to the example at Saone (Sahyun). This section of the outer wall dates from the late 1160s, while the structure behind it is believed to date from the first Crusader castle, built around 1142. (D. Nicolle)

be covered from Saffuriyah. This was, at least initially, what the Crusader Kingdom's army did during Saladin's invasion of 1187. On this occasion King Guy's army camped about 1km south of Saffuriyah, around the largest springs in the area. However, Guy decided that a passive strategy was politically untenable and so marched to meet the invaders – resulting in Saladin's overwhelming victory at the battle of Hattin.

A PLACE OF REFUGE

If the Crusader States lost a battle, or felt unable to risk even shadowing the enemy, then their fortresses became places of refuge. After the defeat at Hattin, much of the Western European settler population and those of its knightly elite who remained were obliged to retreat into their castles, towers or whatever fortifications were available because the local non-Christian populations now rose against them. Some of these castles managed to hold out for a long time, and a few clung on until relieved by what developed into the Third Crusade. In most places, however, the remaining Crusader garrisons were seriously undermanned and perhaps demoralized. On the other hand, the established Middle Eastern Islamic strategy that Saladin adopted (described in Shaykh al-Harawi's military treatise for Saladin or his son) stated that a ruler should not unnecessarily court danger or even a setback. Instead a ruler was advised to mop up the weakest enemy places, thus maintaining the momentum of his campaign as well as the morale of his troops.

It was the intensity rather than the basic nature of siege warfare that changed during the 12th century. Certain features remained the same, the most obvious being a castle's physical location. In 1115 an Islamic army had little difficulty seizing the suburbs of Crusader-ruled Afamia, but their still primitive stone-throwing siege machines were unable to reach or damage the citadel of Afamia, which was on a high hill. That same year the Muslims attacked Crusader-held Kafr Tab. This time the same stone-throwing machines created a gap in the fortified wall – a remarkable feat given the small numbers and limited power of such weapons – through which infantry could make their assault. Four years later Crusader-held Atharib was similarly attacked and this time the Muslims' stone-throwing engines 'deprived the towers of their defences and killed the defenders'. Here it is clear that the mangonels' primary role was to smash wall-head defences and thus clear the garrison from such walls or towers.

The castle of Le Destroit (Qal'at Dustray), was constructed on the low coastal ridge of central Palestine to control a coastal road between Haifa and Jaffa, and it also played a major role during the Third Crusade. It stood on a rock-cut base and many of its internal structures were partially cut from the rock. The narrow coastal ridge was itself cut by a ditch, perhaps during the early 13th century, this serving as a sort of dry moat on the southern side of the castle. (D. Nicolle)

THE CAVE-FORTRESS OF THE CAVE DE SUETH UNDER SIEGE

The Cave de Sueth was often raided, attacked or besieged, and fell to one side or the other several times. Unfortunately the site is also very vulnerable to earthquakes, and has suffered severe damage during its recorded history, both before and since the Crusader period. As a result most of the cliff face has collapsed into the deep valley of the River Yarmouk. Nevertheless, several man-made caves survive: some are still complete, others have only partial remains and a few are only visible now as recesses in the cliff. Consequently, the methods used to attach any outer wooden structures can only be guessed at, though the existence of such external galleries or hoardings is strongly suggested in various accounts of the Cave. In this reconstruction, a timber hoarding has been placed outside what appears to have been the most important caves in the complex, at what has been termed the 'third level'. Their openings led into what seems to have been a water-storage cistern and a series of neatly carved chambers that originally formed part of an Eastern Christian *laura* or monastic retreat. The timber hoarding or gallery itself has been envisaged as a smaller, more cramped and necessarily more flimsy version of the only complete and original timber hoarding to survive in Western Europe, which is located at Laval castle in France and dates from the 13th century. (Adam Hook © Osprey Publishing)

It is also clear that the Crusader garrison of Atharib had intended to make an active defence. However, mining at the base of their walls led the defenders to surrender because, as William of Tyre put it, 'The townsmen, fearing that when the ramparts were undermined the whole fortress would collapse headlong, surrendered the place.'

THE SIEGE OF THE CAVE DE SUETH

Another interesting and well-recorded siege was that of the Cave de Sueth. In 1174 Saladin took control of Damascus, and as a result the Cave de Sueth now faced the same powerful enemy to the north and to the south. But it was not until June 1182 that the storm broke and the Cave fell to a small force commanded by Farukh Shah, Saladin's formidable deputy in Damascus. The fact that this cave-fortress surrendered after only five days led to rumours of treachery within the Christian camp, perhaps on the part of the garrison commander. Farukh Shah's Mamluk troops were, however, an elite. William of Tyre also reported that the enemy mined vertically through the soft rock, thus forcing the garrison to surrender. In fact, a roughly hewn passage still leads almost vertically from a second-level cave to one of the third-level caves. It seems a big excavation for only five days' work, but Syrian military miners were amongst the most respected of their day. Although the vertical tunnel only allowed access to the northernmost third-level cave, this was presumably linked to the more important southern group of third-level caves by external walkways.

Perhaps the psychological impact of this mining operation and a consequent threat to the garrison's water supply prompted a quick surrender. The question of water is clearly important. The waterfall of 'Ain al-Habis only exists following rain and was presumably tapped to supply one or more cisterns within the southern third-level caves. The siege by Farukh Shah took place in late summer, before the rainy season, so the Crusader garrison would have been relying on stored water. If the Christians damaged the cisterns or polluted the water before surrendering, this would be of even greater significance where the second siege of 1182 was concerned, with the Crusaders attempting to retake the Cave. Farukh Shah's seizure of the Cave de Sueth had been the opening move in a major campaign during which Saladin failed to capture Beirut, but went on to conquer substantial territory in northern Iraq. Meanwhile, Crusader forces counterattacked Damascene territory. Farukh Shah also died around this time, weakening Islamic resistance.

One of the most carefully carved chambers in the cave-fortress of the Cave de Sueth was the church. It dated from before the Crusaders arrived, when this site was a Christian monastic retreat. Today most of the front and one of the side walls of the man-made cave have collapsed into the valley. (D. Nicolle)

William of Tyre stated that the Crusaders now brought their own miners to help besiege the cave-fortress, cutting away rocks on top of the cliff, which others then hurled down the precipice. Flints in the soft rock damaged their tools but these were immediately repaired by yet other workers, the whole operation being defended by troops camped on the hilltop. This bombardment continued day and night, perhaps smashing the wooden walkways and eventually demoralizing the Muslim garrison. William of Tyre's description seems remarkably accurate, for there are traces of what appear to be man-made excavations terrifyingly close to the lip of the cliff above the caves. Meanwhile, other warriors ventured along a narrow path leading to a ledge across the cliff-face. There they skirmished using spears, swords, bows and crossbows with a garrison consisting of only 70 picked men. Such skirmishing presumably took place around walls whose remains can still be seen north and south of the lower caves. After three weeks the exhausted garrison surrendered on honourable terms. The Cave de Sueth then remained in Crusader hands for a further five years until the entire area was abandoned following Saladin's great victory at the battle of Hattin. Thereafter its military role apparently disappeared.

VADUM JACOB, SAONE & BOURZAY

Archaeological excavations have shed fascinating light on how the unfinished Crusader castle at Vadum Jacob was lost. Work on Vadum Jacob began in October 1178, the King of Jerusalem reportedly employing the whole army of his kingdom in its construction. However, the workers were attacked by Saladin in August 1179. The Crusaders gathered their livestock into an area inside the southern gate and hastily built archery positions inside a small gate to the east. Saladin's troops attacked from the north, east and south, setting fire to wooden doors in the gates and shooting an astonishingly dense hail of arrows at the defenders within. Mining of the northern wall probably took place near the north-eastern corner of the unfinished fortress. On 30 August 1179, Vadum Jacob fell and its garrison was slain. After this there was no further attempt to fortify the site.

Information from other sieges later in the 12th century adds further details about how such places were both defended and attacked. Following Hattin and the fall of Jerusalem to Saladin, the arrival of Conrad of Monferrat at Tyre inspired its people to refuse Saladin's terms and to defend their city. On this occasion, according to Ibn al-Athir, they strengthened the fortifications and 'dug the moats anew', which suggests that the fosse and perhaps even the wall had been allowed to fall into disrepair. Further north along the coast, Saladin suffered another setback at Tartus in July 1188 where the Crusader garrison's heavy crossbow balistas, mostly installed in the keep, foiled the besiegers.

Very little remains of the 12th-century castle at Kadmos (Qadmus) in the Syrian coastal mountains. Though normally regarded as an Isma'ili or 'Assassin' stronghold, it was built by the Crusaders earlier in the 12th century before being taken by the so-called 'Assassins'. (D. Nicolle)

SALADIN'S CAPTURE OF THE UNFINISHED CASTLE OF VADUM JACOB, 1179

The siege of Vadum Jacob by Saladin's army in 1179 has provided historians with an abundance of information about castle building and siege warfare in the 12th century. Not only was the event well documented, largely from the Islamic side, but the castle was also abandoned after its capture by Saladin. No further work was done on the unfinished fortifications and it was left as a virtual time capsule. Tools and other pieces of equipment remained where the Crusader workmen had dropped them; walls, gates, doors, piles of finished and semi-prepared masonry, lime for mortar and all the other paraphernalia of the 12th-century building trade lay scattered around. Such items have recently been uncovered by Israeli archaeologists, along with evidence confirming various details of the siege as described in the chronicles. The whole army of the Kingdom of Jerusalem is said to have been employed in the construction of Vadum Jacob but, as Saladin's army approached, they gathered their livestock inside the southern gate, including the beasts of burden used in construction work. This was presumably regarded as the easiest part of the unfinished fortress to defend. Another position was hurriedly constructed in a smaller gate on the eastern side. Saladin's troops attacked from the south, east and north, showering the defenders with a massive hail of arrows and managing to burn the wooden structures in and around the gates. Mining was also started, probably against the north-eastern corner of the existing defences, and the castle was overrun on 30 August 1179. (Adam Hook © Osprey Publishing)

The northern part of the fosse or moat around the citadel at Arsus (Arsuf). Massive strengthening piers were only added to this, the longest stretch of outer retaining wall, probably because the pressure of loose sandy earth behind threatened to burst the wall and fill the moat. (D. Nicolle)

Later the same month the fall of the massive Crusader castle of Saone was a great shock to the Crusader States. General Hackett investigated this siege in his Oxford University B. Litt thesis in 1937. Having himself explored the site, he identified what he regarded as 'dead ground' in the south-east, which, he suggested, provided a suitable jumping off point for an assault. The 12th-century Arab chronicler Imad al-Din certainly mentioned 'an angle of the ditch that the Franks had neglected to fortify', perhaps referring to the same spot though in medieval terms. Given the immense effort put into the construction of the Crusader castle of Saone, it seems unlikely that its designers would make such a fundamental error and the truth can probably be found in changes in siege technology over the previous generation or so. This was clearly a time of rapid development, with the adoption of more powerful stone-throwing mangonels, including those powered by the counterweight principle, as well as advances in the design of crossbows.

The Crusader garrison of the mountaintop inland castle of Bourzay similarly relied on their crossbows to keep Saladin's fully armoured assault troops from hauling themselves up the extremely steep slopes when they attacked. Here, in August 1188, a bombardment by even the latest mangonels was impractical, so Saladin used his army's numerical superiority and the length of the Crusaders' walls to wear down the garrison: he conducted a sequence of limited assaults in difficult places throughout the heat of the day. Once again, at Bourzay Saladin's siege tactics closely mirrored advice given in the treatise written by Shaykh al-Harawi. It is also worth noting that both Muslim and Crusader chroniclers sometimes tended to exaggerate the steepness of the slopes upon which some Crusader castles were built. The present author, having clambered up several very steep slopes, and tumbled down a few, knows that they are tiring rather than exhausting, even in the height of summer.

TACTICS & TERRITORY – THE 13TH CENTURY

Despite the development of larger transport ships and better accommodation for horses on board, the Crusader States continued to suffer from a serious shortage of livestock in the 13th century. This applied not only to large war-horses but also to pack animals. The limited territory of the remaining Crusader States also meant that they lacked pasture to maintain large herds. The shortage had several effects, not least of which was to make it difficult for armies to move around between their main fortified centres. Furthermore, huge efforts were made to avoid losses of horses on campaign or in battle. In complete contrast, the Crusaders' Muslim neighbours had access to very large numbers of horses, though more so in Syria than in Egypt. These included not only the relatively small horses traditionally associated with Turkish horse-archers, but also the large, finely bred and hot-blooded mounts used by elite armoured cavalry.

The main entrance into Le Destroit (Qal'at Dustray), on the low coastal ridge next to Atlit castle, was a gateway partially cut through the rock. Another secondary entrance seems to have been approached via an external wooden stair supported on timber beams slotted into a series of holes in the man-made rock face, as seen here. (D. Nicolle)

Given such constraints, it is hardly surprising that the Crusader States – and even those new Crusader forces arriving from Europe – relied on fortifications to an ever increasing extent. Furthermore, castles played a leading role in the Crusaders' rare attempts to regain lost territory. Sometimes land was temporarily abandoned as a result of the enemy's raiding expeditions, which often meant that villages and even towns had to be evacuated. Sometimes Islamic armies attempted to destroy such places, although small-scale raids merely damaged crops, orchards, vineyards, olive groves and other agricultural targets. The destruction of food stores and economic assets, like mills, would be considered a significant success, so the Crusader States placed great emphasis on giving them some degree of fortification. If this failed, the damaged facilities might hopefully be regained, repaired and refortified, as happened to the mills at Recordane during the 13th century.

Meanwhile, the fortified cities served as centres from which such localized reconquests could be launched. The citadels built at Jaffa, Caesarea and Sidon by Emperor Frederick II as nominal ruler of the Kingdom of Jerusalem may have provided secure bases for such limited operations. Certainly the Kingdom of Jerusalem made what were, in the circumstances of the time, considerable efforts to re-establish control over the southern coast of Lebanon in 1227–28, during which period the Sea Castle of Sidon was constructed on a previously uninhabited

During the 12th century the Crusaders extended the hilltop castle of Saone (Sahyun) in two directions. The western end of the spur on which the castle was built was eventually enclosed by these relatively simple fortifications because this part of the site was surrounded by cliffs and very steep slopes, though their date remains unclear. (D. Nicolle)

coastal islet. Only later were serious fortifications added to the town of Sidon itself, which thereafter remained under Crusader control until its evacuation in 1291.

Safad castle, lost to Saladin in 1188, returned to Crusader hands from 1218 to 1220 when it was apparently intended as a base from which to reconquer Galilee. As a result, when the Muslims took it again in 1220, they completely dismantled the existing castle. Safad was handed back to the Kingdom of Jerusalem in 1240, whereupon major efforts were made to refortify it, probably for the same strategic reasons. A few years later the Crusading King Louis IX of France camped as close as possible to Frederick's fortifications at Jaffa, in order to protect the building of a stronger city wall. Louis probably did something similar at Sidon where an apparent hall along the northern face of the Sea Castle served as his headquarters.

However, such rebuilding efforts did not always succeed. For example, the Fifth Crusade, using Acre as its base, failed to retake Mount Tabor in 1217, although the latter was closer to Acre than to any comparable Islamic seat of power. Several efforts launched from Antioch after 1191 similarly failed to regain territory lost by the Principality. The main reason for these uncertain results was the Crusader States' lack of sufficient manpower to undertake proper siege operations. Consequently they largely relied on raiding tactics, and these could regain territory only if an enemy was willing to relinquish it. Full-scale offensives were possible only when

The Galata Tower, built by the Genoese as the keypoint in their defence of Pera (modern Galata) in Istanbul. (D. Nicolle)

large Crusading armies arrived from Western Europe, and these were few and not always successful.

Meanwhile, the upgrading or repair of existing fortifications was essentially defensive. Even the decision to refortify Ascalon in 1239 was initially defensive, to face any threat from Egyptian-held Gaza while the Crusaders planned to attack Damascus. In the event they attacked the Egyptians instead, and suffered catastrophic defeat at the battle of La Forbie in 1244. Thereupon Egyptian forces blockaded Ascalon until it surrendered.

The County of Tripoli enjoyed a better strategic situation, and although it lost some territory to Saladin and his successors, its heartland in what are now northern Lebanon and the southern part of the Syrian coast was strongly protected by the military orders. In fact, this territory remained a substantial and well-fortified base area from which Crusader forces could raid their Muslim neighbours. This caused massive economic damage and kept the Arab villages so subdued that many accepted Crusader suzereinty, even within rugged and inaccessible mountain regions. Hospitaller garrisons from Crac des Chevaliers and Margat often joined forces to raid the hinterland of Hama and other nearby Islamic cities, and the strength of the Hospitaller palatinate in the north of the County of Tripoli even obliged the fearsome Isma'ili 'Assassins' to pay tribute. This tribute only ended with the fall of Crac des Chevaliers to the Mamluks. Even then, some remaining Crusader garrisons remained strong enough to launch further raids; in 1280, 200 knights attacked the fertile Buqai'ah plain near Crac, despite the fact that the latter fortress was now in Islamic hands.

Things seemed quieter in the now tiny Principality of Antioch. However, several Crusader-held ports were already being used as bases from which to launch naval raids against Islamic coasts and shipping. This might be interpreted as 'the wave of the future' in the struggle between Christian and Islamic forces in the Middle East and eastern Mediterranean, something which became a major aspect of 14th-century warfare.

The only large-scale or strategic Crusading expeditions in the Middle East during the 13th century were those launched against Egypt, which was now the centre of regional Islamic power. One of these seaborne invasions provides the only known evidence for a classic motte-style castle from this period. When the Fifth Crusade landed on the western bank of the main eastern Delta branch of the Nile, facing Damietta, on 27 May 1218, they fortified their camp with the usual ditch and rampart.

The campaign dragged on through the summer and autumn, despite the capture of the Chain Tower of Damietta. Operations stagnated during winter when the Crusader army was virtually trapped within its fortified camp on the western bank of the river. However, Damietta finally capitulated in 1219. The Crusaders then seized the fortified town of Tanis. According to James de Vitry, who was eyewitness, the Crusaders built a third fortification in the middle of Lake Manzala, between Damietta and Tanis.

This was followed by a new and separate fourth construction on the west bank facing Damietta. It was on a sort of motte, which, according to de Vitry, was:

> raised on the height of a mound until it resembled a hill, enclosing the sand with a wall of
> clayey soil, for in Egypt stones are not to be found unless they are carried with great labour
> from Cyprus or Syria (by ship) … In the middle they erected a wooden tower of astonishing
> height, not only for the defence of the castle, but also so that from a distance it might appear
> as a beacon to those sailing to Damietta.

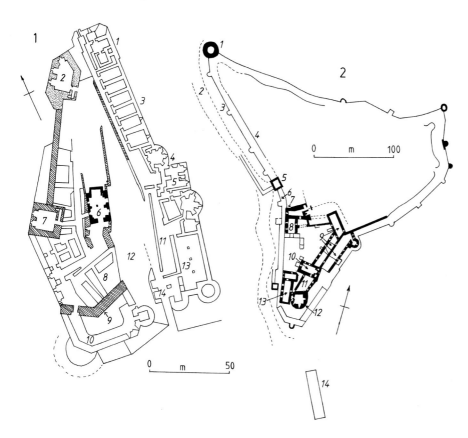

1 – The castle of Belfort (structures built by the Lords of Sagette 1139–90 are hatched, Ayyubid structures 1190–1240 are stippled, Templar structures are black, and Mamluk and Ottoman structures are unshaded): (1) early Mamluk residential tower, (2) Ayyubid great tower, (3) early Mamluk casemates, (4) early Mamluk postern, (5) early Mamluk salient with two towers, (6) Templar chapel, (7) 12th-century Crusader donjon, (8) 17th-century Ottoman buildings, (9) 12th-century Crusader main wall, (10) early Mamluk entrance way, (11) early Mamluk entrance passage, (12) early Mamluk entrance ramp, (13) early Mamluk hall (after Corvisier).

2 – The castle of Margat: (1) north-western great tower, (2) outer fosse, (3) outer enclosure wall, (4) inner enclosure wall, (5) outer entrance tower, (6) forecourt between outer and inner gates, (7) inner gate, (8) substructure of vaulted chapter house, (9) magazine chambers, (10) chapel, (11) two-storied hall, (12) southern great tower rebuilt by the Mamluks, (13) hall, (14) open cistern (after Müller-Wiener).

The castle of Montréal (Shawbak) stands on a steep hill which, being in a broad valley, is lower than the surrounding plateau. Almost all of what can be seen today consists of the later medieval Islamic fortress, while the remains of a much smaller 12th-century Crusader castle are hidden within these massive walls. (D. Nicolle)

Apparently this unusual castle consisted of a mound of sand retained by a clay ringwork with a timber tower on top. The design may have been determined by a lack of building stone in this part of Egypt, where traditional Nile Delta architecture was of brick. However, it is interesting to note the major role played by Germans and Frisians who provided the timber, and the fact that the majority of men on this Crusade came from areas of Western Europe where the old motte style of castle remained common.

The defensive function of Crusader fortifications is obvious, but the precise way in which they operated during the 13th century is not always clear. The many small towers that dotted Crusader territory may, for example, have served as observation posts and local refuges. Nevertheless, warning of the approach of enemy forces did not necessitate fortifications, however small, so perhaps their tiny garrisons were expected to offer suicidal resistance in the hope of delaying an attack upon a major centre. Delays or truces clearly featured prominently in resistance. A short three months' truce with Saladin, after the battle of Hattin, enabled Renaud de Sagette to prepare his castle of Belfort for a prolonged siege. Chroniclers refer to supplies being sent, and to the repair of its walls and gate. Yet when the crisis came, Belfort fell quite easily. The importance of outlying castles was clearly not lost on Saladin, whose biographer Imad al-Din wrote of Antioch after Hattin that 'To take away her fortresses is to take away her life.'

Good visibility was important for a major fortress. A sentry on the inner towers of Atlit, for example, was said to have been able to see an approaching enemy 13km away, but this was merely a result of its coastal location. Furthermore, the site of Atlit could, to some extent, 'control' movement along the vital coastal road. At one time the selection of the site of Amoude in Cilicia as the location for a Teutonic Knights castle was thought to reflect the amount of land beneath its gaze. More importantly the hill of Amoude lay close to a strategic river crossing located in the heart of a fertile and densely populated plain. One of the Teutonic Knights' other important castles in the Kingdom of Cilician Armenia was Haruniya, close to a very important pass through the Amanus Mountains linking Cilicia and the plains of northern Syria. Such considerations were far more important than the distance that could be surveyed from the highest towers.

Despite the development of more powerful siege machines, most notably the counterweight trebuchet, the basic techniques of siege warfare remained the same in the 13th century as they had been during the 12th century. This was as true for the defenders as for the attackers. Given their numerical weakness, the basic strategy adopted by Crusader garrisons when facing a major assault was to retire into their citadel until, hopefully, the raiders withdrew. For several decades this worked well, especially against ill-disciplined foes like the Khwarawzians, who were themselves little more than a 'refugee army' fleeing ahead of Genghis Khan's more determined forces.

The Citadel of Tripoli (Qal'at Sanjil) stands on top of a hill overlooking late medieval Tripoli and the coastal port-suburb of al-Mina on the site of the early medieval and Crusader city. It was considerably modified by both the Mamluks and the Ottomans, though its basic plan and inner keep are essentially Crusader work. (D. Nicolle)

Clearly the construction of powerful defences made the Islamic states consider smaller campaigns as little more than pointless. Major invasions now had to be conducted by sizeable forces and even the hugely powerful Mamluk sultanate of Egypt and Syria could not take all fortified places in a single campaign. Indeed some of the strongest Crusader fortresses were left until last. Furthermore, the Mamluks had to take complete control of major citadels if they wanted to occupy a city or region permanently. The fact that it took the Mamluks over 40 years to subdue what looked like small, isolated, vulnerable and demoralized coastal enclaves demonstrates the soundness of the Crusader States' defensive strategy. That it ultimately failed was a reflection of geopolitical factors, not of the defences, their garrisons or their tactics.

The more warning a garrison received of an impending attack, the better its chances of a successful defence. Yet Crusader garrisons often had little warning. Sultan Baybars, for example, was famous for the care he took to achieve surprise, sometimes not even informing his senior commanders of the real destination of a raid or siege campaign until his army was already on the march. This forced the Crusader States to spread their defences amongst several potential targets, further contributing to the remarkably small size of some garrisons.

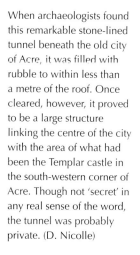

When archaeologists found this remarkable stone-lined tunnel beneath the old city of Acre, it was filled with rubble to within less than a metre of the roof. Once cleared, however, it proved to be a large structure linking the centre of the city with the area of what had been the Templar castle in the south-western corner of Acre. Though not 'secret' in any real sense of the word, the tunnel was probably private. (D. Nicolle)

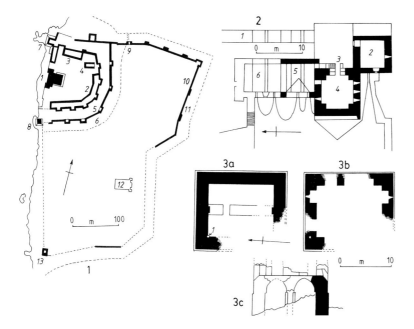

1 – Tartus: (1) donjon,
(2) inner wall of the citadel,
(3) banqueting hall,
(4) chapel, (5) outer citadel
wall, (6) inner fosse,
(7) north-western tower,
(8) south-western tower of
the citadel, (9) north gate
of the city, (10) city wall,
(11) city fosse,
(12) Cathedral of Our Lady
of Tortosa, (13) south-western
corner tower of city walls
(after Deschamps and
Müller-Wiener).

2 – The fortified mill
at Recordane (Khirbat
Kardanah): (1) bridge
across the stream,
(2) first mill, (3) entrance
to the tower protected
by a machicolation,
(4) fortified tower,
(5) second and third mills,
(6) fourth and fifth mills
added during the Ottoman
period (after Pease).

3a–c – Remains of the
fortified tower of Caco
(al-Qaqun): 3a – lower floor
or basement with ceramic
drainage pipe (1) from the
roof; 3b – upper floor with
pipe embedded within the
corner wall; 3c – east–west
section through the existing
structure (after Leach).

Larger towns and cities could summon local militias when threatened, and such communal forces were recorded even before the emergence of real 'communes' with Crusader cities. At the same time, major urban centres like Acre housed relatively large professional forces, yet their effectiveness was not guaranteed; Antioch capitulated in 1268 after a siege of only five days, despite being fully garrisoned.

The large numbers that crowded into a city or its citadel as the outer town and suburbs were abandoned to the enemy must have caused problems. There would have been far more frightened mouths to feed and only a small proportion of such refugees would have been effective fighting men. The final defence of Acre in 1291 drew in many available troops from other coastal enclaves, weakening them to such an extent that, after Acre fell, most other outposts simply surrendered.

When such a city fell much of its population is unlikely to have been able to escape, especially when disciplined and organized conquerors, like the Mamluks, placed guards on the gates to avoid unauthorized looting by their own men. Even on the coast there were not enough ships for everybody to escape. As a result many of the poor, unable to pay for a passage in such ships, with nowhere to go and no family links outside the Crusader States, had no alternative but to remain. A larger number of these usually unrecorded 'poor' were presumably absorbed into what became the Arab-speaking coastal populations of Syria, Lebanon and Palestine.

The lower part of the great fortified tower that rises over Safita (Castel Blanc) consisted of a church, which it has remained to this day throughout the tumultuous history of Syria. The impact of earthquakes, which still sometimes rock this region, can be seen in the cracked semi-dome of the apse. (D. Nicolle)

Although the basic techniques of siege warfare remained largely unchanged, more powerful artillery was available in increasing numbers during the 13th century. The mining operations that had proved so effective against Crusader fortifications in the 12th century continued, but were now supported by massed trebuchets. This combination proved highly effective against Crac des Chevaliers in 1271. The demoralization of Crusader garrisons during these final decades may have been overstated, but constant bombardment by great rocks clearly had an impact that was probably more significant than the physical damage caused.

On the other side, the defenders' use of espringals and 'great crossbows' could prove very effective, because the attackers were more exposed to the massive arrows shot by such weapons than the defenders within their stone walls. 'Great crossbows' were used by the Templars of Atlit in 1220, causing such heavy casualties that the Ayyubid Sultan al-Muazzam withdrew his army. The Templar garrison of Jaffa used the same sort of weapons in defence of Jaffa in 1266.

Other chroniclers add further details about defensive measures, these being particularly abundant in accounts of the final siege of Acre in 1291. For example, Oliver of Paderborn, in his *Historia Damiatina*, described one tower as having huge iron spikes attached to wooden hoardings. Similar obstacles may have been planted in the moat. However, a suggestion that, during the final epic siege, the main wall of Acre was protected by wooden barbicans seems more doubtful.

THE FALL OF ARSUF, 1265

The relatively new citadel of Arsuf was leased to the military order of the Hospitallers by the once-powerful Ibelin family in 1261. The Hospitallers then poured money, materials and effort into strengthening this vital fortification, which formed one of the southernmost coastal outposts of the Crusader Kingdom of Jerusalem. Nevertheless, only four years later, the powerful Mamluk sultanate of Egypt and Syria launched a major offensive under Sultan Baybars, who was one of the most effective military leaders in medieval history. In fact, Baybars pretended to be on a hunting expedition in what is now the occupied West Bank when he and his troops swooped. First they attacked Caesarea, which fell after only a week. Haifa was then destroyed, but Atlit held out, and so Baybars besieged Arsuf. Despite its Hospitaller garrison,

which included 270 knights, the town fell and the citadel capitulated only three days later. Archaeological evidence of this final siege includes not only a thick layer of ash but also an extraordinary number of mangonel stones. Those of the Crusader defenders were mostly found in neat piles, never having been shot. Those of the Mamluks, however, not only included chipped and broken examples of the carefully carved and balanced missiles preferred by mangonel operators, but also large numbers of more roughly shaped rocks. This seems to indicate that the Mamluks launched such a massive bombardment that they ran out of ammunition and had to collect whatever stones were suitable from the neighbouring hills. (After Roll and Smertenko, with additions by Nicolle; Adam Hook © Osprey Publishing)

143

THE FATE OF THE FORTIFICATIONS

The first of the Crusader States to fall was the County of Edessa, the last fortress of which surrended to Nur al-Din in 1151. Having existed for only a little over half a century, and its western regions having already been strongly fortified, few of the County of Edessa's castles had been altered by the Crusaders. Some were then strengthened by the Ayyubid successors of Saladin. This territory then became a battleground between the Mamluk sultanate of Syria-Egypt, and the Mongol or post-Mongol dynasties of Iraq-Iran. Consequently its fortresses, fortified towns and cities were extensively strengthened if not entirely rebuilt, particularly by the Mamluks.

The Principality of Antioch endured for much longer. On the other hand the Principality lost the lands east of the River Orontes – over half of its original territory – even before Saladin virtually destroyed the Kingdom of Jerusalem further south. Consequently, few of the fortifications at Harenc, Ma'arat al-Nu'man, Afamia and Kafr Tab date from the short-lived Crusader occupation. Several large and strategically more important castles, lost by the Crusader States in the later 12th century, then served to defend what had become Islamic frontier territory. Some, like Sahyun, previously called Saone by the Crusaders, were subsequently involved in inter-Islamic civil wars.

Other (mostly small) castles that had briefly been held in the Syrian coastal mountains where the Principality of Antioch and the Country of Tripoli met, were taken over by the Isma'ilis during the mid 12th century. These Isma'ilis were a sect of Shi'a Islam who often felt more threatened by the Sunni Muslim rulers of the great Syrian cities of the interior than by the Crusader invaders on the coast. As a consequence they strove to maintain an armed neutrality between the Crusader States and the Islamic states, basing their power upon small castles that dotted their own tiny mountainous state, several of which had been built or rebuilt by the Crusaders earlier in the 12th century. One such castle was at Qadmus, which had been constructed for a member of the Crusader feudal aristocracy.

Other Crusader fortifications remained in Christian hands for much longer, even after being briefly retaken by Islamic armies. Saladin, for example, spent eight days supervising the careful demolition of the walls of Tartus and the part of the citadel that his army had managed to capture. His

The citadel in the north-western corner of the Crusader port-city of Tartus was surrounded by two massive walls, except where it overlooked the sea. These walls had large rectangular towers, those of the inner wall seen here as quite closely spaced. (D. Nicolle)

effort to make them indefensible in the future failed, however. Having been unable to take all of Tartus' citadel, he moved on; the city was soon retaken by the County of Tripoli, and its defences were greatly strengthened during the 13th century. Yet the castles of Oultrejordain, far to the south, were never regained by the Crusaders after falling to Saladin's troops. Most of them were then greatly enlarged and altered under Islamic rule. Even the small rocky castle of al-Wu'aira was reoccupied during the Ayyubid period, though its fortifications were neither altered nor extended. Under Ayyubid rule, many of the fortifications regained by Saladin were rendered indefensible rather than simply being abandoned. Jerusalem was turned into what could almost be called an open city, with the citadel as the only fortified structure to be maintained and strengthened.

The citadel or upper fortifications of Antioch are almost entirely ruined, though some vaulted chambers from the Crusader castle remain. These were added to the Romano-Byzantine urban defences in the 12th and 13th centuries. They were destroyed when this, the capital of the Crusader Principality of Antioch, fell to the Mamluk sultan Baybars in 1268. (F. Nicolle)

The speed of the collapse of the Crusader-held enclaves along the eastern Mediterranean coast during the 13th century came as a shock to Catholic Christian Europe. The situation was all the more painful because so much effort and expense had been put into the fortifications. Despite the impressive nature of some castles and urban defences, their subsequent fate depended upon their location rather than their strength. In general, those on the coast were demolished and abandoned by the Mamluks whereas many of those sited inland, especially overlooking strategically important passes, continued to be used. In many cases the latter were then considerably strengthened.

Despite several exceptions, the one feature that seems to have been consistent in Mamluk strategy was that the Muslim conquerors demolished those places they felt unable to garrison adequately, and which could become the targets of Crusader counterattacks. If a castle was more vulnerable than useful, it was destroyed. On the other hand, the new Mamluk rulers seem to have tried to maintain existing Western European forms of land tenure and peasant servitude, which had proved very effective in supporting the Crusader military elite. Unfortunately – from the Mamluks' point of view – this was not practical, as under Islamic law it was illegal to enslave fellow Muslims, even the poorest peasants, or tie them to land as serfs.

The fate of Jerusalem, as an important (though small) inland city, was less clear cut. Most Crusader fortifications here were broken down though not entirely demolished, with the exception of the Tower of David citadel. Here the lower parts of the Crusader structure remained largely intact, including the glacis, while the main tower above was rebuilt as the Mamluk garrison's only strong fortification within the city. The 12th-century fortresses in what is now southern Jordan had already been strengthened by the Ayyubids, and this process continued under the Mamluk rulers from the mid 13th to the end of the 15th century. A comparable process was seen in the coastal mountains of Syria where archaeologists have found that more of the famous 'Crusader castle' of Crac des Chevaliers is actually of Mamluk construction. The same has been found at Belfort in southern Lebanon.

Down on the coast of Palestine, the citadel of Arsuf was razed by the Mamluks after its capture in 1265, never to be used again except for a brief period during World War I when British troops established a strongpoint in its ruins. After Tripoli fell to the Mamluks, its new rulers largely abandoned the Crusader coastal city, which declined into the small fishing port of al-Mina. Only later did the Mamluks build some coastal towers to guard the port. Meanwhile, a new Islamic town developed around the Crusader Castle of St Giles, as it was widely known, which was on a steep hill a few kilometres inland. This became modern Tripoli.

There is a joke amongst scholars specializing in medieval Middle Eastern fortifications that the great Mamluk sultan Baybars was 'a great builder of Crusader castles'. A similarity in military building techniques on both sides of the Crusader–Saracen frontier still causes problems when it comes to identifying who exactly built what. There was certainly a flow of technical and stylistic ideas in both directions, but it is often difficult to state who were the instigators of new ideas or the most original developments. What is clear is that during the Crusader period the Middle East served as an important centre for the dissemination of developments within the art of fortification, and did so in all directions. Those directly responsible for transmitting such ideas could range from humble Italian sailors to the Grand Masters of the military orders. Amongst the latter, Hermann von Salza, Grand Master of the Teutonic Knights, is credited with bringing new concepts of castle design from the Middle East to the rather backward province of Thuringia in Germany. He is unlikely to have been alone.

PART II

CRUSADER CASTLES IN CYPRUS, GREECE & THE AEGEAN, 1191–1573

DESIGN & DEVELOPMENT

Beyond the Holy Land, the Crusaders who conquered so much Byzantine territory also seized a variety of fortifications. These they mostly reused and strengthened. Cyprus, despite its seemingly exposed situation in the eastern Mediterranean, had not been strongly fortified by the Byzantines and the important town of Magusa (Famagusta) had only minor defences. The Crusaders now added more, strengthening Famagusta's two or three gates and constructing a tower to control the harbour entrance. Under Lusignan rule there were four types of fortification in Cyprus: isolated mountaintop castles in the north of the island, such as Buffavent (Buffavento), Dieudamour (St Hilarion) and Le Candare (Kantara); coastal towns with citadels, such as Paphos, Limassol and Magusa; inland towns with minimal defences, such as Nicosia; and small rural castles.

In the early Crusader period, the towns did not apparently have properly defensible curtain-walls. European naval superiority and the relative poverty of the Lusignan kingdom might also account for the majority of Cypriot fortifications being old fashioned, with barrel vaulting rather than the ribbed vaulting already seen in many Crusader castles in Syria. This traditionalism continued in the 14th century, despite the increased external threats following the fall of the mainland Crusader states, and instead of being replaced by modern fortifications, the large tower-type castles of Lusignan Cyprus were merely strengthened. Only in the mid 15th century were new fortifications built to face the new threat from gunpowder artillery, often enveloping rather than replacing the earlier structures.

One Cypriot castle did not, however, fit this pattern. Although the 'Castle of Forty Columns' at Paphos is generally believed to have been a new Crusader fortress dating from the very early 13th century, it has also been suggested that the inner enceinte is Byzantine, dating from the late 7th and 8th centuries. Others suggest that a donjon was built immediately after the Crusader conquest, but was replaced by the distinctive concentric castle whose ruins exist today. Attention has also been drawn to the similarities between the castle at Paphos and the earlier concentric castle of Belvoir in Palestine, which was built by the Hospitallers. Paphos may also have a connection with the Hospitallers, who helped defend the new Crusader outpost in 1198. The Castle of Forty Columns remained the only one of its type in Cyprus and, following the Fourth Crusade's conquest of Constantinople in 1204, may have been considered redundant. Although construction was almost complete, work ceased when the site was hit by an earthquake.

The early Crusader rulers of Cyprus did strengthen several coastal towns in the 13th century. At Kyrenia the Lusignans rebuilt the northern and eastern sea-facing walls of a Byzantine fort while new walls were added to the landward sides, each containing a chemin de ronde connecting arrow slits. This Lusignan fortress probably had corner towers, though only one D-shaped example survives. Royal apartments on the west side perhaps strengthened the castle entrance and there was a chapel over the inner gate.

A castle had been constructed at Limassol by 1228, perhaps including the French-style, square, two-storey keep in the centre of town, which is now encased in 14th–15th-century fortifications. It was a small but interesting structure with simple wooden floors in its upper levels. The citadel at Magusa largely dates from after the loss of the Crusaders' remaining mainland enclaves in 1291, but might incorporate the 'sea tower' mentioned during Emperor Frederick II's

The Frankish tower at Markopoulo, north-east of Athens. It is one of the best-preserved of such free-standing towers on the Greek mainland. (P. Lock)

Crusade. The coastal flank of Magusa was defended by a rectangular castle with corner towers built before 1310. From there a chain could close the harbour entrance. By the early 15th century the town defences consisted of a roughly rectangular walled enclosure with at least 15 regularly spaced towers, plus smaller turrets. In 1441 the Genoese added a small fort, the Gripparia, defending a secondary entrance into the port. The sea-wall was pierced by a marine gate close to the Comerc mercantile area and an arsenal gate, which could be walled up in an emergency. However, Magusa had few land gates, the main one being the strongly fortified Limassol Gate, which also included a substantial *bretéche* (projecting machicolation above a gate).

Several Crusader castles in the mountains of northern Cyprus made use of existing Byzantine fortifications, while the new lowland castles were much less dramatic. The Hospitaller keep at Kolossi is neither powerful nor sophisticated, although it was

CRUSADER AND OTHER WESTERN EUROPEAN FORTIFICATIONS IN GREECE AND THE AEGEAN (FRONTIERS C. 1360).

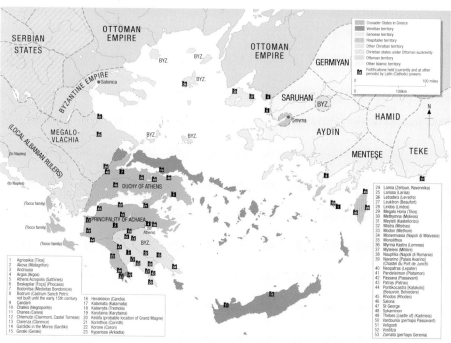

Note that not all the High and Late Medieval fortifications of Greece and Aegean Turkey appear on this map. Medieval European names, where known, are given in parenthesis.

RECONSTRUCTION OF THE 13TH-CENTURY RURAL TOWER AT HALIARTOS, GREECE

The tower at Haliartos is one of the best-preserved examples of this type of isolated Crusader fortification, and enough survives to permit a reasonably reliable reconstruction. Although the masonry of the tower is quite crude, roughly rectangular ashlar blocks form the corners of the structure. The building had five levels, two of which were supported by vaulting (fourth and first – the vault at fourth level runs east–west while that at first level runs north–south) and two by timber beams (second and third levels). Rough wooden stairs or ladders linked each level. The fifth and topmost level (1) could be described as a fighting platform, and its crenellations are based upon those surviving on another tower. The fourth-level chamber is illuminated by the only large arched window (2) in the building. It is immediately above the entrance door (3), perhaps being used to drop missiles upon unwanted visitors. This rectangular entrance at the third level was closed by a wooden door, outside of which is a wooden platform supported by substantial beams thrust into put-log holes. Comparable beams support other external wooden structures. The narrower apertures that allow light into several levels (4) may also have served as arrow slits; in the south walls these are only on

the second and third levels but on the east and west walls there are also slits in the first level. The beams that support the flat ceilings and planked floors are thrust into sequences of holes along the insides of the walls and also rest on ledges. Based on the position of the put-log holes it seems that a central section of the access stairway might have been removable (5), like the lowest stairs or ladder (6). The first level probably served as a storage chamber. Floor plans for four of the levels are shown to the left of the main illustration. (Adam Hook © Osprey Publishing)

sufficient to dominate its rural surroundings and serve as an administrative centre. Similarly, the 13th-century fortifications of the inland city of Nicosia consisted only of a citadel, city walls not being added until the 14th century.

The situation was different in regions closer to Constantinople. Here the existing Byzantine defences were very strong. Nevertheless, the fortifications of Izmit (Nicomedia) had recently been damaged by earthquake and the Crusader occupiers apparently did some limited repair work.

In Greece itself the majority of Crusader fortifications were based upon Byzantine or earlier defences, but this had been a backwater, far from the most threatened frontiers of the Byzantine Empire, and most of the fortifications were simple. Virtually all were reused by the Crusader conquerors, though it is often difficult to identify precisely when. In other places the newly arrived Westerners built castles on new sites such as Veligosti, Geraki, Tremola (Kalavryta), Karytaina, the lower peaks of Corinth, Mistra, Chlemutzi, Old Navarino and Leuktron. Most of this work was done in the first 75 years, but other fortifications mentioned in the documentary sources have either disappeared or not yet been identified. Nevertheless it seems clear that the Crusaders preferred to strengthen what existed, as at the upper site at Corinth, Argos, Kyparissa, Nauphlia (Nafplion), Kalamata, Monemvasia and Patras. Here it is sometimes difficult to confirm whether the newcomers altered the basic plans of such fortifications. At Acrocorinth (upper Corinth) they merely added outworks and a powerful keep. At Patras the rectangular tower and courtyard of a Byzantine archbishop's palace required little to be transformed into a fortress. For example, *The Chronicle of the Morea* stated that, at the time of its capture in 1210, Nauphlia already consisted of 'a castle in two enclosures'.

A study of surviving Crusader fortifications suggests that they were almost entirely defensive rather than offensive bases. Even so, most were lost to the Byzantines in the late 13th and early 14th centuries as a result of negotiation or treachery, very few falling to siege or direct assault. Despite the careful strategic location of key Crusader castles, they remained remarkably old-fashioned in design, reflecting what was, in military terms, a backwater of Western European civilization. Apart from Clairmont, most were also built with limited materials, money and manpower.

The relative unimportance of castles is clear in the description of the *Parlement des Dames* held in the aftermath of a serious military defeat by the Byzantines.

Commenting on how the captured Prince William of Achaea had offered to hand over the fortresses of Mistra, Monemvasia and Grand Maine in exchange for his release, Sir Pierre de Vaux, 'the wisest man in all the principality' and one of only two secular lords present, maintained:

> If the basileus [Byzantine emperor] takes these three castles, he will not hold to the oaths
> which he has sworn. He will send here against us many armies and troops that will throw us
> out of here and disinherit us. Therefore, that you may recognize my good faith, I say and
> affirm I will do this; I will enter prison and the prince, let him come out, or if it be a question
> of ransoming him for sums of hyperpyra [Byzantine coins], I will pledge my land for denarii
> [another form of coinage], and thus let the ransom of my liege lord be paid.

The Lord of Karytaina, who had been released by the Byzantines to act as an emissary, replied (tr. Lurier):

> The castle of Monemvasia, as everyone knows, was won by our lord, the prince, himself.
> Maina and Mistra were built by him, and it would be a sin and a great rebuke for him and his
> followers to die in prison for the sake of castles which he himself had won and built. Just let
> him escape the torment of the prison he is in, and afterwards God will help him to capture
> his castles and to have them as his own.

The castles were handed over – but were never regained.

Crusader castles in Greece fall into clear categories, reflecting the geography of the country. For example, a steep cliff removed the need for anything more than a thin parapet wall on that side of the site, as at Acrocorinth, Nauphlia, Monemvasia, Kalamata, Arkadia, and Old Navarino. Here these 13th-century Greek castles were similar to several 12th-century Crusader castles in Syria and Lebanon. At Monemvasia the hilltop was almost entirely surrounded by cliffs, resulting in a curtain-wall that followed the summit, plus a keep and enclosures to defend the few accessible slopes. A more distinctive feature of several Greek Crusader castles was the huge areas enclosed by their curtain-walls. At Levadia (Livadia) in central Greece this was used for growing crops in the late 14th century. On the other hand large donjons were rarer than in Western Europe or the Crusader Middle East.

The medieval castle (right) dominates the bay of Parga on the Ionian coast of northern Greece. Disputed between the Latin rulers of the offshore islands and the local Orthodox Christian rulers of the mainland, it was ceded to Venice in 1401. (R. Rankin)

Less is known about the organization, costs and manpower of castle-building in Crusader Greece than in Crusader Syria. Most workers were locals and money was almost invariably short. Crusader repairs to the Byzantine fortifications of Izmit (Nicomedia) show no evidence of Western European workmanship. Prisoners of war, both Muslim and fellow Christian, were often forced to work on castle-building; we know that Genoese prisoners were labouring at Nicosia in the late 14th century. On Hospitaller-ruled Rhodes, Greek peasants were obliged to take part in such work, while more skilled Greek masons had higher status and greater responsibility. By the mid 15th century, such Master Wall Builders were exempt from military service and were given grain from the order's own granary. Their high status also meant that they could form part of the committees that inspected castles throughout Hospitaller territory.

While Hospitaller island fortifications were often of the highest quality, Crusader defences on the Greek mainland and some other islands were mostly of very inferior construction, made from poor-quality local limestone and soft (though easily cut) poros. Existing masonry was also used, as at Kalamata where the donjon and part of the inner enceinte seem to have been reconstructed from a derelict Byzantine fortress. Meanwhile, there was widespread continuation of the Byzantine tradition of incorporating bands of thin bricks or tiles between layers of stonework. Ancient Greek or Roman masonry was sometimes used, though for structural rather than decorative reasons, as seen at Salona in central Greece.

Continuity with the Byzantine past, limited Western influence during the Crusader occupation, and comparable continuity into the Ottoman period, often make it difficult to date surviving masonry. Having to rely on local masons and even architects, the Crusaders seemed unable to build in the styles of their homelands, even if they wished. The normal result was a simplified, old-fashioned, late-Romanesque style with provincial Byzantine elements. The regular ashlar blocks favoured in Crusader Syria and Palestine were normally seen only in the corners and sometimes in vaults. Similarly, the way buildings were assembled generally reflected local traditions, and there seem to have been few differences between periods or patrons. Somewhat later at Clairmont large, carefully cut poros blocks were used for gates, the angles of buildings, pilasters and windows, while vaults were constructed from ashlar. Many structures consisted of rough limestone blocks and ceramic tiles set in hard mortar, or of mixed rubble walling; alternatively, as at Patras, Kyparissa, Kalamata and Nauphlia, virtually uncut 'fieldstones' were simply laid horizontally.

The walls of the Kastro or castle on Myteleni enclose a very large area. In comparably extensive castles such land was sometimes used to grow crops, this practice being characteristic of several fortifications built by Western European rulers in later medieval Greece. (D. Nicolle)

Although the Crusaders who conquered Greece in the early 13th century brought with them essentially French ideas of fortification, their successors generally adopted previous Byzantine styles while adding Western European elements, resulting in a varied style of military architecture. Thereafter the main outside influence came from Italy, but a great age of Italian castle-building had actually ended in the mid 13th century. Until the 14th and 15th centuries, the main Italian influence was in the design of water-storage facilities and, perhaps, upon those tall, isolated towers that characterized parts of the Greek Crusader States (see below). A new age of Italian originality emerged in the 14th and 15th centuries, with an emphasis on comfort, magnificence and the resistance to gunpowder artillery.

Meanwhile, the walls of Crusader castles in Greece remained vertical and as high as possible, with an occasional stepped talus at the base, until the later 14th century. After this, walls with a slightly sloped, or battered, outer face appeared, perhaps reflecting later Byzantine ideas. The only 13th-century parapets known to survive were at Clairmont, where the crenellations of the original keep were incorporated into a heightened wall, the merlons being square, without loopholes. The only evidence for an early machicolation has been found at Karytaina, other fortified walls being plain, though a bretéche was sometimes added above the entrance.

Most towers were tall, rectangular, and projected forwards a short distance, but were generally little or no higher than the walls. Many were partially open at the rear or contained a vaulted chamber in their upper storey, as seen in the southern flank of the keep at Patras and part of the curtain-wall of Acrocorinth. A few half-round towers date from the early 13th century – the first to be used in Greece since antiquity – and are strikingly different from the stark squareness of Byzantine fortification.

The donjons of most 13th-century castles were almost square, that at Acrocorinth being built upon a characteristically French base with almost pyramid-like sides, while at Mistra and Clairmont a chemin de ronde runs round the top of the keep. Most entrances consisted of straight-through gates with wooden doors secured by horizontal beams, but portcullises were rare and barbicans almost unknown. Clairmont is again an exception, its outer gate originally being a rectangular building with a portcullis, set into a recess of the enceinte. Most early Crusader gates consisted of simple passages under a vault of arches, as in the east curtain-wall of Clairmont, the keep of Acrocorinth, the inner redoubt of the Crusader castle at Mistra, and the east flank of the summit fort at Monemvasia. The distinctive hexagonal keep at

Clairmont has a more elaborate entrance consisting of broad, inset archways in either face of an entrance chamber masking a tall, round-vaulted inner passage.

Clairmont also includes the greatest variety of early 13th-century windows, the most striking having a tall, wide opening like a passage, with a depressed vault of arches cut from poros stone into which a poros screen pierced with twin lancet windows is fitted. Although these castles date from the same period as the great Gothic structures of Western Europe, pointed Gothic arches only appear at Clairmont, Karytaina and in a few religious buildings.

Carved architectural decoration is extraordinarily rare in surviving Greek Crusader structures, and where it does exist it is old-fashioned and almost minimalist. The incorporation of ceramic tiles or thin bricks usually provided what little surface decoration there was. This was just one example of the mutual artistic influence between the Crusader States and the fragmented remnants of the Byzantine Empire, which was felt more strongly on the mainland than on the Italian-ruled islands. The architectural historian Ramsay Traquair wrote of such artistic developments: 'The conquerors themselves must have become "Byzantinied" and the Gothic influence slowly wanes. Yet at intervals some more homeloving Frank would turn his thoughts westwards, and … import into his building the forms … from which he had come, or which his craftsmen knew best.' This was much more apparent in the design and decoration of tombs than of buildings.

Most Crusader fortifications in Greece have a village nearby, whereas several lowland towns declined or were even abandoned. Even more typical of Crusader-

The combined coats-of-arms of Francesco I Gattilusio, the Genoese ruler of the island of Lesbos (1355–85), and his wife, a Byzantine princess, carved above the entrance of the Kastro of Myteleni. (D. Nicolle)

ruled regions in central if not southern Greece were numerous isolated towers. Few were sited for strategic reasons. Except on Venetian-ruled Euboea, most of these towers were not visible one from another and only a handful were associated with obvious settlements. Their purposes and dates of construction remain a matter of debate, though the majority seem to have been constructed during a period of feudal fragmentation. Most were entered at first-floor level via a removable ladder, they completely lack ornamentation, and were almost certainly built by local craftsmen. The lack of many loopholes, machicolations or hoardings, and the minimal space for supplies, indicate that their military role was limited.

Surprisingly, given the wealth of their 'mother city' and their vital role as a chain of commercial outposts, the fortifications of the Venetian colonial empire were even more inferior in construction. Even at Methoni, which the Venetians retook after a brief Genoese occupation, their new urban defences consisted of small, square, open-backed towers linked by low walls around a peninsula, which was sealed at its northern end by a castle. Inside this walled area stood the town, its port and a cathedral. Meanwhile, the Genoese remained the dominant Western European commercial and naval power in the Black Sea. Here existing coastal fortifications reflected various cultures, the most important being the Byzantine. The military architecture of the rising states of Moldavia and Wallachia (today in Romania and Moldova) used the old Byzantine concept of a walled enclosure, or the traditional earth and timber fortifications of Hungary and the Balkans. During the later 13th and 14th centuries, however, Western European influences reached the north-western coasts of the Black Sea via the Genoese colonial outposts, Hungary and the short-lived Crusader 'Latin Empire of Constantinople'.

The most important Genoese colony was in fact Pera (now Galata), a suburb of Istanbul (Constantinople). Here on the northern side of the Golden Horn, the original Genoese colony was destroyed by its Venetian rivals in 1296. Seven years later the Byzantine authorities gave the Genoese a substantially larger area where they re-established a colony defended by a moat or ditch. In 1313 the *podestà* or local Genoese governor, Montano de Marini, built the first land wall around Pera. A sea-wall was in place before 1324, after which the Genoese added towers to their land walls, the biggest of which, the Galata Tower, still dominates the skyline.

Elsewhere the Genoese seized substantial pieces of ground that they defended with long walls, though the areas enclosed were not necessarily then filled with

Opposite:
The north-eastern corner of the Genoese castle at Molivos on the island of Lesbos. (D. Nicolle)

161

buildings. The biggest of these Genoese outposts were established on or near the Crimean peninsula. Here Kaffa was strongly defended by land and sea-walls, which, by 1352, were 718m long and incorporated numerous towers. Even this was considered inadequate and Genoa proposed strengthening the fortifications while increased reserves of food and weapons were stored inside the walled commune. The fortifications themselves were, however, still Byzantine-style plain walls with tall rectangular towers. Far to the south, on the Aegean island of Chios, a five-sided castrum was erected for the first Genoese rulers in 1346 – with three sides facing the Greek town, one facing the port, and the fifth facing the coast. According to a surviving contract written by the Mahone or local Genoese authorities in 1461, a master mason was to erect a wall 3.46m wide at its base and 2.97m wide at its summit.

The quality of Italian colonial fortifications, particularly those of the Venetians, improved markedly during the gunpowder revolution of the 15th century. Newly strengthened defences emerged as being amongst the most advanced anywhere. In fact the Venetians, who purchased Nauphlia in 1388, refortified it so thoroughly that little trace of previous Crusader construction can be seen. Similarly the new walls that the Venetians built around the promontory of Methoni were designed to resist cannon, while a moat was excavated across the landward side and a *fausse braie* (low-walled outwork) was added in front of the land walls. The fortifications that the Venetians constructed in Cyprus after they took over the island in 1489 demolished many earlier defences and included some notably advanced military architecture, with massive, solid earth bastions in the Italian style, as seen at Magusa, Kyrenia and Limassol.

The southern end of the Acropolis of Athens. This part of the hilltop became a palace under Crusader rule, but the medieval structures were destroyed in the 19th century in an effort to return the site to its supposed classical appearance. (F. Nicolle)

THE PRINCIPLES OF DEFENCE

Until the second half the 15th century, the old principles of defence and attack dominated the Western European outposts in Cyprus, Greece and the Black Sea. While the attackers aimed to get over a wall or to undermine it, the defenders largely relied on the height and thickness of their walls to resist – actively or passively. The increasingly effective stone-throwing siege machines in both attack and defence had their impact upon the design of towers, while the introduction of cannon at first merely speeded up the process of thickening the walls. Later on, however, the power of cannon led to the lowering of fortified walls and resulted in siege warfare involving less physical combat, though more intensive or prolonged bombardment. The excavation of siege entrenchments by besiegers as a defence against counter bombardment, and more sprawling outworks being added by defenders to fortifications to keep attackers at a distance, were also features of this period. The need to protect the flanks of a fortified place from bombardment similarly led to the construction of the strictly geometric fortifications that began to appear in Venetian Greek outposts in the very late 15th and early 16th centuries.

Until almost the end of the period under consideration, crossbows remained the most important anti-personnel weapons in the hands of those defending Crusader and other Western fortifications. Crossbows also became vitally important to later

Byzantine and local Balkan armies, and even to some extent to early Ottoman Turkish forces. The paramount defensive role of crossbows was emphasized by Theodore Palaeologus in his 1326 military treatise, written in Greek but translated into Latin four years later. Its partially Byzantine author was an experienced soldier who was also marquis of Monferrat in early 14th-century Italy. However, little of his book dealt with siege warfare, perhaps reinforcing the impression that siege warfare remained relatively unimportant in these regions.

Apart from in Cyprus, which was under constant threat from the Mamluk sultanate, the Crusader occupiers often cut corners in the design and construction of their castles, especially on mountainous sites where natural geography was as important as man-made structures. Even where fortifications did exist, they were not necessarily defended. For example, in 1311, after the defeat of the local Crusader army by the mercenary Catalan Company, the citizens of Thebes surrendered without a struggle despite the fact that their castle was in good condition and its owner, Count Nicholas II, had survived the battle. In 1331 the Catalans themselves destroyed the castle of Thebes, rather than defending it and thus risking it falling intact into enemy hands. Indeed the castle seems to have been regarded more as a prize to be won or lost than as a strongpoint to be defended. Much the same was seen elsewhere during the early 14th-century struggle for domination in the Principality of Achaea. Castles remained symbols of authority or palaces, but in military terms the issue was decided elsewhere.

The small isolated towers that dotted the Duchy of Athens were even more obviously passive. Though few seem to have been associated with a significant settlement site, most were located in agricultural areas and presumably served as refuges for the local Latin elite. The role of fortified ports and small coastal enclaves is more obvious. Medieval Mediterranean navigation largely consisted of coastal routes and short hops between secure ports whose defences varied according to local circumstances. Old Navarino, built around 1278 by Nicholas II of St Omer, had upper and lower fortified enclosures without a strong donjon, presumably because Old Navarino was itself in such a dominating location. On the other hand the Galata Tower in Istanbul was designed as the key point in the defence of the walled colony of Pera. There seem, in fact, to have been major efforts to construct such central strongpoints from the late 14th century onwards. Several fortified coastal enclaves were characterized by having few gates through their land walls, but a larger number through their sea-walls or those leading to their harbours. These outposts were, in effect, fortified markets and mostly consisted of a good port backed by a strongpoint on a high place, with a walled town developing between the two. Where there was no suitable highpoint to be fortified, a castle could be built next to the coast or the harbour.

At Modon (Methoni), in Greece, a small 'sea fort' on a rocky islet defended the mole, which gave additional shelter to the harbour. The role of its garrison was probably more to inhibit smugglers than to stand up to a serious assault. Crossbowmen based in the sea fort formed a first line of defence against any hostile naval attack, and the tower itself was octagonal to avoid blind spots. The size of the garrison is unknown, but probably included infantry to patrol the mole while crossbowmen defended the tower itself. A garrison on the nearby island of Sapientza could be isolated from the mainland by enemy shipping, so their role was probably only to defend Sapientza itself. There was no mention of a chain across the entrance to Methoni's harbour, but later, on the eve of the Ottoman conquest, Venetian records mention a project to 'narrow its entrance' by building a *porporella* or *argine*, a massive breakwater constructed in the same way as the mole. It was probably intended to run from the southern end of the sea fort towards Sapientza, to narrow the channel, but no remains have been found and the ambitious programme was probably never carried out.

The avoidance of surprise attacks was clearly important for isolated outposts. For this reason the Hospitallers established a chain of fire-beacons between the offshore islet of Castellorizo, Rhodes and Kos. This must have involved otherwise unrecorded beacons on the Turkish mainland, as Castellorizo and Rhodes were too distant for direct line-of-sight. One of the main purposes of such beacons would have been to give

A machicolated tower at the south-eastern corner of the Genoese castle at Methymna (Molivos) on the island of Lesbos. (D. Nicolle)

Rhodes warning of any approaching Mamluk fleet, the Mamluks being the main threat to the Hospitallers before the rise of the Ottomans in the mid 15th century. Large enemy fleets sailing from the eastern Mediterranean normally hugged the coasts and were thus visible from Castellorizo.

Mountaintop castles in Cyprus and Greece were similarly difficult to surprise. Their picturesque locations can sometimes appear puzzling; taking St Hilarion as an example: the castle's sheer northern flank falls approximately 500m, making the man-made defences seem somewhat superflous. On the other hand, the very inaccessibility of these locations meant that their garrisons could not easily swoop down on a foe below.

The rocky summit of the Crusader castle at Livadia in central Greece. (D. Nicolle)

THE SEA TOWER AT MODON, GREECE

The small tower at the far end of the narrow peninsula upon which Modon was built was intended to guard the entrance to the harbour. At its centre was an eight-sided *turris* or tower, which dated from before the Crusader conquest of southern Greece. In 1387 the Venetians, who now controlled Modon, added a lower, outer circuit wall. A new breakwater was probably constructed around the same time, consisting of large stones dropped into the shallow water. A smaller eight-sided turret was added to the top of the turris around 1500.

Key:
A. The fortifications as they looked in the late 13th century.
B. The fortifications as they looked at the end of the 14th century.
C. The fortifications as they looked in the early 16th century.

1. The original eight-sided Byzantine or early Crusader turris (tower) before the addition of the outer defences. Note there was no breakwater at this date.
2. The new eight-sided outer wall constructed in 1387.
3. Outer gate with a partially inset, arched recess above the rectangular doorway.
4. Breakwater made of large stones.
5. Small eight-sided and domed turret added to the top of the original Byzantine or early Crusader turris.
6. The late 14th-century, eight-sided outer wall was modified by the Venetians for firearms and cannon around 1500.
7. Most of the embrasures in the previously crenelled outer wall were removed or filled in, especially on the sides overlooking the harbour. Some of this might have been repair work by the Ottoman Turks after they captured the sea-tower at Methoni. (Adam Hook © Osprey Publishing)

Coastal positions demonstrate the same concern to avoid surprise. Amasra on the Black Sea was a major Byzantine fortification before the Genoese established a colony in 1398. Here communication between the coast and the interior was very difficult because a sequence of steep coastal ranges runs parallel to the shore. Nevertheless, Amasra fell to the Ottomans 60 years later. Other Genoese outposts had fewer natural advantages and were more difficult to protect. The lines of Genoese defences normally followed those of the existing – usually Byzantine – fortifications, which mostly consisted of a single wall with widely spaced towers enclosing the town and port, often with a citadel at the highest point. Some of these urban walls were later extended to enclose new suburbs. Magusa, in Cyprus, was located on a low-lying coastal plain where there are no hills between the city and the interior. However, the coastal plain itself was infertile and unhealthy, thus offering some protection.

If an enemy did manage to besiege such difficult locations, they usually faced a series of defended baillies, which made use of the natural topography of the site. Where the terrain did not lend itself to such designs, more regularly planned castles were constructed. The early 13th-century castle at Paphos fell into this second category, and in 1391 King James I of Cyprus built another rectangular castle with corner towers and a surrounding moat at Sivouri, while a similar castle was constructed at La Cava near Nicosia. This style was practically unknown in Greece where castles on hilltops, high or low, almost all relied on one or more enclosed baillies whose curtain-walls followed the contours of the rocks, with a few towers being added. In many cases the core of this system consisted of a large donjon, as at Mistra. At Pendeskupi near Corinth the donjon was very simple, while at Clairmont it was polygonal with a small, open courtyard inside. In all cases such fortifications contained water cisterns, some of which were substantial.

By the 15th century Crusader and Italian colonial fortifications faced an increasing threat from gunpowder artillery. One of the most interesting early examples of how they responded is the Hospitaller mainland castle at Bodrum. Located on a narrow isthmus, it consists of a large glacis and a deep ditch excavated down to sea level. Between the glacis and the gate were casemates covered with stone and containing guns that could sweep the area between the glacis and gate. The northern side was protected by two towers joined by a curtain-wall and a narrow ditch, while to the west, facing the port, was a broad boulevard.

TOUR OF THE CASTLES

CYPRUS

Kyrenia is amongst the best-surviving Crusader coastal fortifications in Cyprus. The late 12th- and early 13th-century castrum next to the harbour was massively strengthened by the Venetians in the 16th century, but the Crusader outer wall still encloses a barrel-vaulted interior with basement galleries.

The original medieval plan consisted of a large, square court surrounded by structures built against the curtain-walls. At each corner were large, square towers, the north-eastern one being diagonal to the others. There was a postern on the north side, while the main entrance lay across a moat on the west side, defended by a barbican and a drawbridge. The upper of the two storeys above the gate contained a chapel, plus a vestry with an elegant arch over its door. There may originally have been a second, outer barbican or outwork beyond the bridge against the curtain-wall. A little church still survives on a small space forming a continuation of the platform on which the castle is built, overlooking the harbour.

According to R. Fedden in *Crusader Castles: A Brief Study in the Military Architecture of the Crusades*, a royal palace overlooked the entrance to Kyrenia castle and the harbour:

This harbour and the bourg behind it were ringed with their own walls, of which several towers survive. Venetian fortification has obscured much of the earlier work. The Venetians entirely rebuilt the outer west wall and, to protect the west and south of the castle, built three ponderous tower-bastions and filled with earth the space between the inner and the outer walls… On the north and east, where the sea provided its own security and additional fortification seemed superfluous, much Latin work fortunately survives. The fine ashlar masonry speaks of Crusader building. The north curtain, with its two fighting galleries below the parapet whose merlons are pierced for fire, and the elegant horseshoe-shaped tower at the north-east, still indicate the formidable character of the Lusignan fortress.

St Hilarion is a typically dramatic example of a Crusader mountaintop castle in Cyprus. It had already been fortified by the regent Jean of Ibelin around 1228, perhaps as a retreat for the heir apparent and his sisters who felt threatened by Emperor Frederick II. Here the Crusaders improved upon the three separate stages or levels of existing Byzantine fortification. The large outermost bailey lay to the south. Its rather feeble Byzantine rubble wall and circular towers remained largely unchanged, though the gate did have a machicolation. A steep corridor climbed from this outer bailey to the second level. Here it is interesting to note that, at an altitude of around 700m, the medieval builders used pitched roofs to resist heavy winter snowfalls rather than the flat roofs characteristic of most other Crusader architecture in the eastern Mediterranean. The third level of fortification was to the west of the second level and can only be reached by another steep climb. To the north, south and west of the castle breathtaking cliffs and very steep slopes remove the threat of serious assault. Lying between the two rocky summits is a small area of which the eastern or entrance side is protected by fortification. Immediately to the west are buildings whose finely carved doors and windows show that this was the *cour d'honneur* of what was, in effect, both a palace and a castle.

MAINLAND GREECE

Mistra, to the west of the town of Sparti in the Peloponnese, is better known for its late Byzantine wall paintings and churches than for the Crusader castle that dominates the site. The latter was constructed for William of Villehardouin in 1249 and consists of a donjon and inner enceinte on the topmost ridge, with a lower

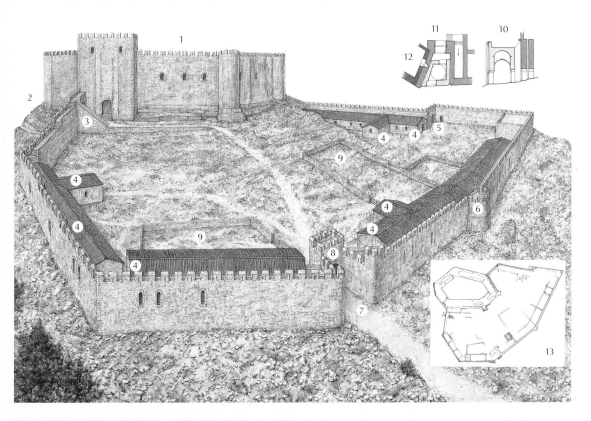

THE CASTLE OF CLAIRMONT

The dating of the castle of Clairmont remains a matter of debate. Most historians believe that it was built by the prince of Achaea in the 13th century, but some suggest that the prince's castle is marked by unexcavated ruins closer to the shore. They also maintain that the existing castle dates from as late as the 15th century. The entrance through the outer wall or enceinte was modified at some time after the original construction, either by the last Crusader lords, the Byzantines, or perhaps the first Ottoman Turkish occupiers.

Key
1. Keep.
2. Path leading to postern gate or secondary entrance in the enceinte outer wall.
3. Stairs from ward to the outer wall of the castle.
4. Storage buildings, barracks and stables.
5. Postern gate or secondary entrance in the enceinte.
6. Small, half-round tower in the outer enceinte.
7. Main gate, twice remodelled and strengthened after the building of the castle.
8. Building housing the portcullis and its mechanism, behind the main gate.
9. Walled enclosures, probably for animals.
10. Section through the remodelled main gate.
11. Plan of the remodelled main gate.
12. Earlier arrow-slit, closed off after the subsequent remodelling of the main gate complex.
13. Plan of the castle.
(Adam Hook © Osprey Publishing)

171

Girne (Kyrenia, Cyprus), known to medieval Western Europeans as Cerina, showing the castle, inner harbour and the Turkish old town as they appeared in the 1950s. (Author's collection)

enceinte beneath. The 13th-century Crusader castle was subsequently repaired by the Byzantine Greeks or the Ottoman Turks. Its main entrance is protected by a large, rectangular tower, and there are semi-circular towers in the circuit walls. The inner enceinte is surrounded by a second wall with a gate into the outer bailey. A small chapel embedded in the southern battlements apparently existed before the castle was built. A substantial round tower on the north-eastern side is near a large underground water cistern, and there was another cistern beneath a massive rectangular building at the eastern end of the upper citadel, which in turn served as the commanders' residence. On the highest part of the western edge of the summit is another semi-circular tower facing a dangerous tribal area in the mountains beyond.

Clairmont is by far the finest fortified structure dating from the Crusader period on the Greek mainland. From here Geoffrey III of Villehardouin commandeered the church revenues, a role that enabled him to spend much more on the site than elsewhere. It took three years to build (1220–23), defended the town of Clarenza, and overlooked the main harbour – though from a distance.

The existing castle of Clairmont consists of a large keep with an inner court on top of the hill, plus an outer bailey on the sides most vulnerable to attack. Accommodation inside the keep appears to have been comfortable and well lit. It was cool in summer, while fireplaces, one above the other on each floor, ensured warmth in winter. Clairmont was, in fact, clearly a centre for courtly life. The outer bailey and its wall were, however, altered during the Ottoman period and have recently been restored. Furthermore, the dating of the keep itself remains a matter of debate. Its plan is very different from other medieval castles in Greece. The method of forming a courtyard by great surrounding halls, the monumental character of this court, the double external staircases to the principal rooms of the main floor, the wooden floors of these rooms and the numerous and well-constructed fireplaces, all seem more characteristic of the 15th century. Ramsay Traquair also noted Clairmont's similarity with the 15th-century Italian castle of Bracciano, and the Ottoman Turkish Anadolu Hisar castle on the Bosphoros.

The castle of Patras was a very strong fortress, which, in 1429, resisted a year-long siege by the Byzantine ruler Constantine – even after he had captured the town. It consists of a keep with a central citadel and a large courtyard. The walls clearly date from at least two separate periods and the lower parts of the keep, particularly on the northern side of the court, incorporate many classical fragments, whereas the upper parts of the structure comprise rubble. On the east wall of the keep are the remains of stone corbels, which originally supported the hoardings of the Crusader castle. According to Traquair in 'Laconia, I: Medieval Fortress', writing just over a hundred years ago before the more recent changes to this site:

> The entrance is on the south side by a fine vaulted gatehouse, the sheeted iron doors are still
> in use, and above the arch is a little huchette on two brackets. The western end of the court, and
> particularly the south-western tower, are fine example of Italian fortification; the tower is
> octagonal… The defence is in two stories, a battlemented rampart above, with under it, a range
> of chambers and loopholes. The plan is typically medieval and is probably very little changed
> from the castle so ruthlessly constructed by Aleman, to whom we may attribute the greater part
> of the keep walls and the northern wall of the court. To Italian influence are due the notched
> battlements, and at some time in the fifteenth century an extensive reconstruction must have
> taken place which included the upper parts of the keep walls, the gatehouse and the southern
> and western walls of the court, with their octagonal towers… The later Turkish repairs are
> easily distinguishable by their plastered surface. Patras is in some ways the most interesting
> of Greek castles; it is still in fairly good preservation and has never been completely rebuilt,
> unlike so many of the famous Frankish castles whose sites are now marked only by crumbling
> Turkish walls.

Platamon (Pandeleimon) is the best-preserved Crusader castle in north-central Greece. It is on a naturally defensible site overlooking a strategic pass. King Boniface of Thessaloniki gave the site to a northern Italian knight named Orlando Pischia and ordered him to build a castle. The resulting fortress has three enclosures, the outermost being particularly large, with its main entrance on the south-eastern side where there was another ruined outer wall or perhaps a barbican. Today the walls are still 7.5–9.5m high and 1.2–2m thick, with towers of varying size and design spaced at irregular intervals where the wall changes direction. Between the inner and outer gates of the main entrance there was once a large tower. The second wall is 6–7m high with, in the north-east corner, an unusual tower that is square outside and round inside, with a Byzantine-style tiled dome on top. Another wall 1m thick and 5.25m high surrounds a large octagonal tower, which served as the central keep. It is 16m high with walls 2m thick, having its entrance 3.45m above the ground and reached by a wooden staircase. This tower has semi-circular windows, one having two openings with a small central column decorated with a cross, and it may date from after the Crusader period when the castle of Platamon was repaired for the Byzantine Despotate of Arta.

THE AEGEAN

The citadel of Chios, on the eponymous island, is a good example of Genoese colonial fortification. Here the Zaccaria family from Genoa built a new fortress under Byzantine suzerainty around 1328, on the site of an existing castrum. This was taken by another Genoese, Simone Vignoso, in 1346, after which the Genoese Mahone, or local colonial authorities, modified its defences still further. The result was a large, five-sided, fortified enclosure of which three sides faced the Greek town, the fourth dominated the port and the fifth overlooked the coast. The walls were improved or repaired in the second half of the 15th century and in its final form the fortress had nine towers equally spaced along all the walls, except that facing the sea. Surviving documents also mention two gates leading to the market area of the town, and one facing the port. The fact that the wall facing the port was also the weakest indicates that the Genoese expected trouble from the land and the open sea, but did not expect to lose control of their harbour.

The arms of Genoa flanked by those of two of the Genoese families which dominated this trading post, carved on the fortified walls of Amasra on the Black Sea. (D. Nicolle)

THE BLACK SEA

Amasra was not the most important fortified Italian commercial outpost in the Black Sea, but it is an interesting example of how a Western European maritime power used existing Byzantine fortifications, only modifying them where it was really necessary to do so. Here the small island of Boz Tepe was so close to the shore, being separated by shallow water and a beach, that it could be linked to the mainland by a fortified bridge. Behind this was a powerful wall and towers to protect the southern side of the island. On the mainland immediately opposite was a citadel now called the Iç Kale. In addition, the walls and towers of the southern or inland-facing fortifications protected the coastal hill on which the town itself sat. Most of the fortifications are Byzantine, dating from before the 14th-century Genoese occupation, and include emplacements for both traction-powered and perhaps also torsion-powered pre-gunpowder artillery. The Genoese then converted some of the arrow slits to make them into gun-ports for early cannon. Since the main threat to Amasra came from inland, the strongest fortifications were located here, comprising at least two lines of walls in the most vulnerable sections. The Genoese colonial authorities also increased the height of some walls and towers. The main inner wall is still well preserved, with projecting rectangular towers of various sizes and shapes, between 6 and 9m wide and projecting 4–6m. One much longer tower near the centre of the wall is nearly 23m across but projects only about 2m. Many of these towers have a solid core. Some alterations to the gates are thought to be Genoese, including the addition of machicolations on the secondary gate. On the

The castle of Bilhorod-Dnistrovsky. Inspired by fear of the Ottoman Turks, the Genoese built the fortification in the 14th century. It featured a rectangular citadel with four massive round corner towers (Author's collection)

Iç Kale the Genoese inserted a new wall to create a sort of keep on the west side. This was entered at first-floor level above a blocked Byzantine door. Here other strengthening included projecting corbels, huchettes and machicolations in the Western European tradition of military architecture, plus further gun-ports. Other than these modifications, the most visible relics of the Italian occupation are a number of carved stone heraldic panels. Those over the entrances to the Iç Kale display the arms of the Republic of Genoa flanked by those of the powerful Poggio and Malaspina families.

The fortifications of Caffa (Kaffa) on the Crimean peninsula of what is now Ukraine were far more extensive. Little remains today, but most seem to be 14th-century Genoese work built upon the foundations or along the lines of earlier Byzantine defences. The outer wall was almost 5.5km long, forming an arc around the town, outside an inner wall, and joining up with the sea-wall. According to the Ottoman Turkish traveller Evliya Celebi, writing in the 17th century, this wall had 117 bastions, with an exterior dry ditch 13.5m deep and 33.5m across. There was no ditch along the coast. Instead the sea gates opened directly onto the beach to make the loading and unloading of goods easier. The Ottomans called the third line of defence at Kaffa the 'land fortress'. Outside the main, strongly defended city the suburbs were protected only by simple embankments during the later Genoese period. These, however, have all but disappeared.

THE LIVING SITES

The Crusader conquest of central and southern Greece was carried by a remarkably small number of knights and mounted sergeants, with infantry rarely mentioned. The states that emerged were even shorter on loyal military manpower than the Crusader States of the Middle East. After the fall of the ephemeral Crusader Kingdom of Thessalonika to the Byzantine Despotate of Epirus, all that remained was the increasingly feeble Latin 'Empire' of Constantinople, which fell in 1261, and the remarkably enduring Principality of Achaea, which also included the Duchy of Athens.

In Greece, fertile land was scarce and few baronies could be created. They ranged in size from four to eight fiefs, though the number of fiefs subsequently increased; by 1377 a list mentioned 51 castles, some of them very small. The exposed nature of these Crusader states meant that feudal military obligations of four months, plus four more on castle guard, were firmly enforced during the 13th century. By the mid 14th century, however, the military enthusiasm of the Latin or Western European aristocracy had declined, and personal military service was gradually replaced by a tax called the *adoha*. There were also differences between various Crusader-ruled regions – for example, a feudal structure never took root in central Greece. In contrast, the conquerors of the south managed to establish a society based upon a French model.

Subsequent Italian and Spanish occupiers introduced other, later variations of the feudal model. At the same time the ex-Byzantine elites, not all of them Greek, increased in influence because they were more numerous than the Westerners, and their military allegiance had to be encouraged. Nevertheless, there is no evidence that these indigenous groups had specific associations with local fortifications – even with the small rural towers.

In Cyprus the ownership of fortifications remained a royal prerogative, except for a few castles built by the military orders. Instead, the Latin aristocracy largely lived in towns, and their rural manors were rarely fortified. There were similarly few castles in Crusader-ruled central Greece, despite this being an exposed and vulnerable frontier area. Instead, it seems to have been dominated by an anarchic elite of knights and sergeants who could only afford to build modest towers.

Castles were more abundant in southern Greece, where their primary function was apparently to store and display wealth. At first the hugely outnumbered Crusaders mostly lived in isolated mountaintop castles and fortified rural mansions, confident in their military superiority, though many also had town houses. Most of the major citadels were controlled by the ruler rather than the barons, the Castle of Sathines on the Acropolis of Athens and the Kadmeia fortress in Thebes being under military governors appointed by the prince. After the Angevin rulers of southern Italy took over Achaea in 1278, the area was governed by officials, who were in charge of the main castles and garrisons.

Once the Crusader aristocracy started paying the adoha tax rather than offering personal military service, castle garrisons increasingly consisted of mercenaries. Their pay varied according to circumstances, but an ordnance of Nicolas of Joinville (1323–25) was seemingly intended to fix the pay for men-at-arms at 800 *hyperperes* per year if the soldier came from overseas, and 600 if he was local. Squires would be paid 400 and 300 respectively. Many 'local' troops were now Greek in culture and military tradition, though some converted to Catholic Christianity to be accepted by the ruling elite. The latter were now increasingly Italian

Small Greek mainland fortifications: A – The Crusader tower at Thebes: (1) modern entrance, not existing in the medieval period (after Bon).
B – The interior of the Southern Sea Gate at Methoni, 15th-century Venetian (after Andrews).

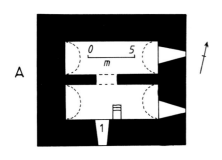

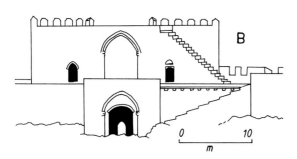

The small Hospitaller-ruled Aegean island of Tilos had several castles. They served as refuges for the local population during a period of sometimes intensive naval raiding and retaliation during the 14th and 15th centuries. Here the ruins of Mikro Horio still look out across the largely abandoned village beneath, while in the distance is the Turkish coast. (R. Rankin)

in origin and outlook, being much less feudally minded than the previous French aristocracy. Large military contingents were sent from Italy after the Angevin takeover, along with specialists like doctors and military engineers, though some garrisons were still not paid for a long time. It is interesting to note that amongst the troops the Angevin ruler sent to his garrisons in Albania in the 1270s were hundreds of Muslim 'Saracens from Lucera', mostly archers and crossbowmen. But as a shortage of troops became more serious, the Angevins increasingly recruited Greeks and Albanians – a pool of manpower that was also vital to the Byzantine rulers of this region.

Little is known about the arsenals that clearly existed in several fortresses. Archaeologists uncovered a large store of crossbow boltheads in the castle at Paphos, along with about 1,500 stone mangonel balls, seemingly stored on a terrace that collapsed during the earthquake. Documentary sources mention crossbows being manufactured in an arsenal on Corfu under Angevin rule, while the Angevins certainly established an armoury in the castle of Clarenza in 1281, to maintain weaponry shipped from Italy.

While the castle at Thebes was usually the main residence of the duke of Athens, the entrance complex of the Acropolis of Athens was eventually converted into a ducal palace. Known as the Mnesikles, it was described as a fine palazzo by the later

Italian dukes. How strongly it was fortified is much less clear. In complete contrast were the isolated towers that dotted the Duchy of Athens. There were many others on the Venetian-ruled island of Euboea and in the Peloponnese. Such towers may have expressed the power and status of the non-noble but militarily significant sergeant level of Crusader society. Most were small and simple, but some resembled small castles with curtain-walls. The little documentary evidence that survives includes a reference to the tower at Krestena being repaired in 1354 when it was said to have had a gilded roof, a drawbridge and a private residential apartment.

In addition to a few fortified towns and cities, the Crusader States also included some fortified monasteries, including Dafni, which was inhabited by Cistercian monks during the Crusader period. They demolished the upper floor of what had been a library or abbot's residence at the western end of the church, and added defensive battlements. The Ottoman sultan returned the monastery to Greek Orthodox monks in 1458, and it is unclear whether the fortified curtain-wall dates from this or from the Crusader occupation.

Where Crusader fortresses were used as residences, they could be remarkably comfortable. In Cyprus the mountaintop castle of Kyrenia may have been used as a summer retreat from the sultry lowlands. In Greece some early 13th-century castles reflected the home life of the knightly elite of France from which most of the conquerors came. Clermont, which dated from rather later, contained an unusual number of fireplaces, latrines and water cisterns, which made life more comfortable.

Residential castles certainly helped the new military rulers retain their cultural and physical separation from the Greek Orthodox majority. In Cyprus this separation remained almost complete until the second half of the 14th century, the dominant Latins using costume, military ceremonial, and military architecture to proclaim their distinctiveness. In late 13th-century Greece, the castle at Thebes was described as being highly decorated and 'big enough for an emperor and his court'. French remained the language of the knightly class in Cyprus and Greece until partially replaced by Italian in the 14th century.

The culture and society of the new rulers were, according to contemporary sources, extremely refined. Raymond Muntaner wrote that 'the most noble French knights were the knights of the Morea [Peloponnese] who spoke as good French as that of Paris.' Early 13th-century literature from Cyprus was in the same tradition as that of both France and the Crusader States of the Holy Land, while literary works from later 13th-century Crusader Greece were similar to those of French-ruled southern Italy. In both areas there was a strong interest in the history of the Crusades as well as Arthurian legends and ancient Greek myths, particularly those concerning battles against the Amazons. On the other hand, this cultural brilliance faded in the 14th century in Crusader Greece, which became little more than a collection of outposts dominated by powers from Italy and Spain.

Wall paintings similarly helped the Crusaders keep in touch with their Western European cultural roots. The 'Destruction of Troy' decorated the Catholic archbishop's palace at Patras, while the 'Conquest of Syria' by the First Crusaders was painted on some walls in the Kadmeia castle in Thebes; the artists may actually have been brought from northern Syria by Mary of Antioch, wife of Nicholas II of St Omer.

Some of the earliest wall painting from Crusader-ruled Cyprus has interesting similarities with the art of the ex-Byzantine provinces of what is now Turkey, rather than that of the Byzantine capital. Very little art survives from Crusader Greece, and what does is mostly primitive, a few churches being decorated with geometric or simplified scroll patterns. Crudely carved heraldic animals within circles and heraldic shields were popular and there are also decorative elements drawn from Islamic art, though it is unclear whether these came from Crusader Syria, or from the residual Muslim communities of southern Italy, or reflected the influence of Muslim mercenary soldiers hired by some Crusaders from the mid 13th century onwards.

One might have expected the new rulers to make use of the ancient Greek statues and relief carvings, and the well-cut architectural fragments scattered across the country. However, the Crusader occupiers of Corinth did not apparently reuse such artefacts in a visible way; instead, they used ancient statues as building material. Only in the 15th century did attitudes begin to change, but even at this later date, most marble carvings and statues were rendered down as lime for mortar or concrete. Only a few scholars and travellers, influenced by new Humanist ideas, tried to preserve relics of Classical civilization.

There was a Byzantine influence on the home life of the Crusader aristocracy in both Greece and Cyprus, just as there was an Islamic influence in the Crusader States of the Middle East. The one sphere in which this influence was rejected was, of course, religion since it was the newcomers' Catholic identity that set them apart.

The Genoese fort at Çesme, on the Aegean coast of Turkey, was subsequently repaired by the Ottoman Turks. (D. Nicolle)

At the same time there was a localized Crusader influence on the ruling classes of neighbouring Byzantine states, the cultural and political situation being especially complex in Epirus in what is now north-western Greece and southern Albania. This was feudalized under later Italianized or Italian despots like Leonardo III Tocco, who held three castles on the mainland plus several off-shore islands. As a result, several castles became the hereditary property of Greek, Serb, Albanian and Italian soldiers in the late 14th and 15th centuries.

Life in the fortified outposts of the Italian maritime empires had different priorities. We also know more about it because detailed records survive in Venice and Genoa. The situation was, however, complicated by the fact that some places changed hands several times. The island of Lemnos was in Crusader hands from 1204 to 1279. Thereafter it was disputed between Venetians, Genoese and Byzantines until the Byzantines gave authority to the autonomous Genoese Gattilusi family in 1414. From 1462 until 1479, it was disputed by the Venetians and Ottoman Turks. With such a history it is hardly surprising that Lemnos is dotted with castles, watch towers and fortified monasteries. The castles at Kotsinas and Palaiokastro were then damaged by earthquake in 1470, after which Kotsinas was not rebuilt.

DESTRUCTION OF THE CASTLE OF FORTY COLUMNS AT PAPHOS BY AN EARTHQUAKE, 1222

The ruined castle that overlooks the bay and town of Paphos in Cyprus was badly damaged by an earthquake even before its construction was finished. How much work remained to be done is unclear, and much of the fallen masonry was subsequently taken as building material for the town of Paphos itself. Clearly the castle was no longer considered important enough for work to be restarted, presumably because the conquest of the Byzantine capital of Constantinople by the Fourth Crusade removed the threat from Byzantium. In this reconstruction the main walls and towers are virtually complete, showing the castle to have been of a classic concentric design. Although some historians suggest that the basic design of at least the central part of this castle was Byzantine, dating from as early as the 7th or 8th centuries, any existing Byzantine structures would be embedded

within or beneath the inner keep. This keep consisted of four massive towers around a small inner courtyard, plus a semi-circular entrance tower projecting a considerable distance from one side. The outer walls and towers were separate from the inner complex, making Paphos castle genuinely concentric. The corner towers of the outer defences were relatively small, including three round and one polygonal design. There were also triangular or prow-shaped towers in the middle of two sides of the outer wall, with a small rectangular tower in the middle of the third. Slightly offset from the centre of the fourth side (on the left in our reconstruction) was a massive rectangular entrance tower. Behind this was an entrance bridge across the dry moat, abutting the outer wall at a point where the wall itself was slightly angled.
(Adam Hook © Osprey Publishing)

Venice and Genoa governed their colonial outposts in different ways, the Venetian colonial authorities generally following central government orders closely and reflecting the centralized character of the Venetian Republic. Venetian colonies, with the exception of Crete, also often had small populations and initially archaic fortifications, but these were well maintained. For example, the Venetian merchant quarter at Tana (Azov) north of the Black Sea was fortified in the early 14th century, being given a small garrison under a consul and two counsellors, a system similar to that in other outposts under direct Venetian rule.

Most Venetian fortresses in Greece differed from those of the Crusaders, mostly being on the coasts and usually guarding harbours. They were intended to resist attack from land or sea, and sometimes an entire bay was encircled by walls that extended into moles, virtually enclosing the harbour. At Kyrenia, Herakleion and Chanea the Venetians built a wall facing the sea and ramparts facing the land. At Naupaktos two defensive walls descended from a cliff-edged hill straight to the shore then curved out into the water to form a tiny harbour. In several other places the Venetians occupied a peninsula and, using any fortifications that existed, walled it from end to end and constructed moles to shelter ships. Later they cut off some peninsulas with moats, backed by massive fortifications.

Pay for garrisons depended on rank, the importance of the fortress and the current military situation. Initially, mercenaries in Venetian Greece received two or three ducats a month, the same as an oarsman in a galley, though this later rose to three to four ducats. The chatelain of a small town like Argos might be paid five ducats, whereas the commanders of important garrisons like Coron (Korone) and Methoni received 16 and a half ducats a month in 1341. Seventeen years later the Venetian Senate authorized the châtelain of Methoni to hire 300 mercenaries. Methoni is an interesting example of how Venetian colonists were settled, and their subsequent way of life. In 1293 the Senate ordered the walls of Methoni and Coron to be rebuilt and the towns to be populated by 24 families sent from Venice. Inside the *burgus*, or fortified town, of Methoni were commercial warehouses. There were market places inside the burgus and the castrum, supplying food and drink for passing pilgrims, travellers and sailors. Lodgings were reserved for Jewish travellers, and a hospital dedicated to St Iohannes looked after sick pilgrims and merchants.

Although Methoni was of only secondary importance, considerable efforts were made to keep its harbour operational. However, the mole was often damaged by storms, and this impressive structure could not entirely protect ships from severe weather. One 15th-century map called the *Parma Magliabecchi* recommended that only small craft anchor inside the mole, and in 1477 a Venetian admiral and the castellan of Methoni jointly reported that, due to the previous winter's storms, the port was so silted up that even shallow-draught war-galleys could not enter. Orders of 1395 that a new gate be built linking the castrum to the port caused further difficulties; several houses were demolished and replaced by lodgings for the soldiers guarding the new gate, plus a *platea* (open space) was created, probably with a customs house and public warehouses.

The troops garrisoning the fortresses of the four military districts of Venetian Crete usually numbered about 30 men each. Their primary role was to combat pirates and bandits while the inhabitants of the main colonial towns defended their own walls. In 1394 the *baillo* in Durazzo (now Dürres in Albania) also had 30 'new' crossbowmen in the two castles under his control.

As the threat from Ottoman raiders increased in the 15th century, small local defences were built to protect Greek villages close to the main Venetian fortresses in the southern Peloponnese. By late summer 1410, the Senate recorded that several small forts on the Korone peninsula had towers, walls and burghi, in addition to work done on the existing burghi and *isola* (or fortified island) of Korone itself. These enabled local peasants to store their corn, wine, and oil in safety before all such stores were brought into Korone during November.

The account of a pilgrimage to the Holy Land supposedly made by Arnold von Harff in 1496–99 is sometimes dismissed as a fable, but its German author clearly drew upon travellers' observations even if he never went on pilgrimage himself. In his description of Methoni he stated (tr. M. Letts):

> This town of Modon is very strong. It is subject to the Venetians, and the land belonging to it is called Morea, which lies near to Turkey (the territory of the Turkish Ottoman Sultan)… I found there a German master-gunner called Peter Bombadere, who gave me good company and friendship. He showed me the strength of the town and the artillery, and it is in truth a small town but strong. On the land side it has three suburbs with three walls and three ditches hewn out of the natural rock, on which they are building daily. He took me round the innermost wall which was very thick and built of rough stones; in addition there is a rampart against the wall on which stand many fine cannon, great carthouns [meaning unknown] and slings.

At Karaman in Turkey, the local museum has a very early bronze cannon, which was probably one of those supplied by Venice to their ally, the Turkish Aq Qoyunlu, ruler of eastern Turkey, around 1470. A document in the Venice State Archives notes:

> There are in our Arsenal three moulds for bombards made by Bartolomeo da Cremona, which throw 100 lb. stones, and to cast them are needed 18 milliara [1,000 lb.] of copper and 240 lb. of tin. And, as everybody knows, it is necessary to provide because of our obligations with his highness Ussani Cassani … [The rest of this document concerns the order to cast 50 small guns][1]

Genoese colonial outposts were governed in a different way, reflecting the fragmented nature of authority in the Republic of Genoa. They tended to be largely autonomous, with local governors or almost independent feudal lords having their own small garrisons. These troops maintained internal security while Genoese fleets kept trade flowing. The Mahone or local Genoese authorities preferred a minimal garrison to avoid alienating the local inhabitants, most of whom were Orthodox Christian Greeks, Armenians and others. In dealings with their powerful neighbours, these tiny outposts normally relied on money and diplomacy to maintain good relations. While the soldiers in their garrisons rarely remained in one place for long, those who lived in such Genoese enclaves often had houses in the unfortified suburbs, where there were also mills, orchards and vineyards.

By the late 14th century, Genoa had about 11 castles to defend its scattered possessions, but the large island of Chios remained the only colony with a sizeable population of Genoese origin. Here the Gattilusi family, which also ruled Lesbos and some smaller enclaves, relied on the goodwill of the more numerous indigenous population, real Gattilusio power being confined to the fortress overlooking the main town. Genoese enclaves on the northern coast of Turkey often had tense relations with the Byzantine emperor of Trebizond (Trabzon), who usually favoured Venice. They were also exposed to attack by Turkish rulers of the interior.

The Genoese presence at Kaffa in the Crimea dated from the 1270s, when the Mongol Khan gave the Genoese and Venetians joint permission to establish a settlement. The Venetians eventually lost their foothold after the Byzantines regained

---

1. Archivio di Stato di Venezia – Senato – Deliberazioni Terra, Reg., 191v – 21 December 1472. I am grateful for Prof. Marco Morin for supplying this previously unpublished information.

Constantinople and gave privileges to the Genoese. Kaffa now grew into a prosperous city, and by the start of the 15th century the captured Crusader squire, Iohan Schiltberger, claimed it had 6,000 houses within its fortified wall, with 11,000 outside and a further 4,000 houses in a more distant suburb. The true population of Kaffa in the late 14th century was around 20,000 people, including Greeks, Armenians

Inside one of the massive vaulted chambers of the donjon of Chlemutzi or Clairmont castle. This space would have been divided into two floors. (I. Meigh)

and Russians who lived outside the fortified castrum and *civitas*. At the start of the 14th century, the Caput Gazarie local governor was under the Genoese consul in Pera, but later the governor of Kaffa became responsible for the defence of all the Genoese outposts around the Black Sea in addition to the gate-guards, military equipment, naval construction facilities and galleys based in Kaffa.

The extraordinarily detailed Genoese colonial records emphasize the importance of fully trained crossbowmen – a man capable of repairing as well as using crossbows being even more valued – and such skills were a useful qualification for anyone wanting to find work in Kaffa. Crossbowmen also indulged in local trading, sometimes pledging their weapons and ammunition as collateral in commercial agreements. Given the size of Kaffa, and the length of the coastal strip dominated by Genoa, garrisons in the Crimea seem surprisingly small. In 1369 the podestà, or senior military officer, had only 25 crossbowmen in Kaffa while in 1386 the population of Kaffa included Greeks building ships, and blacksmiths making arrowheads and bombards, or early cannon. The Genoese podestà at Pera had 12 sergeants in 1390 and a year later there were a mere 40 soldiers in the Genoese garrison of Magusa in Cyprus.

On the north-western side of the Black Sea another group of fortified Genoese commercial outposts included Bilhorod-Dnistrovsky, which the Genoese knew as Moncastro, Licostomo (Kiliya) and perhaps a third on the island of Giurgiu further up the River Danube. Early Genoese documents show that Genoese formed a third of the residents of Western European origin around 1300, other Italians including Corsicans, Piedmontese and Lombards. At first there seemed little need for serious fortifications, but after the middle of the 14th century the local Genoese began to feel threatened by the rising power of the Ottoman Turks. At Bilhorod-Dnistrovsky they built a rectangular citadel with four massive round corner towers. This still exists, although it is difficult to differentiate between Genoese construction of the 14th and 15th centuries, and the substantial strengthening done by Moldavian rulers like Alexandru the Good and Steven the Great. At Kiliya a ruined island fortress in the Danube was probably the Genoese castle, while fragmentary fortifications on the left bank were the fortress of Steven the Great. In fact, the Genoese lost Kiliya to the Wallachians, from whom Steven the Great took the fortress in 1465, though most of the population remained Italian merchants. Eventually Genoese and Moldavians attempted to cooperate against the looming Ottoman Empire, but failed.

THE CASTLES AT WAR

Although many Crusader castles outside the Middle East seem to have had a more symbolic than military value, many were of course used in war. In Cyprus only the coastal fortifications could be described as strong, and there was little threat from the interior as long as the Greek population were cowed into accepting Western domination. In contrast, the coasts were exposed to attack from Mamluks, rival Christian powers, and Ottoman Turks.

Things were different in the Latin Empire of Constantinople. There was no attempt to build castles during the failed attempts to conquer Thrace and north-western Anatolia. Instead, the invaders fortified some churches or took over existing Byzantine fortifications. During the initial invasion of Greece a small fort was erected at Pendeskupi in the Crusader siege of 1205–10, but the primary role of castles was consolidation rather than conquest. Thereafter, wars between the Crusader States and the rival Byzantine rulers mostly consisted of raids, naval skirmishes and small-scale sieges, with few major battles.

BASES FOR OFFENSIVE OPERATIONS

Following the fall of the last Crusader enclaves on the Middle Eastern mainland in

One of the last additions that the Hospitallers made to their already powerful fortifications around the city of Rhodes was this polygonal artillery bastion, built around a taller, round tower that still rises out of the centre of the massive artillery position. (D. Nicolle)

1291, fear spread of a Mamluk invasion of Cyprus. This threat failed to materialize, and instead Cyprus remained a Crusader base close to the heart of the Islamic world. While European fleets dominated the eastern Mediterranean, the region needed little fortification. Instead, attempts were made to re-establish a bridgehead on the Syrian coast, to impose an economic blockade on the Mamluk sultanate, and to support the Christian kingdom of Cilician Armenia.

Charles of Anjou, king of southern Italy, was the only major Western monarch seriously interested in rolling back the Byzantine advances that overran so much Crusader territory in Greece during the mid 13th century – principally because he himself had ambitions in the area. Otherwise, the Castle of Thebes was built for Nicholas II of St Omer in 1287, at a time when the Crusaders of central Greece were returning to the offensive in southern Thessaly. The castle of Chastelneuf (possibly the site known as Veligosti), built around 1297, might have protected surrounding villages against Byzantine raiders from Gardiki, but this was built over 30 years earlier, so it is possible that Chastelneuf was actually part of a Crusader counter-offensive. An offensive strategy was clearer at Smyrna, which was held by the Hospitallers from 1346 to 1402 and successfully crippled the previously threatening naval power of the Turkish *beylik* of Aydin.

DECORATING THE GREAT HALL OF KADMEIA CASTLE AT THEBES, LATE 13TH CENTURY

The Kadmeia fortress or castle at Thebes was built between 1258 and 1280 for Nicholas II of St Omer. Most of this castle has been destroyed, including the famous hall, which was originally decorated with wall paintings illustrating the conquest of Syria by the First Crusade. These may have been made, or at least designed, by artists from the Crusader Principality of Antioch in northern Syria, brought to Thebes by Nicholas' wife, Mary of Antioch. This reconstruction is based upon written evidence, upon comparable but surviving Crusader architecture from the same period, and upon late 13th-century manuscript illustrations of various sieges during the First Crusade. The traditional method of making wall paintings shown in our reconstruction is illustrated in many medieval manuscripts and is still practised in various parts of the Balkans and Greece. A senior artist paints over the initial sketches while his assistants mix plaster in a wooden vat and add the fibrous material that strengthens the layer of plaster. (Adam Hook © Osprey Publishing)

COMMERCIAL OUTPOSTS

The shortage of military manpower was particularly acute in the Italian colonial outposts, with around five local inhabitants of dubious loyalty for every one Venetian or Genoese. Theoretically, Westerners lived inside walled towns dominated by a fortified castrum while locals inhabited the suburbs. In reality, however, many Westerners also lived in the suburbs, although at Magusa in Cyprus there appears to have been a specifically Latin suburb close to the city walls.

Life in the Aegean was complicated by almost continuous naval conflicts following the Italian seizure of numerous islands in the aftermath of the Fourth Crusade. Many became meeting places for Christian pirates from all over the Mediterranean. Such pirates also had bases on the mainland coasts, and operating from here, or arriving as naval landing forces, they raided deep inland, sometimes capturing peasants for ransom or enslavement.

In a more peaceful vein, the Crusader and Italian commercial outposts served as recruitment centres for local and foreign oarsmen seeking employment in the galleys. Skilled local pilots would also be available, while the ports themselves supplied food to passing ships, wine from Tenedos (probably sweet and red, like modern Mavrodafne), and dried figs from Foça (Phocaea). Huge quantities of ships' biscuit were made in neighbouring countries like Bulgaria, and were then sold in bulk to ships that called at the major fortified harbours. Captured ships may also have been up for sale, though most were sold back to Italy. It is unclear whether prisoners of war were sold as slaves or, if they were fellow Western European Christians, were sold to dealers who then extracted ransom from families or governments.

In 1386 only one or two large Venetian war-galleys were based at Corfu, two or four at Herakleion, one at Euboea, and one at Coron or Methoni, though there was also a larger number of smaller galliots. As the power of the Ottoman Empire grew on land and at sea during the 15th century, some Venetian colonial fortifications, which had merely provided defence and refuge against pirates, now became major military and naval centres. Meanwhile, the Venetian government continued to foster good relations with the Ottoman sultan through trade and negotiation wherever possible.

It is possible that a Turkish fleet from Aydin in the Aegean penetrated the Black Sea to attack Kiliya in the 1330s. Within a generation or so the Genoese outposts in this region were threatened not only by the Ottomans but also by the nearby

Despot Dobrotitch, both of whom now had fleets. In contrast, the Genoese fleet overcame a temporary threat by the Mongol Golden Horde to Genoese outposts on the northern coasts of the Black Sea, because the Mongols had no ships.

BASES FOR DEFENSIVE OPERATIONS

Defensive circumstances differed between regions. In Cyprus there was less urgency to modernize Byzantine fortifications, and little money to do so anyway. The only large new castle from the early period, overlooking Paphos, was built to defend a strategic harbour, but it lost its importance after the Fourth Crusade. Destroyed by earthquake in 1222, it was subsequently used for building material. Other Cypriot fortifications upgraded in the early years were primarily to counter local Greek rebellion, but this danger also diminished after the Fourth Crusade. With a Byzantine revival in the mid 13th century, fear of an attempt to retake Cyprus resurfaced, but never seems to have reached a serious level.

The disappearance of the Crusader States on the Middle Eastern mainland did, however, increase the threat of Islamic raiding, if not invasion. This became serious from the mid 14th century onwards and consequently harbour defences were the strongest type of fortification in Cyprus. Nevertheless, mountaintop citadels were more than mere refuges. St Hilarion overlooked the main pass between the port of Kyrenia and the capital of Nicosia, and in 1374 its garrison harassed Genoese supply columns during the siege of Kyrenia.

Greece was inhabited not only by settled Greek peasants and townsfolk, but also by sheep-raising semi-nomads. Most of these people did not speak Greek, and they dominated several mountainous regions. They also tended to raid the settled peoples of the plains – and were practically impossible for any government to control. In fact, the Crusader States that emerged in the wake of the Fourth Crusade certainly did not truly 'rule' all the territory that appears as 'Crusader' in modern historical atlases. Many Crusader fortifications in Greece were probably designed to deal with these warlike tribal peoples, which included Albanians, Rumanian-speaking Vlachs, and Slavs such as the Melings of the Taygetos Mountains in the deep south of the Peloponnese. Mistra, Maina and Leuktron were apparently built for this purpose, and the location of Vardounia suggests that it had a similar role. There were usually two castles, one at each end of a vulnerable pass, but instead of serving as bases from which to attack the tribes in their own mountains, their garrisons usually attacked raiders as they returned laden with spoil and pursued by Crusader troops from the plains.

Mistra was the most important link in the defensive system established by William of Villehardouin, who chose this site in 1249. According to P. Burridge:

> By examining the function of each castle and its relationship with its neighbours a picture of the medieval military strategy of the area begins to present itself. To the north the Langhada pass was protected at its western end by the castle of Kalamata and to the east by Mistra. Each castle also guaranteed the security of the productive plain in its vicinity. To the south the main pass between present-day Areopolis and Gytheion was guarded by Passava to the east and Oitylon/Kelefa to the west, the latter also protecting the principal harbour on the west coast. Any fortifications at Porto-Kayio and Tigani must have been designed to secure the anchorages adjacent to these sites. Zarnata – whenever it was built – as well as protecting

The north-eastern tower of the Citadel (now the Iç Kale) of the Genoese fortified outpost of Amasra on the Black Sea coast of Turkey. It appears to be the only round tower in the entire defensive system (D. Nicolle)

THE CASTLE OF SATHINES (ATHENS ACROPOLIS) IN THE LATE 14TH CENTURY

The world famous Parthenon Temple on the Acropolis (upper city) of Athens had been converted into a Christian church in the 6th century; it served as the cathedral of the Crusader Duchy of Athens from 1208 to 1458. However, virtually every fragment of post-Classical architecture on the Acropolis was removed during the 19th century in an almost fanatical attempt to recreate what had existed in the Golden Age of Classical Greece. This meant that not only the Ottoman Turkish mosque, houses and other structures were demolished, but also what remained from the Byzantine and Crusader periods. One of the last items to go was a tall stone tower (1), similar to those that still dot the countryside of Attica. It survived long enough to be photographed and had at least one overhanging box-machicolation (2) above its only entrance door. Facing it, the north wing of the Propylaea or main entrance complex of the ancient Acropolis (3) had been raised in height and was used as the chancellery of the Duchy of Athens. When the Italian banker Nerio Acciaioli, Lord of Corinth, became duke of Athens in 1388 he converted the Propylaea into a fine Italian-style palace known as the Mnesikles. Acciaioli is also sometimes credited with constructing the fortified tower. To what extent the rest of the site was fortified remains unknown, though crenellated walls (4) were built around various parts of the ancient Acropolis, and fallen drums of ancient columns were often used as defences or obstructions in subsequent fortifications (5). Serious defences were certainly added during the Ottoman period. In the 17th century the palace, which was currently being used as the Ottoman governor's residence, was struck by lightning; a magazine exploded and part of the Classical portico collapsed. (Adam Hook © Osprey Publishing)

the Kampos valley will have guarded the track southwards into the Mani. Control would also have been exercised over a rough, but passable, route from Anavryti (south of Mistra, on the eastern flanks of the Taygetos) to Kampos.

Where the specific function of the Crusader castle of Beaufort was concerned, Burridge continues:

> It would be remarkable if, after securing two of the major passes over the Taygetos, William failed to control the eastern side of the third pass either by strengthening an already existing defence or by building a new castle. To have built Beaufort without securing the eastern side of the pass would have left Beaufort and its fertile plain open to attack.

Although the Crusader States in Greece were in an almost constant state of war with one or other of their Byzantine neighbours, the chroniclers rarely mention castles being attacked. Having played virtually no role in the initial conquest, they did little more than slow down the subsequent Byzantine reconquests. The garrisons were not only tiny, but probably contained many Greeks whose loyalty to their Crusader rulers was shallow. As noted previously, in 1311 the castle of Thebes was surrendered to a marauding army of Catalan mercenaries after its field army had been defeated in open battle; the Catalans later destroyed it rather than let it fall into the hands of Gautier II of Brienne.

The threat from the sea was perhaps more significant, though even here there was a tendency for garrisons to fight in the open before retreating within their walls. During the 13th century the main problem was caused by rivalry between Genoese, Pisans, Venetians and Byzantines. Turkish-Islamic naval raiding increased in the 14th century. Several Crusader expeditions were launched in response, but had only a short-lived impact, with the beyliks of Karasi, Saruhan, Mentese and above all Aydin soon reviving to dominate much of the Aegean. Most Turkish fleets consisted of large numbers of small ships rather than the great war-galleys preferred by Christian naval powers. Turkish naval tactics also focused on transporting men and horses as raiding parties – sometimes even carrying siege machines to attack coastal fortifications. Such fleets were very vulnerable to the large Christian galleys and tended to avoid combat at sea, enabling the Christian powers to claim 'naval domination', which, however, only existed when and where their war-galleys were present.

The military orders were active in defence of the Crusader States in Greece, initially against the Byzantines but later focusing on the Turks. In 1402 the Hospitallers twice sent their senior admiral, Buffilo Panizati, to inspect the defensive works being carried out at Smyrna. The Christians had 20 years to strengthen this vital outpost and its garrison now consisted of 200 brother knights. The construction cost the Hospitallers a great deal of money, as did the maintenance of each knight in Smyrna – nevertheless, the effort was considered worthwhile.

The main threat faced by the Venetian colonial authorities came from internal rebellion in Crete and savage guerrilla warfare. Then came the Ottoman Turks' combined army and naval campaign that conquered Euboea (Negroponte) in 1470. This was a terrible shock to the Italians who had, until then, not feared the Ottoman fleet. By that date the remnants of the Crusader States had already fallen, but, being on the mainland, they had been overrun by the Ottoman army, not the navy. Small wonder that Venice, which took over Cyprus in 1489, concentrated on defending its coast while largely abandoning inland castles, many of which were dismantled.

The Genoese outposts in the Crimea faced different problems. Here the Italian colonial governors controlled a long but narrow coastal strip, which was backed by ranges of mountains that lay between the fortified ports and the steppe Khanates of the interior. These mountains were also the powerbase of a little-known, essentially Byzantine Christian people who maintained their own series of fortresses, some carved from the mountain rock itself. Nevertheless, the vast Mongol Khanate of the Golden Horde remained the dominant land power in this region, and it was the temporarily anti-Christian policy adopted by its ruler that caused the Genoese to refortify Kaffa in 1313.

THE FORTIFICATIONS UNDER ATTACK

Until the arrival of the Ottomans, armies in late medieval Greece tended to be small with little siege equipment. During the 13th century the Crusader States' most pressing enemy was the revived Byzantine 'Empire of Nicea', which subsequently re-established itself as the main, though not the only, claimant to be *the* Byzantine Empire. The Despotate of Mistra in southern Greece formed part of this revived empire and was a constant threat to the Crusader Principality of Achaea. Until the

This 13th-century tower is virtually all that remains of the once luxurious Crusader castle of Kadmeia at Thebes. (D. Nicolle)

mid 14th century its armies were very mixed, including many Western mercenaries as well as Turks, Albanians and local tribal forces.

These were effective in open warfare, but their siege capabilities are virtually unknown. According to the *Chronicle of the Morea*, the Byzantine 'Grand Domestikos' senior army commander considered attacking the castle of Andravida after being defeated in a skirmish, but a European mercenary advised trying to lure the Crusader Prince William into the open:

> I have learned that the prince has returned to Andravida and that the armies that he brought have gone home; let us go straight to him there in Andravida; and if he should have such misfortune as to come out to battle, do not set to fighting him with arrogance, but only fighting him with skill and cunning.

However, those who knew this area well advised the Byzantine commander not to go to Andravida 'because the approaches were too narrow for the balistas [tzagratoros, crossbows] and their crews'. After an inconclusive skirmish the Byzantines withdrew and the Grand Domestikos instead besieged the castle of Nikli, where his Turkish mercenaries changed sides because they had not been paid. Half a century later the Byzantine army proved much more effective and in 1316 Andonikos Asen, the emperor's governor in the Peloponnese, defeated the Crusaders' field army in open battle near the castle of St George – though again the fortress itself played only a minimal role.

Events concerning minor fortifications and isolated towers were usually too insignificant to warrant mention in the chronicles. Nevertheless, the people of the Archangelos area of Rhodes petitioned the Hospitaller Grand Master for a small castle in 1399 because of the increasing danger of naval raids. Instead, they were permitted to seek refuge in the existing castle of Feraklos 5km away. Some time after 1399 a castle was constructed at Archangelos, but was stormed with ease by the Ottomans in 1457. Thirteen years earlier the citadel of Lindos was more successful in sheltering the inhabitants when a substantial Mamluk army invaded Rhodes. In 1395 the whole population of the island of Leros retreated into the castle every night for fear of raiders.

Most early Ottoman conquests in Greece and the Balkans were achieved by persistent raiding and once the surrounding countryside had been subdued, the remaining fortified places eventually came to terms with the Ottoman invaders. Only coastal enclaves, resupplied by ship, could withstand such tactics, but once the Turks took to the seas they too came under serious threat. To make matters worse, the local Greek island populations were often hostile to their Latin-Catholic rulers and frequently helped the Muslim Turks.

Seen from the Muslim perspective, however, the garrisons of Crusader castles could seem large and remarkably well equipped, especially when Turkish naval raiders lacked cavalry. The Turkish epic

An internal passage with archery embrasures, inside one of the walls of Kantara or Le Candare castle in Cyprus. (M. Youden)

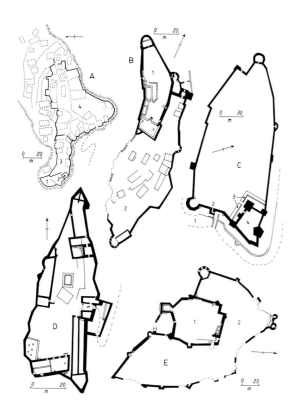

Large Greek mainland
fortifications:
A – Vardounia castle:
(1) keep, (2) tower, (3) inner
court, (4) outer court,
(5) lower gate
(after Burridge).
B – The castle of Mistra:
(1) citadel, (2) lower ward
(after Bon).
C – The citadel of Patras:
(1) outer moat, (2) main
gate, (3) inner moat, (4) keep
(after Bon).
D – The castle of Karytaina
(after Bon).
E – The citadel of Argos:
(1) keep, (2) outer ward
(after Bon).

Destan of Umur Pasha describes one such attack on Chios: 'The Franks numbered ten thousand, all covered in iron they came to give combat', and emerged to fight the raiders in open battle. The major role of crossbows in defence of Christian fortification is reflected in another Turkish epic, the *Danishmand-name*, which survives in a mid 14th century form. These weapons apparently included frame-mounted versions, which were used alongside stone-throwing mangonels, Greek-fire incendiary devices, simple fire-arrows and the *tufenk*, which was an early form of musket.

The most catastrophic siege was Timur-i Lenk's (Tamerlane's) assault on Smyrna in 1402. While Timur's troops ravaged the area, largely focusing on Turkish rather than Christian-held localities, preparations continued in Smyrna. The defences were concentrated on the rugged peninsula, which included a castle that 'closed' the port and was separated from the mainland by a recently excavated deep ditch. Smyrna was, in fact, thought impregnable and the Hospitaller garrison felt confident. Munitions, food supplies, money and troops continued to arrive. Timur led his own 'central' army towards Smyrna on 2 December 1402, where his left and right 'flank' armies were ordered to join him. Almost immediately his siege machines and miners set to work on several parts of the fortifications. Timur also ordered a senior officer to construct a massive platform on wooden piles to stop enemy ships entering the port. A few days later the armies of the left and right wings joined the siege. Timur now ordered a full-scale bombardment, which survivors compared to a 'Second Deluge'. After two days Timur's miners weakened a stretch of the outer walls; the props were burned, the wall collapsed and a general assault swept into Smyrna. Resistance was scattered; the Hospitaller knights fled to their ships, and the population was slaughtered while several ships, which had come to support the city, turned and fled, fearing Timur's stone-throwing machines. Meanwhile, the nearby Genoese outpost at Foça (Old Phocaea) surrendered, following the example of Yeni Foça (New Phocaea), which had sent a peace ambassador to Timur. When Francesco II

Gattilusio, the Genoese ruler of Lesbos, also surrendered and, like the Genoese authorities on Chios, offered to pay tribute, Timur-i Lenk won temporary control over two large Aegean islands – without launching a single warship.

Western historians have tended to dismiss the Mamluk sultanate of Egypt and Syria as having little interest in naval affairs. This is not true, as those on the receiving end of several Mamluk attacks could testify. However, such assaults were raids in force rather than attempts at conquest. One of the most effective took place during the reign of the Sultan al-Ashraf Barsbey and was in retaliation for Cypriot piracy against Mamluk merchant vessels.

In 1424 five ships, two of which were brigandines with 80 elite Mamluk soldiers on board, set out from Cairo down the Nile. At Dumyat (Damietta) they were joined by a galley manned by Egyptian volunteers. Two more ships joined the fleet at Beirut and Sidon, substantially increasing the number of troops involved. They reached the Cypriot coast south of Limassol where they captured a Christian merchant ship whose crew had fled as they approached. After looting then burning this vessel, the Mamluk fleet sailed to Limassol. King Janus of Cyprus had been warned of their approach, so the Muslim squadron was met by three fully armed warships, but these were soon defeated and burned. As soon as they landed, the raiders were attacked by the vanguard of the Cypriot army, which they again drove off, killing its commander, Philippe of Picquingni. After raiding the area, the Mamluks considered attacking the castle of Limassol, but, lacking siege equipment, they instead sailed towards Paphos, capturing one and burning a second enemy galley on their way. After devastating the region of Kouklia, they returned home with one captured galley, 23 prisoners for ransom and considerable booty (see Ziada, 1933).

On this occasion the fortifications at Limassol had done what they were supposed to do, but the limitations of such urban defences became apparent

Cypriot fortifications:
A. The upper citadel of St Hilarion Castle showing Byzantine, plus 13th- and 14th-century Crusader, structures: 1 – great hall; 2 – kitchen; 3 – gateway; 4 – redoubt (after Enlart).
B. Kantara castle (after Enlart).
C. The Hospitaller castle at Kolossi: 1 – donjon; 2 – outbuildings (after Megaw).
D. The fortified town and castle at Kyrenia: 1 – remains of the city wall; 2 – citadel; 3 – harbour (after Enlart).

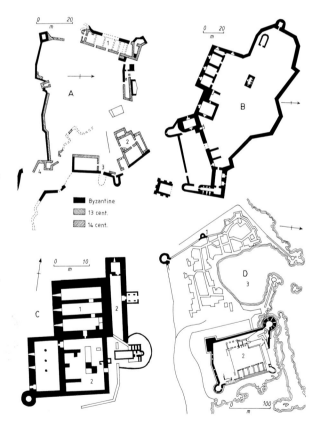

during the next Mamluk raid in 1425. This involved eight Mamluk vessels from Egypt supported by smaller ships from Lebanon carrying volunteers. Eventually the fleet, commanded by Jirbash al-Karimi, consisted of five large war-galleys, 19 smaller galleys, six horse transports and 12 galliots. It set sail from Tripoli on 30 July. Genoese-held Magusa surrendered immediately, raising the sultan's flag on 4 August. The Genoese also provided information about Cypriot defences. Next came a full-scale naval battle within sight of Larnaca, which the Muslim fleet won, after which the Mamluks ravaged a wide area. On 15 August they landed a mere 150 men, who stormed Limassol town and castle with relative ease after escaped Muslim slaves told them about a poorly guarded stretch of wall. Nevertheless, news now arrived that the Venetians were sending substantial support to the Cypriot king, who had also assembled a large army to attack the raiders. So the Mamluks abandoned Limassol, defeated the Cypriot army in several small skirmishes, then sailed home with much more booty than before and over a thousand prisoners.

Gunpowder artillery was now having a major influence upon both defence and attack. In fact the Venetian fortifications in Greece, including those at Methoni, Korone and Nauphlia, are amongst the best examples from this period. Until 1470 the Venetians had continued the medieval reliance on height, but this gave way to lower, thicker earth-filled ramparts with broad terrepleines on top for cannon. The earliest-dated Venetian artillery constructions are those designed by Vettore Pasqualigo at Nauphlia. They were primarily designed to face Ottoman Turkish attack, but even before this the struggles between rival Christian powers in late

Platamon (Pandeleimon) castle, built between 1204 and 1222 with later additions. It is one of the best-preserved Crusader castle in central Greece. (D. Nicolle)

medieval Greece, including Catalans and Aragonese, might be reflected in the deeply anti-Genoese Catalan epic *Tirant lo Blanc*. This was written in the mid 15th century. In one description of the defence of a castle, the hero Tirant ordered that a bulwark be built inside the gate, which was itself left open. When the enemy charged in they were trapped and killed. Fearing enemy mining beneath the walls, Tirant also ordered countermines to be dug and filled with brass bowls, which rattled when enemy miners used pickaxes. Next the enemy tried to attack through these tunnels, but Tirant fired bombards into the entrances.

Though fictitious and exaggerated, Tirant's adventures probably reflected reality. The first unsuccessful Ottoman siege of Hospitaller-held Rhodes in 1480 was, however, brutally real. Sultan Mehmet tried to keep news of his fleet's departure secret, but the Grand Master had an effective intelligence network and was able to get the local inhabitants and their animals inside various castles before the Turks arrived. The small Hospitaller fleet did not challenge the enemy at sea, but allowed them to establish a bridgehead almost unopposed. The Ottomans then attempted to take the city of Rhodes at a rush, but failed. Next the Turks bombarded the Tower of St Nicholas, which protected the shallower Mandraki or northern harbour. This resulted in a duel between three large Ottoman mangonels in the garden and orchard of the Church of St Anthony, hurling stones across the Mandraki harbour, and three Hospitaller bombards in the garden of the Inn of Auvergne (the hostel of Hospitaller brothers from central France). Subsequently the Turks established several other mangonel and cannon batteries, the struggle continuing to focus on the vulnerable Tower of St Nicholas throughout June and most of July. In fact this tower was badly damaged, though the Hospitaller defenders constructed a timber stockade to protect the damaged sections. After unsuccessfully attacking the Tower of St Nicholas from the sea, the Turks tried to anchor a pontoon supported by barrels across the Mandraki harbour. This enabled them to take the mole and isolate the tower, but the pontoon's mooring ropes were cut by swimmers at night. Part of the Turkish fleet now sailed into the Mandraki and bombarded the tower while the pontoon was towed back into position, followed by an assault. But the defenders' artillery destroyed many of the attackers' boats and eventually the Ottoman attack on Rhodes was abandoned after another assault on the other side of the town failed. It would be another 42 years before Sultan Mehmet's grandson, Sulaiman the Magnificent, finally conquered Rhodes in 1522.

AFTERMATH

Several Crusader castles in Greece lost their strategic significance after being reconquered by the Byzantines, but, being distant from major towns, were not pillaged as sources of building material – as happened to the Castle of Forty Columns in Cyprus. Consequently these Greek castles remained virtually unchanged. Other fortified locations of Crusader origin remained important or even increased in military significance. The most famous was Mistra, which became the capital of the Byzantine Despotate in the Peloponnese. Its superb late Byzantine churches and their wall paintings date from this later Byzantine period. Mistra remained locally important under Ottoman Turkish rule, the castle again being slightly altered while several charming but now utterly ruined Islamic buildings were added to the town. The greatest damage to Mistra occurred in the 19th century, when it was burned and then devastated by Russians and Albanians.

The Byzantine despots of Mistra also modified several other inland Crusader castles, while the coastal fortresses were even more substantially altered by the Venetians. For example, the existing castle of Vardounia incorporates elements from many different periods, both before and after the introduction of gunpowder. Alterations from the age of firearms are mostly visible on the highest parts of the existing structures, though in fact the walls and towers were probably higher in the Crusader era than in subsequent centuries.

Constantine Palaiologos, the Despot of Mistra and subsequently the last Byzantine emperor, took up residence at Clairmont in 1427. In 1430 he destroyed the Crusader castle of Clarence (Clarenza) and, perhaps, the neighbouring town, while his army may also have devastated Beauvoir (Pontikocastro). It has, however, been suggested that the present castle of Clairmont is not actually a Crusader structure at all, but was built by Constantine Palaiologos to replace the Crusader castle that he destroyed some distance away. Having been regained by the Byzantines from the Latins in 1429, Patras was certainly rebuilt during this period in a final effort by Constantine to stem the Ottoman advance. In the event the castle of Patras did hold out when the Turks first took the town, obliging them to retreat. Only in 1458 did both the town and the castle of Patras surrender to Sultan Mehmet the Conqueror.

The fate of those of Western European origin and Catholic religion who had held Crusader castles in Greece was varied. As the Latins lost territory to Byzantine reconquest, the senior aristocracy was either killed or returned to France or Italy. Lower-ranking members of Crusader society found it more difficult to leave, many migrating to the Venetian colonies or being absorbed into the Byzantine military elite. In southern Greece many families were clearly assimilated in this way, and became loyal military supporters of the Byzantine Empire. Whether they retained any connection with the ex-Crusader fortifications is unknown, as is the fate of their descendants under Turkish rule. Many were probably incorporated into the Ottoman military system, along with so many of the Byzantine military class.

The Ottoman impact upon castles of Crusader origin was similarly varied. During the early decades the Turks strengthened some fortifications, but most were now irrelevant and were consequently abandoned. Where the early Ottomans did make changes, these were mostly a continuation of Byzantine military architectural trends, although stronger towers in the Arab-Islamic tradition were added to incorporate or resist firearms.

Genoese outposts in the Aegean survived slightly longer than those around the Black Sea. Although the Ottoman sultans were more sympathetic towards Orthodox Christians, especially Greeks, than towards Latin or Western Catholics, they allowed the Genoese Gattilusi to retain control of Lemnos under Ottoman suzerainty following the fall of Constantinople. This was probably when the Gattilusi added gun emplacements to Myrina Kastro, strong enough to bear the weight and recoil of modern firearms, though these may also be later Ottoman Turkish improvements.

After several years of chaos and oppression the local Greeks appealed to the sultan, who handed the island to a member of the ex-Byzantine imperial family in 1457. Finally, in 1467, Ottoman direct rule was imposed, though the Venetians continued to dispute the island until 1478. Thereafter there was little need for fortifications, as the Aegean Sea was now effectively an Ottoman lake. The Gattilusi rulers of Lesbos paid tribute to the sultan until 1462 and the Genoese Mahone on Chios survived as late as 1566, the same year that the sultan gave the ex-Crusader island and Duchy of Naxos to the famous Jewish governor, Joseph Nasi.

The fate of the Venetian outposts tended to be more clearcut. At Monemvasia, most of the Crusader and Byzantine fortifications were on the summit, forming an acropolis. Under later Venetian rule these were abandoned and a new town called Ghefira was built on the shore, within Venetian fortifications that extended from the acropolis to the sea. However, much of the existing urban walls date from the first Ottoman and second Venetian periods in the later 16th to early 18th centuries.

The substantially restored 14th- and 15th-century walls of the Italian colonial outpost of Soldaia (Sudak) in the Crimea. (Author's collection)

The fort of Palamede at Nauphlia was similarly rebuilt by the Venetians in 1711, virtually enclosing the Crusader structures within new ones designed to resist modern artillery.

THE CITADEL AND TOWN WALLS OF SOLDAIA (SUDAK), CRIMEA, IN THE 15TH CENTURY

Today Soldaia is the best-preserved medieval fortified city on the Crimean coast, though it was not the most important during the period of Genoese rule. Its fortifications were made of red sandstone and much of these has been restored in modern times. The oldest part of the defences was probably a simple Byzantine tower on the top of the hill (1), but the line and perhaps the foundations of the curtain walls (2) might also date from the Byzantine period. The summits of at least two of the larger towers were decorated with rows of blind arches in what would seem to have been an Italian fashion (3). Many of the smaller rectangular towers were much simpler, being partially open at the back (4) and with wooden floors, in a style common in Byzantine, Balkan and some early Ottoman military architecture. There also seems to have been a group of substantial towers or fortified structures where the land walls met those facing the sea, perhaps creating a strongly defended entrance complex (5). How much of the interior of the walled town was built up with commercial premises, houses, orchards and gardens (6) is unclear. Outside the walled town there were also suburbs or scattered houses. (Adam Hook © Osprey Publishing)

The Ottomans took and garrisoned the island fortress of Giurgiu in the River Danube in 1394, and 50 years later the ex-Genoese enclave of Licostomo (Kiliya) on the Black Sea coast was occupied by Hungary's local allies. Twenty or so years after the Ottoman conquest of Istanbul, all the Genoese outposts around the Black Sea had fallen, and in the end Kaffa sought protection from Poland – but this also failed. Most of the local inhabitants refused to fight for Genoa and instead made terms with the Ottomans, who took control in 1479. The fall of Kaffa led to a brief attempt at a Genoese-Moldavian alliance against the Ottoman Empire, and the same year Steven the Great of Moldavia sent a force of 800 masons and over 17,000 labourers to strengthen the defences of Kiliya. Only Kiliya and Moncastro now remained, but their Moldavian garrisons surrendered to a major Ottoman land and sea campaign in 1484.

VISITING THE
FORTIFICATIONS TODAY

MIDDLE EAST

The historian or visitor who wants to explore 'untouched' 12th-century Crusader fortifications will find himself exploring shattered ruins. If the enthusiast wants to find more than this, he or she will almost inevitably be drawn to some of the less accessible and mountainous, though not necessarily least populated, regions of what were once the Crusader States of Edessa, Antioch, Tripoli and Jerusalem.

As we have already seen, the names given to cities, castles, villages and practically every other feature of the Middle Eastern landscape have changed over the centuries. Furthermore, they were known by different names by different peoples during the period of the Crusades. The list of alternative names given below includes most of the sites mentioned in this book, but Turkish and Hebrew names only apply to locations that lie within the modern states of Turkey or Israel. Cities that are commonly known by variations of their correct or ancient names are given these within the text. This is not, however, a full list of sites fortified by the Crusaders during the 12th and 13th centuries.

Names of Holy Land Castles

Medieval French or Latin	Arabic	Turkish or Hebrew
Aintab	'Ayn Tab	Gaziantep
Albara	al-Barah	—
Alexandretta	Iskandariyah	Iskerderun
Amoude	Khan 'Amudah	Amuda
Anamour	—	Anamur
Anazarbus	—	Anavarza
Apamea	Afamiyah (also Qal'at al-Mudiq)	—
Aqua Bella	—	'En Hemed
Aradus	Ruad or Arwad	—
Arima	al-Araymah	—
Arsur (Apollonia)	Arsuf	—
Ascalon	'Asqalan	Ashqelon
Ayla	'Aqabah & Jazirat Fara'un	—
Balatonos	Balatun (or Qal'at al-Mahalbah)	—
Belfort (or Beaufort)	Shaqif Arnun (or Qal'at al-Shaqif)	—
Belhacem	Qal'at Abu'l-Hasan	—
Belinas	Banyas	—
Belmont	Suba	Zoba
Belvoir	Kawkab al-Hawa	—
Bethany	al-'Azariyah	—
Bethgibelin	Bayt Jibrin	Bet Guvrin
Bethsan	Baysan	Bet She'an
Bira	al-Bira	Birecik
Blanchegarde	Tal al-Safiyah	—
Bokebais	Abu Qubais	—
Botron (or Le Boutron)	al-Batrun	—
Caco	al-Qaqun	—
Caesarea	al-Qaisariyah	Sedot Yam
Cafarlet	Kfar Lam	Habonim
Calansue	al-Qalansuwa	—
Casal des Plains	Yazur	Azor
Casal Imbert	al-Zib	Akhziv
Castel Blanc	Burj Safita	—
Castel Neuf	Hunin	—
Castel Rouge	al-Qal'at Yahmur	—
Castellum Beroart	Minat al-Qal'a	Ashdod Yam
Castellum Regis	al-Mi'ilyah	Ma'alot
Cave de Sueth	'Ain al-Habis (or Habis Jaldak)	—
Cave de Tyron	Shaqif Tirun	—
Cavea	al-Mughayir	—
Caymont	Tal Qaimun	Yoqne'am
Celle	al-Habis	—
Château de la Vieille	Bikisra'il	—

Château Pelerin	Atlit	—
Châteauneuf	Hunin	—
Cisterna Rubea (see Maldoim)	Qal'at al-Damm	—
Coliat	al-Qulai'ah	—
Crac des Chevaliers	Hisn al-Akrad	—
Cursat	Qusair	—
Daron	al-Darum	—
Edessa	al-Ruha	Urfa
Emmaus	Abu Ghosh (or Amwas)	—
Forbelet	al-Taiyiba	—
Gaston	Baghras	Bagra
Gibelcar	'Akkar (Jabal 'Akkar)	—
Gibelet (or Byblos)	Jubayl	—
Harenc	Harim	—
Hormuz	al-Naqa II	—
Ibelin	Yibna	Yavne
Judin	Qal'at Jiddin	—
Kadmos	Qadmus	—
Karak des Moabites	al-Karak	—
La Forbie	Harbiyah	—
La Tor de l'Opital	Burj al-Shamali	—

The embrasures in the outer wall of the Crusader citadel at Mistrus (Mistra) loom above the later Palace of the Byzantine Despots. (D. Nicolle)

Le Destroit	Qal'at Dustray	—
Le Petit Gerin	Zirrin	—
Le Toron des Chevaliers	al-Atrun	—
Le Vaux Moise	al-Wu'aira	—
Maldoim (see Cisterna Rubea)	Qal'at al-Damm	—
Maraclea	Maraqiyah	—
Margat	al-Marqab	—
Mirabel	Mijdal Afiq	Migdal Afeq
Montferrand	Ba'rin	—
Montfort	Qal'at al-Qurayn	—
Montréal (Krak de Montréal)	Shawbak	—
Nephin	Anafah	—
Ranculat	Qal'at al-Rum	—
Ravendel	Ravanda	Ravanda
Recordane	Khirbat Kardanah	—
Roche de Roussel	Hajar Shuglan	Chilvan Kale
Rochefort	Qal'at al-Barzah (Burzay)	—
Ruad	Arwad	—
Saone	Sahyun	—
Saphet	Safad	Zefat
Selucia Trachea	—	Silifke
Sephorie	Saffuriyah	—
St Simeon	—	Süveydiye
Subeibeh	Qal'at Subayba	—
Toprak	Tal Hamdun	Toprakkale
Tortosa	Tartus	—
Trapesac	Darbsak	—
Turbessel	Tal Bashir	—
Turris Rubea	Burj al-Ahmar	—
Turris Sallnarum	Tal Tananim	—
Vadum Jacob	Jisr Ya'kub	Gesher Benot Ya'acov
Villejargon	'Arqah	—

TURKEY

The northern regions of the County of Edessa and the Principality of Antioch covered part of what are now the Turkish provinces of Antakya (also called the Hatay), Adana, Maras, Gaziantep, Adiyaman and Urfa. Within this rugged and rather under-developed territory the easiest Crusader fortifications to reach are the Citadel of Antioch (Antakya) itself, the Citadel of Edessa (Urfa) which, like the walls of the city, contains very little Crusader work, and the castle of Baghras which, though rebuilt by the Byzantines in 968, is now largely Crusader and Armenian. Other castles that are more difficult to reach are Ravendel and Haruniya, though both of these are largely Islamic rather than Crusader. Amoude (Khan 'Amudah), between Kozan and the great Cilician Armenian fortress of Toprakkale, appears only on the most detailed maps.

SYRIA

Generally speaking the Crusader castles of Syria are more numerous and easier to reach, particularly those of the 13th century. The largest and most dramatic are Saone, Margat and Crac des Chevaliers, all of which have been opened up and developed for tourists. Fortunately this development has been done in such a way that the castles themselves have been neither spoiled nor over-restored. South of Margat, the historic port city of Tartus contains several Crusader buildings and fortifications, some of which are still inhabited by local people. The tiny island of Arwad, a few minutes' journey in an open boat from Tartus, still has a fort dating from the Crusader period and – perhaps more importantly – also has some of the best fish restaurants in Syria.

The dog-leg turning halfway up the entrance ramp inside the castle of Crac des Chevaliers (Hisn al-Akrad). Horses are, of course, no longer permitted inside this Syrian national monument, but the animal seen here being ridden down towards the main gate was brought in for a filming shoot. (D. Nicolle)

Although much of the Qal'at Sinjil citadel overlooking Tripoli was rebuilt several times under Mamluk and Ottoman rule, much of the lower parts of its fortifications dates from the Crusader period, perhaps including some 12th-century construction. The large chamber and embrasure seen here are in the ground-floor outer wall of a large tower on the eastern side of the castle. (D. Nicolle)

Amongst the more difficult fortifications to reach, but still worthwhile, is Bourzay, which was probably the Rochefort of the Crusaders, standing in a wonderfully dramatic location overlooking the northern part of the Orontes valley. The citadel of Apamea (Afamia) is similarly dramatic, though located on the lower eastern side of the Orontes valley. It also has the advantage of not having been turned into an uninhabited archaeological site or architectural relic. The old town still fills most of the area within the city walls while the main or newer part of the town stands where the outer and lower suburbs of the medieval town once stood. In terms of its fortifications, however, most of what can now be seen at Apamea dates from after the earthquakes of the mid 12th century and is therefore Islamic.

LEBANON

The citadel of Trablus (Tripoli) includes both 12th- and 13th-century Crusader work, as well as fragments of the previous 11th-century Islamic palace-fortress. It is in a good state of repair, though its external appearance is more Ottoman than medieval. Gibelet and the southern coastal cities like Sidon (Saida) and Tyre (Sur) similarly include both Crusader and later Islamic work. It is certainly possible to visit the latter two, and the effort is worthwhile because so much remains from the Crusader period; however, southern Lebanon, though theoretically open to visitors, remains rather tense at the time of writing. In the very north of Lebanon the small but dramatic castle of Gibelcar is again well worth visiting. However, it remains difficult to reach not only in terms of roads to the site but in a very strenuous climb (without a path) to enter the castle itself. At the other end of the country, in the deep south, the castle of Belfort (Qal'at al-Shaqif) again includes identifiable 12th-century structures.

ISRAEL & THE PALESTINIAN TERRITORIES

Further south in Israel and the Palestinian autonomous areas, many castles and fortifications dating from the Crusader period have been excavated and restored to such an extent that they resemble historical theme parks. None of the Crusader-period walls of Jerusalem survive to their original height, and most of today's city walls were rebuilt under the sway of the Ottoman Empire. In the Citadel, Crusader elements that survived the destruction of 1239 can be found in the talus, the eastern tower, the eastern curtain-wall (including the remains of stables), a postern gate, the base of the south-western tower (again including stables), the southern postern, the western gateway, the north-western curtain-wall (including the lower parts of some arrow slits) and the north-eastern curtain-wall. Archaeological excavations in the 'Armenian Garden' south of the Citadel have revealed part of the city's western wall, including a tower, and a barrel-vaulted cistern that may originally have been underneath a southern part of the royal palace of the kings of Jerusalem.

In addition to the best-known Crusader sites, such as the fully excavated castle at Belvoir overlooking the Jordan valley, and the mixed Crusader and Islamic urban fortifications of the abandoned city of Ascalon, there are many other Crusader fortifications in Israel and the Palestinian territories. For example, the tower or

The only remaining sections of the seaward-facing wall of the city of Ascalon are in the south-eastern corner. Even here, around what was originally the Sea Gate, some structures teeter on the brink of collapse. (D. Nicolle)

donjon at Saffuriyah includes ancient and medieval masonry, but was considerably altered in later centuries and has been inaccurately restored in more recent years. The remains of another tower-keep have been exposed in Baysan and are still two storeys high. Its enclosure wall is also very unusual because it was surrounded by a water-filled moat – most inland moats in the Middle East were dry. The existence of such a moat was noted by the medieval Arab chronicler Ibn al-Furat, and was confirmed when archaeologists found the remains of freshwater snails. On a rather smaller scale, the Templar tower at Khirbat Dustray stands on a cut-to-shape rock base and contained a cistern. A rock-cut courtyard enclosed the tower on its southern and eastern sides with stables containing rock-cut mangers. Other rock-cut features include further courtyards, reservoirs, mangers and cisterns.

The Old City of Acre was one of the few Palestinian towns to retain its Arab population following the mass expulsions of 1948. This, when added to the skilful, sensitive and restrained manner in which Israeli archaeologists are still uncovering the ruins of the medieval city, makes Acre a top priority for those seeking Crusader fortifications in the Holy Land. Pilgrims' Castle at Atlit, south of Haifa, is still out of bounds because the location has been used as a training base for Israeli Naval Commandos. However, the dramatic fortress is clearly visible from the coast. Southward again, the excavated site of Caesarea contains remarkable remains from many periods, of which the 13th-century Crusader fortifications are the best preserved. The equally remarkable but smaller and less known site of Arsuf lies on the coast just north of Herzliya. It was another closed military zone until a series of explosions and chemical leaks convinced the Israeli Defense Forces to move their weapons development facility from the site. Nevertheless, until the existing toxic pollution is removed, archaeological excavations and public access to the remains of medieval Arsuf will remain restricted.

JORDAN

Jordan has perhaps the greatest variety of different sorts of 12th-century Crusader fortifications, with the notable exception of a walled Crusader city. The cave-fortress of Cave de Sueth in the north of Jordan has already been described. In the south the existing fortifications of the town of Kerak date from the post-Crusader, Ayyubid or Mamluk centuries. The castle of Kerak, however, is on a steep promontory separated from the town by a rock-cut ditch 30m wide. Again many of the visible fortifications were built after the Crusader castle had been taken by Saladin, but the interior contains many Crusader structures. There are now believed to have been two main phases of construction under Crusader occupation in the 12th century. The first consisted of a castle built around 1142. At this time there also seems to have been a local or indigenous Christian monastery at the eastern end of the site, beneath what are now the ruins of a Mamluk *madrasa* or Islamic school. A second phase of building in the late 1160s doubled the size of the castle by adding a new outer wall and huge glacis. This was probably done around the time the Latin Catholic or Crusader metropolitan see (a centre of local ecclesiastical administration) was transferred from Shawback to Kerak. Shawback was modified around the same time, but most of what can now be seen there dates from the late 13th-century Mamluk period. Earlier Crusader structures are encased within this later fortress and seem to indicate that the 12th-century Crusader castle of Montréal was not particularly strong. It may have consisted only of a donjon. Very little remains of the Crusader castle at Tafila, between Shawbak and Kerak, other than some foundations beneath a much later rectangular Ottoman fort.

Petra in the deep south of Jordan is the most important archaeological and tourist site in the country, and is surely one of the most astonishing places in the

The reasons why the designers and builders of the Hospitaller castle of Belvoir (Kawkab al-Hawa), on the western escarpment of the Jordan valley in Palestine, used black basalt and white limestone in their construction were practical as well as aesthetic. Here, in an arrow-slit next to the south-eastern tower of Belvoir castle, imported but more easily worked limestone has been used for the complicated shape of a tapering arch, while black basalt forms the bulk of the structure. (D. Nicolle)

217

world. So perhaps it is not suprising that few visitors to Petra make a detour to look at the remains of three Crusader castles, which consist of little more than tumbled rocks. On the other hand, al-Wu'aira is worth the effort. It dominates the eastern summit of al-Wu'aira ridge overlooking the al-Wu'aira gorge. Al-Habis consists of the tumbledown remains of a small castle and tower on a rocky height overlooking the centre of ancient Petra. The third recently identified Crusader castle at al-Naq'a is, unfortunately, very difficult to reach without specialized transport and a knowledgeable guide.

CYPRUS, THE NEAR EAST & BLACK SEA

Fortifications associated with the Crusaders and their Italian trading allies outside the Middle East are generally easy to reach, though sometimes well off the beaten track. Political problems only interfere in Cyprus, while the emergence of the Ukraine as an independent state has largely removed the problems previously associated with independent travel within the Soviet Union.

Names of Crusader fortifications outside the Holy Land

Modern Names	Medieval Western European Names
Agriosikia (Tilos)	—
Akçaabat	—
Akova	Matagrifon
Amasra	Amastris
Anamur	Stallimuri
Androusa	—
Argos	Argos
Athens Acropolis	Sathines
Beskapilar (Foça)	Phocaea
Bilhorod-Dnistrovsky	Moncastro
Bodonitsa	Medietas Bondonicie
Bodrum	Castrum Sancti Petri
Boudonitsa	—
Buffavento	Bufevent
Çandarli	—
Chalkis	Negroponte
Chanea	Canea
Chlemutzi	Clairmont [Castel Tornese]
Clarenza	Clarence
Dafni	Daphne
Galata (Istanbul)	Pera

Gardiki	Gardiki
Gastria	Gastria
Geraki	Geraki
Giresun	—
Girne (Kyrenia)	Cerina
Herakleion	Candia
Izmit	Nicomedia
Kaffa	Caffa
Kalamat	Kalamata
Kalavryta	Tremola
Kantara	Le Candare
Karytaina	Karytaina
Kelafa (Oitylon)	Grand Magne
Khirokitia	—
Kiliya	Licostomo [Kilia]
Kolossi	Le Colos
Korikos	Corycus
Korinthos	Corinth
Korone	Coron
Kotsinas (Lemnos)	—
Kyparissa	Arkadia
Kyrenia	Kyrenia

The late medieval Hospitaller castles on the island of Tilos are mostly of quite simple, and occasionally quite crude, construction when compared to the sophisticated fortifications of the city of Rhodes itself. However, they clearly served their purpose. The example seen here is Megalo Horio. (B. Rankin)

219

Lamia	Zeitoun [Ravennika]
Larissa	Larisa
Leuktron	Beaufort
Lebadeia	Levadia
Limassol	Limassol
Lindos (Rhodos)	Lindos
Livadia	Levadia
Magusa (Famagusta)	Famagusta
Methymna (Lesbos)	Molivos
Meyisti	Kastellorizo
Mistra	Mistras
Megalo Horio (Tilos)	—
Methoni	Modon
Monemvasia	Napoli di Malvasia
Monolithos (Rhodos)	—
Myrina Kastro (Lemnos)	Lemnos
Myteleni (Lesbos)	Mitilini
Nauphlia	Napoli di Romania
Navarino (Palaia Avarino)	Chastel du Port de Junch
Neopatras	Lepater
Nicosia/Lefkosa	Nicosia
Palaiokastro (Lemnos)	—
Pandeleimon	Platamon
Paphos	Paphos
Parga	—
Patras	Patras
Pendeskupi	—
Pontikocastra (Katakolo)	Beauvoir (Belvedere)
Ravennika	—
Rhodos	Rhodes
Salona	—
Silifke	Selef
Sivouri	—
St George	—
St Hilarion	Dieudamour
Sudak	Soldaia
Sykaminon	—
Thebes, castle of	Kadmeia
Tirebolu	—
Vardounia	Passavant (?)
Veligosti	Chastelneuf (?)
Vordonia	Verdognia (Verdonia)
Vostitza	—
Yermasoyia	—
Zarnata	Gerenia (?)
Zeitoun	Lamia

CYPRUS

Almost all the medieval fortifications on Cyprus are easily accessible. However, some are located in the Greek south and others in the Turkish north of the island. Both 'states' have well-developed tourist industries, hotel accommodation of all grades and efficient transport systems. What is missing is an open frontier between the two, which in reality means that separate trips are probably needed if castles on both sides of the divide are to be seen.

GREECE

Greece has all the facilities required by a major tourist destination. Unfortunately, Greek 'cultural tourism' has concentrated on the country's Classical past, with some attention also being given to its Byzantine heritage. Relics from the medieval Crusader period are largely neglected, while the Ottoman heritage sometimes seems to be deliberately hidden from view. Several Crusader castles are actually more closely associated with the Turks than with the 'Latins', and are thus not made easily accessible. Furthermore, most Crusader fortifications are well off the normal tourist routes – in several cases off any routes whatsoever. So those wishing to visit them are almost obliged to hire a sturdy self-drive car, motorbike or bicycle, and then to expect a hard walk or climb to follow.

TURKEY

Like Greece, those coastal parts of Turkey where Crusader and medieval Italian colonial fortifications exist have a fully developed tourist trade. The Crusader fortifications on Turkey's Aegean coast have, in fact, become major features of their regional tourist industries. The Black Sea coast is less known to European visitors, but has good hotels and transport facilities, which largely cater for Turkish rather than foreign visitors.

GLOSSARY

ablaq	Middle Eastern tradition of architectural decoration combining different coloured stone, usually black basalt and white limestone.
antemurabilus	Second or outer walls.
ashlar	Stone cut into rectangular blocks and laid in regular rows.
bailey, bailli	Fortified enclosure with a castle.
balista	A crossbow, usually of a large form.
barbican	Outer defensive enclosure of a castle or city, usually outside a gate.
barrel vault	Vaulting in the form of an elongated arch.
bastion	Projecting or additional part of a fortification.
batter	Slope, usually on the outer face, of a fortified wall.
bezant	High-value Byzantine currency.
boulevard	Low and extended platform to form an artillery emplacement in front of a fortified wall.
bovaria	A farmstead or animal pen, sometimes fortified.
bretéche	Projecting machicolation above a gate.
casemate	Covered emplacement for cannon.
castrum (pl: castra)	Fortified enclosure, usually rectangular.

châtelain	Commander of a castle.
chemin de ronde	A raised walkway around the circuit or curtain-walls of a fortified place.
concentric castle	A fortification with two or more circuit walls.
corbel	Stone bracket to support another structure.
counter-fort, counter-tower	A fortification, usually small, to blockade or isolate another fortification.
cour d'honneur	Central or ceremonial court of a castle-palace.
crenellation	Tooth-like projection along the top of a fortified wall to provide protection for the defenders as well as spaces through which they can observe or shoot.
cubit	Unclear unit of measure, about half a metre.
curtain-wall	A continuous defensive wall around a fortified location.
donjon	Main tower of a fortified location, or a single isolated tower.
double-castrum	Fortified enclosure with two concentric defensive walls.
drawbridge	An entrance bridge, usually over a moat, which can be raised out of position, usually also blocking the gate behind.
église-donjon	A fortified church.
embossed masonry	Blocks of stone in which the centre is raised and usually roughly cut.
embrasure	An opening in a fortified wall, tower, crenellation or other structure through which the defenders can shoot.
enceinte	A curtain-wall.
fausse braie	Low-walled outwork.
fieldstones	Naturally available rocks or small boulders.
forewalls	Additional defensive walls in front of the main defensive walls and towers.
fosse	Defensive ditch.
gallery	A passage, usually within a defensive wall, sometimes with embrasures through which defenders can observe or shoot.
glacis	Smooth, open slope leading up to the base of a fortified wall.
grange	A building to store agricultural produce, usually from a specific feudal fief.
hoarding	A wooden structure in the form of a gallery mounted on top of, and also ahead of, a defensive wall.
huchette	A form of machicolation above an entrance.
keep	The main tower of a fortified position (see also donjon).

machicolation	Overhanging structure on a tower or fortified wall, down which arrows could be shot or missiles dropped.
mahone	Local Genoese authorities in one of the Genoese colonial outposts.
mangonel	A stone-throwing siege weapon based upon the beamsling principle, either man powered or counterweight powered.
march	A frontier province with a primary military-defensive function.
masonry marks	A symbol or design scratched or simply carved into a piece of masonry to identify the stone-mason who had cut the stone in question.
merlons	Raised masonry forming a crenellation (see above).
moat	Ditch or fosse forming an obstruction outside a defensive wall, sometimes but not necessarily filled with water.
motte and bailey	A castle consisting of a tower on a small man-made hill (motte), with an outer fortified enclosure (bailey).
palatinate	An autonomous or semi-autonomous province, often under ecclesiastical control.
portcullis	Grid-like gate or iron of iron and wood, usually raised and lowered into position inside a gateway.
posterns	Small doors or gates in the defences of a fortified position.
presidium, praesidium	A defended place.
put-log	Holes in masonry into which supporting beams are thrust.
redoubt	An outwork of a fortified place.
salient towers	Towers thrust forward from a fortified wall.
sénéchal	A senior medieval military official in charge of inspections of the king's castles.
slot machicolation	An aperture or broad groove down the face of a tower or fortified wall, through which arrows could be shot or missiles dropped.
spur-castle	A castle built on a spur or promontory, usually on the side of a hill.
talus	Additional sloping front along the lower part of a wall and tower.
terrepleine	Open area on top of a rampart as an emplacement for cannon through which the defenders can shoot.
undercroft	Lowest chamber of a multi-storey building or structure.
ward	Open area surrounded by a curtain-wall.

FURTHER READING

Andrews, K. *Castles of the Morea* (Princeton, 1953).

Anghel, G. 'Les forteresses moldaves de l'époque d'Etienne le Grand', *Château Gaillard*, 7 (1975) 21–34.

Antaki, P. 'Le château Croisé de Beyrouth; étude préliminaire', ARAM Periodical 13/14 (2001/2) 323–53.

Avissar, M. & Stern, E. 'Akko, the Citadel,' *Excavations and Surveys in Israel*, XIV (1994) 22–25.

Balard, M. 'Les formes militaires de la colonisation Génoise (XIIIe–XVe siècles)', *Castrum*, 3 (Madrid, 1988) 67–78.

Beldiceanu, N. 'La conquête des cités marchandes de Kilia et de Cetatea Alba par Bayezid II', *Südost-Forschungen*, 22 (1964) 36–90.

Biller, T. 'Der Crac des Chevaliers – neue Forschungen,' *Château Gaillard*, 20 (2002) 51–55.

Blin, R. 'Châteaux croisés de Grèce: Fortifications franques de Morée', *Histoire Médiévale*, 56 (August 2004) 58–67.

Boaz, A. 'Bet Shean, Crusader Fortress – Area Z', *Excavations and Surveys in Israel*, IX (1989-90) 129.

Bon, A. 'Forteresses médiévales de la Grèce centrale,' *Bulletin de Correspondance Hellénique*, 61 (1937) 136–209.

Bon, A. *La Morée Franque* (Paris, 1969).

Brown, R.M. 'A 12th century A.D. Sequence from Southern Transjordan; Crusader and Ayyubid Occupation at El-Wueira', *Annual of the Department of Antiquities of Jordan*, XXXI (1987) 267–287.

Burridge, P. 'The Castle of Vardounia and Defence in the Southern Mani', in P. Lock & G.D.R. Sanders (eds), *The Archaeology of Medieval Greece* (Oxford, 1996) 19–28.

Chevedden, P.E. 'Fortification and the Development of Defensive Planning in the Latin East,' in D. Kagay & L.J.A. Villalon (eds), *The Circle of War in the Middle Ages* (Woodbridge, 1999) 33–43.

Cohen, A. 'The Walls of Jerusalem', in C.E. Bosworth (ed.), *Essays in Honor of Bernard Lewis; The Islamic World from Classical to Modern Times* (Princeton, 1989) 467–77.

Crow, J. & Hill, S. 'Amasra, a Byzantine and Genoese Fortress', *Fortress*, 15 (1990) 3–13.

Dean, B. 'A Crusader Fortress in Palestine (Montfort)', *Bulletin of the Metropolitan Museum of Art*, XXII/2 (1927) 91–97.

Deschamps, P. 'Deux Positions Stratégiques des croisés à l'Est du Jourdain: Ahamant et el Habis', *Revues Historiques*, CLXXII (1933) 42–57.

Deschamps, P. *Les Châteaux des Croisés en Terre Sainte: le Crac des Chevaliers* (Paris, 1934).

Edbury, P.W. 'Castles, towns and rural settlements in the Crusader kingdom,' *Medieval Archaeology*, XLII (1998) 191–93.

Edwards, R.W. *The Fortifications of Armenian Cilicia* (Washington, 1987).

Ellenblum, R. 'Three generations of Frankish castle-building in the Latin Kingdom of Jerusalem', in M. Balard (ed.), *Autour de la Première Croisade* (Paris, 1996) 517–51.

Ellenblum, R. 'Frankish and Muslim Siege Warfare and the construction of Frankish concentric castles', in M. Balard (ed.), *Die Gesta per Francos* (Aldershot, 2001) 187–98.

Elliott, R. 'Lemnos and its Castle', *Fortress*, 17 (1993) 28–36.

Eydoux, H-P. 'L'architecture militaire des Francs en Orient', in J.P. Babelon (ed.), *Le Château en France* (Paris, 1986) 61–77.

Faucherre, N. et al (eds), *La Fortification au Temps des Croisades* (Rennes, 2004).

Fedden, R. *Crusader castles, a brief study in the military architecture of the Crusades* (London, 1950).

Fiene, E. *St. Hilarion, Buffavento, Kantara: Bergburgen in Nordzypern* (Hannover, 1992).

Fiene, E. *Die Burg von Kyrenia* (Hannover, 1993).

Folda, J. 'Crusaders Frescoes at Crac des Chevaliers and Marqab Castles', *Dumbarton Oaks Papers*, XXXVI (1982) 177–210.

Fournet, T. 'Le château de Aakar al-Atiqa (Nord-Liban)', *Bulletin d'Archéologie et d'Architecture Libanaises*, 4 (2000) 149–63.

Gertwagen, R. 'The Crusader Port of Acre: Layout and Problems of Maintenance', in M. Balard (ed.), *Autour de la Première Croisade* (Paris, 1996) 553–82.

Gertwagen, R. 'Venetian Modon and its Port (1358–1500)', in Cowan, A. (ed.) *Mediterranean Urban Culture 1400–1700* (Exeter, 2000) 128–48.Gertwagen, R. 'The Venetian Colonies in the Ionian Sea and the Aegean in Venetian Defence Policy in the Fifteenth Century', *Journal of Mediterranean Studies*, 12 (2002) 351–84.

Hamma, Z. *Syria: The Castles and Archaeological Sites in Tartous (Governorate)* (Damascus, 1994).

Harper, R.P. 'Belmont Castle (Suba) – 1987', *Excavations and Surveys in Israel*, CII–VIII (1988–89) 13–14.

Hartal, M. 'Excavations of the Courthouse Site at 'Akko' (three parts) '*Atiqot XXXI* (1997) 1–2, 3–30, 109–14.

Hodgetts, C. and Lock, P. 'Some Village Fortifications in the Venetian Peloponnese', in P. Lock & G.D.R. Sanders (eds), *The Archaeology of Medieval Greece* (Oxford, 1996) 77–90.

Jacoby, D. 'Crusader Acre in the Thirteenth Century; urban layout and topography,' *Studi Medievali*, 3 ser. XX (979) 1–45.

Jacoby, D. 'Montmussard, Suburb of Crusader Acre: The First Stages of its Development', in *Outremer: Studies in the History of the Crusading Kingdom of Jerusalem presented to Joshua Prawer* (Jerusalem, 1982) 205–17.

Jawish, H. *Krak des Chevaliers und die Kreuzfahrer* (Damascus, 1999).

Jeffery, G.H. *Cyprus Monuments: Historical and Architectural Buildings* (Nicosia, 1937).

Johns, C.N. 'Excavations of Pilgrim's Castle, 'Atlit (1932-3): Stables at the south-west of the suburbs', *Quarterly of the Department of Antiquities of Palestine*, V (1935) 31–60.

Karasava-Tsilingiri, F. 'Fifteenth Century Hospitaller Architecture on Rhodes: Patrons and Master Builders', in Nicholson, H. (ed.), *The Military Orders, Volume 2: Welfare and Warfare* (Aldershot, 1998) 259–65.

Kedar, B.Z. 'The Outer Walls of Frankish Acre', '*Atiqot, XXXI* (1997) 157–80.

Kennedy, H. *Crusader Castles* (Cambridge, 1994).

Kloner, A. 'Bet Govrin: Crusader Church and Fortifications', *Explorations and Surveys in Israel*, II (1983) 12–13.

Lindner, M. 'Search for Medieval Hormuz: The Lost Crusader Fortress of Petra', *Occident & Orient* (Amman, December 1999) 59–61.

Lock, P. 'The Frankish Towers of Central Greece', *Annual of the British School of Archaeology at Athens*, 81 (1986) 101–23.

Lock, P. 'The Frankish Tower on the Acropolis, Athens; the Photographs of William J. Stillman', *Annual of the British School at Athens*, 82 (1987) 131–33 (pls. 46–8).

Lock, P. 'The Medieval Towers of Greece: A Problem of Chronology and Function', in B. Arbel, B. Hamilton & D. Jacoby (eds), *Latins and Greece in the Eastern Mediterranean after 1204* (London, 1989) 129–45.

Lock, P. 'The Towers of Euboea: Lombard or Venetian, Agrarian or Strategic?' in P. Lock & G.D.R. Sanders (eds), *The Archaeology of Medieval Greece* (Oxford, 1996) 107–26.

Lock, P. 'Castles and Seigneurial Influence in Latin Greece', in A.V. Murray (ed.), *From Clermont to Jerusalem: The Crusades and Crusader Societies 1095–1500* (Turnhout, 1998) 173–86.

Lurier, H.E. (tr.) *Crusaders as Conquerors: The Chronicle of the Morea* (New York, 1964).

Luttrell, A. 'Lindos and the Defence of Rhodes; 1306–1522', *Rivista di Studi Byzantini e Neoellenici*, 22–3 (1985–86) 317–32.

Luttrell, A. 'The Later History of the Maussolleion and its Utilization in the Hospitaller Castle at Bodrum', *Jutland Archaeological Society Publications*, 15 (1986) 117–222.

Luttrell, A. 'English Contributions to the Hospitaller Castle at Bodrum in Turkey; 1407–1437', in H. Nicholson (ed.) *The Military Orders, Volume 2: Welfare and Warfare* (Aldershot, 1998) 163–72.

Marino, L. (ed.) *La fabbrica dei Castelli Crociati in Terra Santa* (Florence, 1997).

Marino, L. 'The making of the Crusader Castels [sic.]', in L. Marino (ed.), *La fabbrica dei castelli crociati in Terra Santa* (Florence, 1997).

Megaw, A.H.S. 'Supplementary Excavations on a Castle Site at Paphos, Cyprus, 1970–1971', *Dumbarton Oaks Papers*, 26 (1972) 322–45.

Megaw, A.H.S. 'The Arts of Cyprus, B: Military Architecture', in H.W. Hazard & K.M. Setton (eds), *A History of the Crusades, Volume 4: The Art and Architecture of the Crusader States* (Madison, 1977) 196 207.

Megaw, P. 'A Castle in Cyprus Attributable to the Hospital?' in M. Barber (ed.), *The Military Orders: Fighting for the Faith and Caring for the Sick* (Aldershot, 1994) 42–51.

Mesqui, J. *Châteaux d'Orient, Liban, Syrie* (Paris, 2001).

Molin, K. 'Fortifications and Internal Security in the Kingdom of Cyprus, 1191–1426', in Molin, K. 'The non-military functions of Crusader fortifications, 1187–circa 1380', *Journal of Medieval History*, XXIII (1997) 367–88.

Molin, K. *Unknown Crusader Castles* (London, 2001).

Morray, D. 'Then and Now: A Medieval Visit to the Castle of al-Rawandan Recalled', *Anatolian Studies*, XLIII (1993) 137–42.

Müller-Wiener, W. *Castles of the Crusaders* (London, 1966).

A.V. Murray (ed.), *From Clermont to Jerusalem: The Crusades and Crusader Societies 1095–1500* (Turnhout, 1998), 187–99.

Nicolle, D. 'Ain al Habis. La Cave de Sueth', *Archéologie Médiévale*, XVIII (1988) 113–28.

Nordiguian, L. and Voisin, J-C *Châteaux et églises du moyen âge au Liban* (Beirut, 1999).

Paradissis, A. *Fortresses and Castles of Greece* (Athens & Thessaloniki, 1972–82).

Pringle, D. 'Reconstructing the Castle of Safad,' *Palestine Exploration Quarterly*, CXVII (1985) 139–49.

Pringle, D. 'A Thirteenth Century Hall at Montfort Castle in Western Galilee,' *The Antiquaries Journal*, LXVI (1986) 52–81.

Pringle, D. *The Red Tower (al Burj al Ahmar): Settlement on the Plain of Sharon at the time of the Crusades and Mamluks*, British School of Archaeology Monographs 1 (London, 1986).

Pringle, D. 'Towers in Crusader Palestine,' *Château Gaillard 1992*, XVI (Caen, 1994) 335–70.Pringle, D. 'Architecture in the Latin East', in J.S.C. Riley-Smith (ed.), *Oxford Illustrated History of the Crusades* (Oxford, 1995) 160–83.

Pringle, D. 'Town Defences in the Crusader Kingdom of Jerusalem', in I.A. Corfis and M. Wolfe (eds.), *The Medieval City under Siege* (Woodbridge, 1995) 69–121.

Pringle, D. *Secular Buildings in the Crusader Kingdom of Jerusalem; An Archaeological Gazetteer* (Cambridge, 1997).

Pringle, D. 'The Castle and Lordship of Mirabel', in B.Z. Kedar (ed.), *Montjoie – Studies in Crusader History in Honour of Hans Eberhard Mayer* (Aldershot, 1997) 91–112.

Pringle, D. and De Meulemeester, J. *The Castle of al-Karak, Jordan* (Namur, 2000).

Pringle, D. and Harper, R. *Belmont Castle, the Excavation of a Crusader Stronghold in the Kingdom of Jerusalem*, British Academy Monographs in Archaeology 10 (Oxford, 2000).

Pringle, D. *Fortification and Settlement in Crusader Palestine* (reprints, Aldershot, 2000).

Rihaoui, A. *The Krak of the Knights* (Damascus, 1996).

Riley-Smith, J. 'The Templars and the castle of Tortosa in Syria; an unknown document concerning the acquisition of the fortress', *English Historical Review*, LXXXIV (1969) 278–288.

Roll, I. 'Medieval Apollonia – Arsuf; A Fortified Coastal Town in the Levant of the Early Muslim and Crusader Periods', in M. Balard (ed.), *Autour de la Première Croisade* (Paris, 1996) 595–606.

Rosser, J. 'Excavations at Saranda Kolones, Paphos, Cyprus, 1981–1983', *Dumbarton Oaks Papers*, 39 (1985) 80–97.

Rosser, J. 'Crusader Castles of Cyprus', *Archaeology*, 39/4 (July–August 1986) 40–7.

Rubio y Lluch, A. 'Els castells catalans de la Grècia continentale', *Annuari de l'Institut d'estudis catalans*, 2 (1908) 364–425.

Saade, G. 'Le Chateau de Bourzey: Fortresses Oubliées', *Annales Archéologiques de Syria*, VI (1956) 139–62.

Smail, R.C. 'Crusaders' Castles in the Twelfth Century', *Cambridge Historical Journal*, X (1950–52) 133–49.

Sort, R. 'Two Hospitaller Castles on the Island of Tilos, on the Southern Dodecanese (Megalo Horio & Agriosikia)', *Castles Studies Group*, Newsletter, 15 (2001–02) 96–100.

Traquair, R. 'Laconia, I: Medieval Fortresses', *Annual of the British School at Athens*, 12 (1905–06) 259–76 (pls. II–VI).

Traquair, R. 'Medieval Fortresses of the North-Western Peloponnesus', *Annual of the British School at Athens*, 13 (1906–07) 268–84 (pls VIII–IX).

Traquair, R. 'Frankish Architects in Greece', *Journal of the Royal Institute of British Architects*, 31 (1923–24) 33–48 and 73–86.

Ziada, M.M. 'The Mamluk Conquest of Cyprus in the Fifteenth Century' (two parts), *Bulletin of the Faculty of Arts*, Cairo University, 1 (1933) 90–113; 2 (1934), 37–57.

INDEX

Figures in **bold** refer to illustrations